# DEATH OR GLORY

# DEATH
# OR
# GLORY

*The Legacy of
the Crimean War*

R OBERT  B.  E DGERTON

Westview Press
A Member of the Perseus Books Group

Copyright © 1999 by Westview Press, A Member of the Perseus Books Group

Published in 1999 in the United States of America by Westview Press, 5500 Central Avenue, Boulder, Colorado 80301-2877, and in the United Kingdom by Westview Press, 12 Hid's Copse Road, Cumnor Hill, Oxford OX2 9JJ
Library of Congress Cataloging-in-Publication Data


A CIP catalog record for this book is available from the Library of Congress.
ISBN 0-8133-3570-1 (hc)—ISBN 0-8133-3789-5 (pb)


The paper used in this publication meets the requirements of the American National Standard for Permanence of Paper for Printed Library Materials Z39.48-1984.

10    9    8    7    6    5    4    3    2    1

# CONTENTS

# ILLUSTRATIONS

# ACKNOWLEDGMENTS

I want first of all to thank the reference librarians at UCLA's University Research and Louise M. Darling Biomedical Libraries for their assistance in procuring books from libraries around the country. I am also grateful to the staff of the Public Record Office in London and the Bodleian Library of Oxford University. For their help in translating certain passages in Russian, French, and Italian, I thank Lev Polinsky, Janet Wojcicki, and Natalie Yamashita.

I thank Sharon Belkin of Morphographics for drawing the maps. For comments that helped me to develop this book, I want to thank Alan Fiske, Wally Goldschmidt, Marvin Karno, Keith Otterbein, and Tom Weisner, among many others. To several helpful anonymous reviewers, I also send my thanks. For their enormous help in preparing the manuscript, I am most grateful to Dana Stulberg, Paula Wilkinson, and Cynthia Brooks. Not least, I thank my editor, Rob Williams, for his support and editorial guidance.

*Robert B. Edgerton*

# DEATH OR GLORY

# INTRODUCTION

S OMEONE BROWSING THROUGH this volume in a bookstore could well be excused for wondering why the Crimean War of a century and a half ago, a war that ended five years before the American Civil War began, should attract readers today, especially since so much has already been written about it. Scores of personal accounts in several languages were published soon after the war ended, followed by numerous book-length descriptions of the war, several of them appearing as recently as the last few years in England. There are also several biographies of prominent figures who took part in this war, not least the reminiscences of Count Leo Tolstoy, who was there as a young Russian artillery officer, and whose experiences in Sevastopol did much to shape *War and Peace*. This war gave the world raglan sleeves, the cardigan sweater, the balaclava cap, Florence Nightingale, and the "charge of the Light Brigade," immortalized by Alfred, Lord Tennyson. But why another book about all this?

Historians might answer that this war deserves continuing attention because it changed the balance of power in Europe, weakening Russia, strengthening the imperiled Ottoman Empire, and leaving France the greatest military force in Europe, while Britain remained the greatest naval power. Austria gained strength, both Germany and Italy achieved long-awaited unification, and the United States, hardly an innocent bystander in this conflict, used its friendship with Russia to take possession of Alaska and Hawaii. Military historians might add that this war deserves our attention because despite claims by American Civil War historians to the contrary, it was the first one to be reasonably well documented by photographers; the first to take place in the age of the telegraph, the railroad, and steam-driven ships; the first in which mines played a significant role

I

in naval warfare; and the first to propose a major use of chemical warfare. There were even plans for a submarine and a prototank. Historians might also note that it should be studied by today's readers because it was the first war for which we have reasonably full information about the day-to-day actualities of armies fighting brutal battles at long range and face to face; cavalries fighting one another and charging into enemy cannons; soldiers, sailors, and civilians enduring a year of siege warfare; and all armies being subjected to heavy artillery fire as well as brutal hand-to-hand fighting in which thousands were bayoneted, clubbed, stoned, and even bitten to death. This book is about how the participants endured this war and all that went with it.

There is clearly no need for another book describing the battles of this war; that has been done and overdone. But the key to understanding the human experience of war, and therefore war itself, lies less in the details of the battles than in the realities of life that confronted those who took part in the conflict. Despite the graphic dispatches of British newspaper correspondents and bitter letters by disgruntled officers in several armies, the crucial role of exhaustion, weather, hunger, disease, poor medical care, and bungled military and civilian leadership is still not adequately understood. Neither is the role of women or the Turks, both of whom have been neglected by historians even though what they did was often heroic.

Because the British allowed newspaper correspondents to witness what went on and to write about it without censorship, the British public, and later much of the world, knew what was happening as in no previous war ever fought. Soon after, British officers, sergeants, and civilian visitors added their voices. The French imposed strict censorship during the war, but later, a number of French officers managed to write about their experiences, as did Sardinians who joined the allied cause later in the war. The Turks wrote little about their part in the war, but the Russians left many vivid firsthand accounts. As a result, this war was not only the first great conflict that was reasonably well described but also the first that had a large civilian audience while it was being fought.

This is not to say that the Crimean War was the most horrible war ever fought. The great conquests of the Mongols and the Turks led to incomprehensible slaughter and suffering, as did the Napoleonic wars of more recent times. And difficult as it may be to believe after reading about the Crimean War, it was not even the war most badly bungled by its leaders. To take but one example, in July 1809 the British sent an army of over 40,000 men to attack Antwerp and chose to encamp them on the nearby but notoriously malarial island of Walcheren in Zeeland. By October 10, less than three months later, only 5,616 men were fit for duty, and many thousands had died. Needless to say, the expedition accomplished nothing but the wholesale destruction of its own army.

The distant mirror of the Crimean War of 1853–1856 reflects the experiences of men, and sometimes women, of five culturally different nationalities: the British, French, Russians, Sardinians, and Turks. This cultural diversity allows us to ask an important and as yet unanswered question: In a war as long, horrible, and deadly as this one, does culture—people's traditional beliefs and practices—make a difference in how the war is experienced, or was this war so intense that all people, no matter their backgrounds, reacted to it in the same way? By a comparison of their experiences with those of Northern and Southern soldiers in the well-documented American Civil War, it will be possible to add further perspectives about how soldiers in the mid-nineteenth century experienced war.

The Crimean War was a showcase for bad generalship, bureaucratic bungling, and inept medical care. As a result, men and women died of hunger, cold, and disease many times more often than they were killed by the long-range rifles just introduced into war or the most massive artillery barrages the world had ever seen. Acts of astonishing bravery, many of them by doctors, women, and children, were commonplace, but so was callousness and brutality. Nothing stands out more starkly than the toughness of the soldiers who fought so savagely, seldom complained, and only rarely collapsed under the war's terrible and relentless stresses. It began as an intensely romantic war with officers and soldiers alike shouting phrases like "Death or glory," but it soon became largely an impersonal, long-range killing match that in many ways resembled the trench warfare of World War I. Except for the fifteen-year-long Tai-Ping Rebellion in China, it was the deadliest war ever fought before World War I, costlier in lives lost than the American Civil War, the Franco-Prussian War, or the Russo-Japanese War of 1904–1905.

In 1976, Britain's justly celebrated war historian John Keegan wrote that he suspected that battle had "already abolished itself."

Only six years later, British troops were in deadly combat in the Falklands. Since then, we have seen war in such places as Afghanistan, Bosnia, Chechnya, Iran, Iraq, Israel, Liberia, Mozambique, Sudan, Nigeria, Rwanda, and the Persian Gulf, and the threat of armed conflict hangs over many other parts of the world. The Cold War may be over, but war is not. As we make ready to enter the twenty-first century, we would do well to learn all we can from humankind's earlier wars.

As Samuel Taylor Coleridge, the English poet, wrote well before the Crimean War took place, "If men could only learn from history, what lessons it might teach us."

# 1

# THE CRIMEAN WAR

## *"Curious and Unnecessary"*

THE BUTCHER'S BILL for the Crimean War of 1853–1856 will never be known exactly, but it probably amounted to over 1 million deaths, in addition to an untold number of men, women, and children left permanently disabled by wounds or debilitated by disease. Probably close to half a million of the lives lost were Russian, and a comparable number were Turkish. France probably lost 100,000, Britain perhaps 25,000, and Italy about 2,000. Not until World War I would more people die as victims of war.[1] Considering the small number of people alive at that time, the magnitude of this death toll is all the more appalling. No more than 1.2 billion people lived on earth, a number less than the present-day population of China alone. In 1850, a mere 23 million people lived in the United States (although by 1860 this figure would rise to 31 million); only 26 million lived in Britain and 35 million in France. The entire Ottoman Empire held only some 25 million, and even the vast Russian Empire numbered only around 60 million people, less than two-thirds of Mexico's population today.

Although the earth's population during the Crimean War was only one-sixth its present size, the social divisions among people then had much greater force than they do today, and those divisions played an important part in this war. By the 1850s, there had been some growth of middle classes, especially in France and the United States, but the rich and the poor still lived in profoundly different worlds.

5

Enormous wealth remained in the hands of a relatively few sultans, nobles, bankers, and industrialists. In Britain, for example, forty-four dukes each owned over 100,000 acres. One of these, the Duke of Sutherland, owned 1,358,000 acres, an area larger than the counties of Bedfordshire, Berkshire, and Buckinghamshire put together, and he was not even the richest man in England.[2] In the United States, the differences between wealthy, slaveholding southern planters, who were said to speak "exactly like English gentlemen," and poor white farmers, whose speech was virtually incomprehensible to English gentlemen, and whose malnourished wives and young daughters chewed tobacco incessantly, were also vast.[3] So, too, were the differences between railroad barons and Irish immigrants in the North.

Most of the rural poor in Europe, America, and the Ottoman Empire continued to spend most of their lives eking out a living through mind-numbing drudgery. But more than ever before, large numbers of impoverished people flocked to cities. In Britain, the urban poor had already begun to outnumber people living in the countryside. British cities led the world's industrial revolution, but cities grew everywhere, even in backward Russia and Turkey, and 400,000 workers lived in Paris.[4] Huddled together in overcrowded slums covered with smoke and soot, most impoverished city dwellers endured miserable lives. Whether in France, Britain, or Russia, slum dwellers had so little food that they became physically stunted. Much of the food that they did have was contaminated, and they often drank polluted water. Fleas, flies, mosquitoes, and rats were commonplace, and so were killer diseases such as typhus, malaria, smallpox, and cholera.

Thanks to city dwellers' reliance on horse-drawn transportation, foul-smelling manure blanketed the streets of many cities. For example, each one of New York's 150,000 horses produced twenty to twenty-five pounds of manure every day.[5] Streets also lay strewn with piles of manure produced by pigs, which were allowed to run loose because they would eat the garbage that otherwise rotted on the sidewalks where it was dumped. Most men, women, and children worked long hours under appalling conditions for little pay. Sweatshops and child labor created ghastly conditions, but perhaps no one suffered more than miners. The growing demand for coal led to terrible abuses of miners, who typically worked in dangerous and degrading conditions. In England, for example, both sexes often worked in the nude because of the terrific heat, and children often worked for hours in total darkness, operating trap doors to ventilate the mines. Women and children also worked as draft animals, pulling coal carts through tunnels so low they had to crawl, the carts chained around their necks.[6] Conditions were no better in other parts of Europe or in the silver mines of Nevada.

Despite a continued reliance on horse-drawn transportation, much of the Western world had begun to experience a revolution in transportation. The world's first steamship, invented by American Robert Fulton, appeared on the Hudson River in 1807. By 1853, when the Crimean War began, steam-driven ships had supplanted most of their sail-powered ancestors throughout the West, but not yet in Russia or Turkey. In that same year, Commodore Matthew Perry's coal-burning steam armada from the U.S. Navy made its first visit to Japan, hoping to open that long-isolated nation to American trade. Railroad transportation had become important, too. Except in the Russian and Ottoman Empires, which were slow to change in this regard as well as others, railroads had already spread over much of Europe and North America. In 1850, the United States had almost 9,000 miles of track and Britain close to 7,000, but Russia had only 410 miles and Turkey almost none.[7] By 1860, there were 31,000 miles of track in the United States; all but 9,000 of them were in northern states and therefore retained by the Union when civil war broke out a year later.[8] Most trains were still noisy, filthy, and uncomfortable for passengers, but they carried people and freight at the then-astounding speed of thirty miles an hour in all kinds of weather.

Transformation of communication was taking place, too. Samuel F.B. Morse's telegraph had been in use for ten years before the Crimean War broke out, and newspapers had greatly increased their circulation despite censorship in some countries, including Russia and France. The world's largest newspaper, *The Times,* of London, had a circulation of 40,000, more than all its competitors combined, but newspapers were read widely in many other countries as well. Although fewer than 20 percent of Russian men were literate and even fewer Turks could read, 40 percent of British men could read, as could 80 to 90 percent of white American men.[9] Growing numbers of people read books at home as well as in libraries, and by the time of the war, Pushkin, Turgenev, Gogol, Flaubert, Racine, Dickens, Scott, Longfellow, Tennyson, Shakespeare, and others had been translated into several languages.

Rural areas, however, saw little change. In Russia and Turkey as well as in France, the agricultural cycle still dominated life, and most farmers faced low yields, uncertain markets, and dismal living conditions. Although market days and occasional festivals relieved some of the tedium, and some lucky villagers in the West occasionally enjoyed traveling singers, small theater groups, ventriloquists, circuses, and monologue artists, rural life had changed little since earlier times. In the United States, for example, except for a ragged Italian hurdy-gurdy or a few seedy German bands consisting of a drummer and some raucous horns, rural Americans continued to rely on British entertainers, as their forebears had done. American theater was almost exclusively British, and with the exception of a handful of songs such as "Dixie," "Yankee Doodle," and "Sucking Cider Through a Straw," most popular songs came from Britain, too. Even "Home Sweet Home" was written by an Englishman, who set it to an Italian tune.[10]

In cities throughout the West, the newly arrived urban poor had little money to spend, but many men spent what they had during long weekends of drinking, whoring, and attending sexually explicit burlesque shows. The new middle classes were distancing themselves from this sort of debauchery by flaunting their "Victorian" restraint. British men sported mustaches and side whiskers, slicking down their hair with macassar oil, but they dressed in black. Women still wore corsets to achieve hourglass figures, but they no longer flaunted their breasts in low-cut dresses. They continued to wear colorful dresses, but now buttoned to the neck and with skirts reaching the ground.

People of wealth and high social rank, however, indulged themselves in extravagant pleasures. For example, British country houses provided scenes of lavish luxury, as servants prepared immense dinners for guests who devoted long weekends to manly sports, classical music, and frequent sexual liaisons. London offered exclusive men's clubs, fine restaurants, theater, sporting events, and grand balls. The British gentry, joined by members of the growing middle class, flocked to the southern beaches on warm summer days. While their children paddled in the water, dug in the sand, and played with trained mice and rabbits in cages, adults remained fully dressed, often shaded by parasols. They ate whelk and jellied eels washed down by ginger beer. While women wearing straw bonnets sat about doing embroidery and chatting, men read newspapers, peered at passing ships through telescopes, or enjoyed the antics of "Negro" minstrels. The problems of the urban poor stayed far from sight.[11]

Russia offered even starker contrasts. Its vast serf population remained as ignorant and impoverished as ever, its middle class still very small, while its nobles lived as grandly as they had always done, whether enjoying their vast country estates or the many temptations of St. Petersburg's glittering social life.

St. Petersburg served as a magnet for Russia's party-loving nobility, but Paris served as the center of Europe's gas-lit, dazzlingly wicked world. Russian noblemen flocked there to gorge themselves on oysters and champagne between bouts of sexual frenzy with France's many beautiful courtesans, who went from Russian princes to French counts to guards' officers and back again in a dizzying whirl of gala parties and frequently changing lovers. Paris also provided thousands of prostitutes, and its newly introduced high-kicking cancan—danced by beautiful women who wore no underpants—reputedly did much to increase demand for the prostitutes' services. In 1854, much of Paris was the "gay Paree" of modern parody, the ultimate in frivolity where the so-called *dandys* sought and found every pleasure, and where the downfall of Gustave Flaubert's Madame Bovary became a reality for many women.[12]

In that same year, as the Crimean War had begun in earnest, Emperor Napoléon III ordered Baron Georges Haussmann to transform the narrow, winding, filth-encrusted streets of Paris into a world showcase of his only-two-year-old imperial regime. To beautify the city, and also to allow troops easy access through it in times of civil unrest, Haussmann began the task of tearing down medieval buildings to permit the construction of 805 kilometers of the wide, tree-lined boulevards that have come to epitomize Paris. He also built hundreds of formal parks and gardens, developed a sewer system, and brought running water to much of the city. While this extraordinary transformation was taking place, Paris remained the city of social radicals and turbulent spirits of all sorts. Paris meant Jacques Offenbach, comic opera, and artists like Gustave Courbet, who each day drank a good bit of absinthe washed down by ten bottles of

Swiss white wine, yet continued to paint masterpieces like *Woman with a Parrot*.

The new industrialization of the mid-nineteenth century brought misery to millions of urban poor around the world, and hope to some, but the technological advances that resulted changed the face of war. Except for most Russian and Turkish troops, soldiers now carried mass-produced rifles that could kill at over a mile rather than traditional short-ranged, smooth-bore muskets able to kill at no more than 100 yards or so. These new rifles could also be fired twice as rapidly as the old muskets. Artillery could now fire 200-pound explosive shells for distances of several miles. New weapons killed with such long-range efficiency that war would never again be the same, but doctors were not yet capable of preventing wholesale deaths from wounds and disease.

Steam-driven warships and railroads made the world shrink, while telegraph stations now linked governments with their military field commanders. For the first time, the press made populations aware of world events soon after they took place, because newspaper correspondents could now report by telegraph directly from the battlefield. A few photographs had been taken of the war between Mexico and the United States in 1846–1848, as well as in Burma during 1852, but never in such quantity or with such success as during the Crimean War. Before the war ended, thanks to the wide circulation of newspapers and the presence at the front of war correspondents, the world would learn more about the toll of warfare than had ever been known before. Despite all of this widely shared knowledge, the Confederate States of America expected a short, painless war after seceding from the Union in 1861.

It cannot be said of many wars—or indeed, perhaps, of any— that they simply had to be fought. General William T. Sherman described the U.S. Civil War as "one of the more causeless, foolish wars ever devised by the brain of man." Historians are still debating the relative importance of economic competition, culture conflict, slavery, and other factors in bringing this war about. But of all the wars that could easily have been avoided, the Crimean War must stand very near the top of the list. As one historian recently noted, the development of this war was nothing less than "bizarre," and another described it as "the world's most curious and unnecessary struggle."[13] To be sure, long-standing tensions between Russia and the Ottoman

Empire still rankled. The two empires had gone to war several times in the past, and Russia still coveted access to the Mediterranean through the Turkish-held Dardanelles and Bosporus because Russian trade, and with it, Russian power, were constrained by the ice that closed Russian ports in the Baltic and the Far East for half the year. The religious hatreds between Christians and Muslims remained profound as well. Yet no one at the time believed that any of this was reason enough for another war, not even Tsar Nicholas I, who eventually proved most responsible for starting it.

Russian dominance of eastern Europe at that time was both a blessing and curse for Europe: a curse for Poland, to be sure, as Polish hopes for independence were crushed; a problem for the fragmented German and Italian people, as they sought to unify; and a curse and a blessing alike for Austria. When much of eastern Europe rose in rebellion against Austrian rule in 1848 and 1849, Russia intervened, brutally crushing Hungarian rebels, and once again threatened Turkish control of Moldavia and Wallachia (what is now known as Romania). Five thousand defeated Polish, Hungarian, and Romanian leaders, including many army officers, fled to Turkey, taking with them military and technological skills as well as a burning hatred of Russia. At first, Russia demanded their extradition but finally agreed to let them remain in Turkey as long as they made no attempt to challenge Russian rule in their home countries.[14]

Troubled by these growing tensions, western Europe began to concentrate on what it had for some years called the Eastern Question. For its part, Britain grew increasingly hostile to Russia's autocratic tsar, Nicholas I, largely because Britain believed—wrongly as it happened—that the tsar intended to move south to wrench India out of Britain's colonial grasp.[15] Russian and British imperial competition had become so overt that it was known at the time as the *Great Game*. Large Russian exports of wheat had cut into British trade worldwide, while trade with the Ottoman Empire became another source of contention between the two powers. Like Britain, France had important and growing trade relationships with the Turkish government that Russian expansion would threaten. As the Great Game grew in scale, Tsar Nicholas repeatedly tried to forge an agreement with Britain to carve up the Ottoman Empire because, as he forcefully argued, it was so "sick" that it would soon collapse under the weight of its own corruption, and to prevent conflict in the area, he believed it vital that the two powers agree beforehand what to do with the empire when collapse came. The British listened, but no formal agreement to cooperate came.

Russian and British competition for control of the Mediterranean, India, and the Middle East had grown into a vital concern for both imperial countries and, of course, for Turkey, while French interests became deeply involved, too, but the incident that began the drift into the Crimean War was so trivial as, even at the time, to seem ridiculous. In 1850, Greek Orthodox and Roman Catholic priests in the Ottoman-protected holy cities of Jerusalem and Bethlehem began to quarrel about such arcane issues as which of them should possess the right of first access to certain holy Christian places, who should enter through which door, who should have custody to the keys to that door, and who should have primary access to the Holy Manger. The Vatican paid virtually no mind to the affair, perhaps because almost no Roman Catholics made pilgrimages to the Holy Land, but Greek Orthodox monks, whose faithful did make pilgrimages there, became concerned, and they appealed to the tsar. Always eager to reinforce his traditional role as protector of Christians in the Ottoman Empire, he demanded that the Turks officially grant him the right to protect the interests of the Christian minority in the Ottoman Empire as well as of the thousands of Orthodox Russians who made pilgrimages to Jerusalem every year.

Charles Louis Napoléon Bonaparte, since 1848 France's president, and in late 1852 its newly chosen Emperor Napoléon III, quickly became involved. France had growing mercantile and financial interests in Turkey as well as a long-standing interest in adding Egypt and other portions of the Ottomans' North African empire to French North African possessions. Napoléon III now saw his chance to increase his influence with the Turks by offering to serve as the defender of Europe's Roman Catholics, only a handful of whom ever made the pilgrimage to Jerusalem. He also saw an opportunity to increase France's influence, not to mention his own, throughout Europe. After much consultation and no little dithering, the beleaguered Turkish government ruled against the Greek Orthodox monks, an action that infuriated the tsar. In January 1853, Tsar Nicholas told the British ambassador to Turkey, Sir Hamilton Seymour, that Russia had the right and duty to protect all Christians in the Ottoman Empire and that if necessary, he would occupy Constantinople to do so.

Tsar Nicholas I is often dismissed by historians as a stupid, brutal autocrat bent on using his huge army for territorial expansion. Although not well educated, Nicholas was hardly as unintelligent as he is usually portrayed. He spoke several languages well and could be quite cunning. It is true that he was the ultimate autocrat, but he also had a social conscience, actually instituting a good many reforms, including one that might well have abolished serfdom if Russia's nobles had not objected so strenuously. He also had little desire for more territory, often saying that Russia was already too big.[16] He did not even hate the "wretched" Turks, as he always referred to them, with anything like the intensity of his hostility toward Tatars, Jews, and Poles. He detested Islam, to be sure, but his principal goal was access through the Dardanelles to the Mediterranean, not the destruction of the Ottoman Empire. To achieve this Mediterranean access, he had to reach an agreement with the Turks, but even that would be meaningless if Britain's all-powerful navy chose to block the way.

As a young man, the stern, unsmiling, six-foot four-inch Nicholas I had spent four months in England, where he came to love the lifestyle of the English country gentleman, but he could not quite fathom English freedoms or Britain's parliamentary government. As tsar, he said exactly what he thought and kept his word. He could not understand why British political leaders could not do the same without the consent of Parliament. The tsar was also no longer a war lover. He still adored the pageantry of parades and cavalry drill, but three years after his accession to the throne, he had accompanied his army to war against Turkey. Expecting parades and glory, he found instead an intimate acquaintance with the death, disease, and horror of actual war. Hoping to avert another war with Turkey, as tensions rose he traveled to England to craft an alliance that would achieve his goals without war. The tsar wanted a Turkey too weak to threaten him in any way but just strong enough so that the Western powers could not divide up the country. The British wanted the same thing but did not altogether trust the tsar. Later, Viscount Stratford Canning de Redcliffe, Britain's terrible-tempered, imperious ambassador in Constantinople, detested Russia and did much to prevent

MAP 1: THE WAR ZONE
1853 – 1856

NORWAY
&
SWEDEN

FINLAND

Archangel

Gulf of Finland

Kronstadt

St. Petersburg

DENMARK

Baltic Sea

RUSSIAN    EMPIRE

Volga

Berlin

PRUSSIA

Moscow

Warsaw

POLAND

Danube

Vienna

AUSTRIAN

EMPIRE

Dniester

MOLDAVIA

Kiev

Bug

Dnieper

Don

Odessa

WALLACHIA

Bucharest

Danube

Silistria

Varna

Sevastopol

Kerch

TURKEY

Black Sea

ITALY

Constantinople

Sinope

Gallipoli

Scutari

Erzerum

Kars

GREECE

Athens

TURKEY

Mediterranean Sea

Euphrates

Tigris

OTTOMAN    EMPIRE

Cairo

Nile

0          500 Miles

an accord. Stratford achieved such power in foreign affairs that he sometimes dominated the Turkish government.

Frustrated by his failure to convince the British to join him, as well as by Turkish intransigence, the tsar next sent Prince Alexander S. Menshikov to convince the Turks to accept a Russian protectorate over the holy cities, a role that singularly ill suited the acid-tongued elderly nobleman, who hated the Turks. The prince began his mission by intentionally ignoring Turkey's foreign minister, forcing this unfortunate to resign. He then profoundly insulted Turkish protocol by refusing to wear formal ambassadorial dress. His arrogance and sarcasm, laced with caustic jokes, quickly offended everyone else in the Turkish government and the sultan's court. The Turks also took offense because Menshikov delighted in following the tsar's orders to threaten war whenever the Turks proved difficult.

To counter Menshikov's unceasing threats, both France and Britain sent fleets to the Dardanelles. Tsar Nicholas then threatened to occupy the "Principalities" (of Moldavia and Wallachia, now Romania) if the Turks did not give in to Menshikov's demands. Convinced that British and French naval presence would deter the Russians, the Turks ignored the tsar's demand. To their surprise, on the July 3, 1853, Russian troops marched into the Turkish "Principalities" heading for the Danube River. This area was under something akin to joint rule. The Turks had governors there but no troops, yet received tribute from the populace, some 2.3 million people.

Russia's invasion was clearly provocative—Russia now claimed the tribute for itself—but no fighting was involved. Fearful that its important trade route down the Danube to the Black Sea would be endangered, Austria called a conference at Vienna attended by representatives from Britain, France, and Prussia, but not Turkey or Russia. The conference produced an agreement acceptable to all in attendance, but not to the absent Turks, who, following Stratford's advice, added some minor amendments to the note sent to them. The tsar rejected the mild Turkish changes, whereupon Turkey surprised most observers by issuing an ultimatum. When Russia did not respond by withdrawing its troops from the "Principalities," Turkey declared war on October 5, 1853, sending a formidable army of 90,000 men toward the Danube, and another less capable one of 75,000 east toward the Caucasus.

The reaction to Turkey's mobilization was decidedly mixed. Tsar Nicholas at first wavered, seemingly willing to accept the mediation that Austria proposed. Meanwhile, the French people had so little appetite for war that many French farmers and workers openly opposed it. But the British public grew ever more belligerent, encouraging the government to take a hard stand. They had not experienced war for some forty years, and many seemed to relish the prospect. While cables flew from one European capital to another, Russian forces were unable to advance against unexpectedly fierce Turkish resistance along the Danube. They were defeated in their one great offensive and then harried endlessly as the Turks extended the front inland for some 300 miles, before attacking all along it in small-scale raids that the Russians could not repulse. The tsar's armies fared somewhat better along the mountainous borderlands between Turkey and Russia. No quarter was given as wounded on both sides routinely received a bayonet thrust. At this early stage of the war, a Romanian photographer took over 300 photographs on both sides of the lines, but only one has survived, that of a gray-bearded Turkish irregular reclining next to a bare-breasted woman.[17] The atrocities committed by irregular Turkish troops were too terrible for anyone—then or now—to photograph.

In late November, heavy winds forced a small fleet of Turkish ships under sail for eastern Turkey to put into the Turkish Black Sea port of Sinope. What happened is still not entirely clear, but a larger Russian fleet from the soon-to-be embattled port city of Sevastopol had been tracking the Turks, and when the weather permitted, the Russians opened fire with their 720 long-range guns, destroying the now-becalmed Turks, whose mostly shorter-range guns could not effectively reach the Russian ships. As one Turkish ship after another burst into flames, the Russian ships moved in closer to fire grapeshot at Turkish sailors attempting to escape the flames by climbing the rigging. Most Turks fought ferociously only to die because when fire finally forced them to jump into the sea they could not swim. Between 2,700 and 3,000 Turks died, with only a handful of losses for the Russians. One Turkish ship, a steamer, managed to escape with a British naval officer on board who survived to tell the story.[18]

Tsar Nicholas exulted! After the tsar sent rapturous praise to his brave seamen for upholding the honor of "holy" Russia, St. Petersburg erupted into a frenzy of grand balls, festivals, light shows, and toast after toast while a re-creation of the battle, called "The Pageant of Sinope," played to a packed house.[19] The reaction in France and Britain was altogether different. Although Russia and Turkey were at war, and the doomed Turkish ships had been carrying reinforcements and supplies for Turkey's army, the British and French had warned Russia against attacking Turkish shipping. The French erupted in anger and the British expressed utter outrage. Branding the attack a "massacre," the British public demanded war. Lord Tennyson joined the chorus by calling for the "blood-red blossom of war," a welcome alternative, he added, to Britain's unending and unseemly lust for gold.[20] He would soon enough have occasion to celebrate the shedding of British blood when he memorialized the charge of the Light Brigade.

War involving Britain, France, and Russia now seemed unavoidable, but as telegrams passed between Europe's statesmen and St. Petersburg, and worried diplomats met in Vienna, France and Britain held back. They had no reason to fear that the tsar's armies would soon march into Constantinople, gaining him his long-dreamed-of access to the Mediterranean, because Turkish troops had stalemated the Russians in the east, and in the west the Turks had actually driven them back across the Danube after a series of brutal battles. The winter of 1853–1854 passed without action by France or Britain except to send some troops to stations in the Mediterranean. Meanwhile, Emperor Napoléon III took it upon himself to cable the tsar asking for peace but threatening terrible destruction if war should come. Nicholas responded with imperial indignation, promising to thrash the French in 1854 as his country had thrashed the first Bonaparte in 1812.[21] Still, nothing happened until March 1854, when, for no compelling reason, a joint Anglo-French ultimatum was sent to the tsar demanding that he withdraw entirely from the "Principalities." Nicholas did not deign to reply, and the drift toward war became a free fall. At the end of March, again for no compelling reason, Britain and France declared war.

The French people displayed little enthusiasm as troopships left Marseilles for Constantinople, but crowds in England went wild with joy as Britain's tall, magnificently uniformed Coldstream, Grenadier, and 1st Scots Fusilier Guards joined green- and scarlet-coated regiments "of the line," as most non-Guardsmen were known, in their march toward the ships that would take them to the glories of war.

Cheered on by their bands featuring fifes and drums, they sang "Annie Laurie" and "The Girl I Left Behind Me." While large crowds roared their approval, grateful pickpockets made a profit, and a good many prostitutes, who would suffer a dramatic loss of income after the soldiers' departure, looked on glumly. Queen Victoria observed that "the war was popular beyond belief," declaring that her soldiers would fight to protect all of Europe, then waved and bowed to them as they marched away to board waiting ships.[22] A few wives accompanied them, but most stayed behind to an uncertain fate without any hope of assistance from the government. One wife, determined not to be abandoned, marched alongside her husband in the 2nd Rifle Brigade, her hair cut short, in full green-jacketed uniform and shouldering a rifle.[23] No one stopped her.

When the troops arrived in Turkey, the British set up makeshift camps near Gallipoli, while the much better organized French camped in relative luxury nearby. British officers delightedly patronized a shop they discovered in Constantinople that sold Tennant's Pale Ale, Harvey's steak sauce, Stilton cheese, and Windsor soap, but the allies were horrified by the filth of Gallipoli, where garbage and dead dogs, cats, and rats lay everywhere underfoot. Even so, they were quite taken by what they described as large-breasted, heavily made-up, and thinly veiled Turkish women, who, they said, ogled them openly and giggled at the kilted Highlanders. Some had dyed their hair blond, a common practice among Turkish women. But the British soon learned a Turkish saying: "A blond for your eyes but an Egyptian for your pleasure"[24] (the "Egyptian" women in Turkey were black slaves from the Sudan, which was then a part of Egypt). It took no time at all for the men to be surrounded by Turkish boys offering to sell them anything—horses, sherbet, their sisters. The troops also encountered Greeks with lemonade, as well as Armenian prostitutes approvingly said to be capable of feats of "astonishing agility."[25] There were also Jewish money changers who walked among them, rattling coins in leather purses and shouting, "I say, John, change da monnish."[26] It was soon said, and not always with regret, that Turkey was a place where a soldier or sailor could get drunk for sixpence and syphilis for a shilling. In a short time, most of the French and British troops took advantage of both opportunities.

For some reason, the short, muscular Zouaves, originally Algerian tribesmen, but now mostly elite troops from France, hit it off with the tall, kilted 93rd Highlanders. Drunkenly reeling down the wretched streets arm in arm, groups of Zouaves and Highlanders happily sang "Auld Lang Syne" and "Mourir pour la Patrie" without understanding a word their new friends sang. While the revelry continued, it was so hot in Gallipoli that the pale British soldiers suffered badly from heatstroke and their horses became so miserable that cavalrymen swam them into the cool sea and rubbed their muzzles with vinegar. One officer successfully fried an egg on top of his patent-leather shako, commenting sourly, "We have wonderfully wise men at the head of our War Department."[27] A British surgeon described Gallipoli this way: "Of all the uncivilized, uncultivated, miserable places you have ever seen or heard of, I should think Gallipoli would surpass all. They seem to be at least three centuries behind any place I have ever seen."[28] As dreadful as the British found Gallipoli, they would soon experience very much worse.

While the allied armies languished in Turkey, the French and British navies bombarded Kamchatka in the Far East for little reason beyond a sense of revenge for Sinope, and with so little success that an embarrassed British admiral committed suicide. A British fleet also viciously blew up a good portion of the largely defenseless Russian Black Sea port city of Odessa, firing 4,000 explosive shells into it, many of them at nonmilitary targets. The British press avoided referring to this as a "massacre," like Sinope, but the French, who refused to take part, made it clear that they thought the attack excessive.[29]

The allied armies did not move until later in the summer, when they left the fleshpots of Gallipoli for the even greater filth and squalor of the Bulgarian Black Sea port city of Varna. While the French and British attempted to clean up Varna—the French with considerable success, the British with almost none at all—Tsar Nicholas I responded with undisguised rage when Austrian emperor Franz Josef I, whose hold over Hungary had been saved only by the intervention of Russian troops in 1849, moved 50,000 men to his border near the Russian troops invading Romania. After turning Franz Josef's portrait around to face his wall and cursing mightily at the "ingrate," as he called him, the tsar realized that he had no choice but to withdraw from Romania, the so-called Principalities. His troops recrossed the border on August 2, 1854. With this withdrawal, fighting stopped in the east as well. There appeared to be no reason for this senseless war to continue.

*French Zouaves. The Zouaves were originally native troops from Algeria, but by the time of the Crimean War, their ranks were almost entirely European, although their uniform was distinctly North African in appearance. (Photo courtesy of National Army Museum)*

While the French and British governments tried to decide what to do next, their troops in Varna began to die of cholera. Through August and into September, first the French (who believed that they had brought the deadly disease with them from Marseilles) and then the British died by the thousands in terrible agony. To escape the cholera (thought to be caused by the "miasma" around Varna) and also to punish Russia while salvaging British and French honor, the allied commanders finally decided to invade the Crimean Peninsula as their governments had earlier authorized them to do. They would seize the offending Russian naval base at Sevastopol that had launched the fleet responsible for the Sinope "massacre," destroy its forts and dockyards, then quickly withdraw.

The combined French and British armada consisted of no fewer than eight triple-decked battleships, twenty-two double-decked battleships, seven frigates, thirty paddle-driven warships, and several hundred troop transports. In all, there were over 60,000 troops and 35,000 sailors. So many of the ships were steam-driven that as the fleet sailed east toward Sevastopol, the sky literally turned black. Although the allies lacked maps of the Crimea, or any knowledge of its defenses or of the numbers of Russian troops there, they nevertheless forged ahead, managing to land some 30,000 French, 27,000 British, and 7,000 Turkish troops north of Sevastopol without Russian opposition. The sea voyage had actually improved the men's health, and the French and British navies succeeded in landing the troops and supplies despite rough surf. The atmosphere was almost festive as the British sailors ferrying the troops ashore gleefully teased the kilted Highlanders, yelling, "Come on, girls."[30]

A few days later, the war's first great battle took place at the Alma River north of Sevastopol. Over 33,000 Russian infantry, 3,400 cavalry, and some eighty-four guns waited on the heights south of the river. Ironically, Prince Menshikov, whose failed mission to Turkey had done much to start the war, was given command of the Russian forces. After several hours of preliminary sparring and delay, it took only ninety minutes for the allies to drive the Russians into full retreat, leaving some 6,000 of their men dead or dying behind them. The allies, who had attacked over open ground and across the shallow river before charging up a steep ridge, surprisingly had fewer than half as many casualties, almost all of them British. For a time, the Russian infantry fought hard, stopping the French attacks and actually driving some British regiments back before the British Guardsmen stormed into them, sending the battered Russians reeling back in full retreat. The Russians had learned painful lessons. The allies would fight bravely, and their new long-range rifles could cut down entire ranks of Russian soldiers long before the Russians' short-range muskets could return fire.

The Russians' retreat could easily have become a rout, but the allied commanders did not pursue them. Some of the Russians reached the dubious safety of Sevastopol, but the majority of Menshikov's broken army took up positions well to the east of the city. Instead of

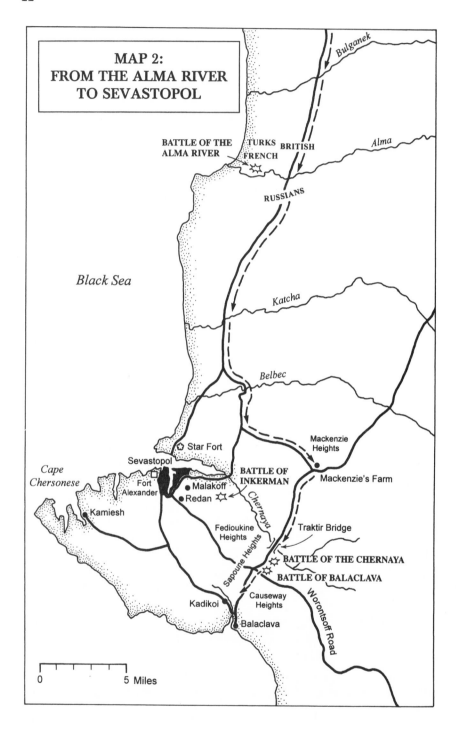

MAP 2:
FROM THE ALMA RIVER
TO SEVASTOPOL

*Bulganek*

*Alma*

BATTLE OF THE
ALMA RIVER
TURKS BRITISH
FRENCH
RUSSIANS

*Black Sea*

*Katcha*

*Belbec*

Mackenzie
Heights

Star Fort

Sevastopol

*Cape Chersonese*

Fort Alexander
Malakoff
Redan
BATTLE OF
INKERMAN

Mackenzie's Farm

*Chernaya*

Kamiesh

Fedioukine
Heights

Traktir Bridge

Sapoune Heights

BATTLE OF THE CHERNAYA

BATTLE OF BALACLAVA

Kadikoi

Causeway
Heights

Worontsoff Road

Balaclava

0            5 Miles

attacking the city from the north, where only a few undermanned fortifications stood in the way, the allies next marched around the city to the east and prepared to attack it from the south. It was a clumsy maneuver across unknown territory, and the long allied columns were dangerously exposed to Russian attack, but Menshikov did nothing and the allies safely took up positions to the south of Sevastopol.

Because the southern approaches to the port city were completely unfortified, it appeared to many British officers that they could walk into Sevastopol without opposition. But instead of agreeing to launch an immediate attack that the Russians later said they could not have resisted, the French commander developed second thoughts. He decided that he could not ask his battle-shy troops to attack a "fortress," and he chose instead to besiege the city. The French on the west and the British to the east dug trenches and slowly brought up their heavy artillery, and a siege began. The British took possession of the small harbor of Balaclava to the south of Sevastopol, while the French occupied two larger harbors to the west. Amazed by a three-week reprieve from attack but immensely grateful for it, Russian men, women, and children worked around the clock to build fortifications designed by a talented, and soon-to-be-famous, young engineer, Colonel Franz Eduard Ivanovich Todleben. This was September 1854. Sevastopol would not fall until a full year of almost unimaginable suffering had passed.

The second major battle of the war took place on October 25, 1854, before extreme winter weather had set in. By now, the Russians had been reinforced sufficiently that Menshikov believed he might be able to drive the British off the heights above the harbor of Balaclava before the French, several hours' march away to the west, could come to their support. The battle began with infantry skirmishes on a misty, foggy morning and ended with several memorable cavalry charges. First, the British Heavy Brigade of large men on huge horses charged into the flank of a much larger mass of Russian cavalrymen, driving them into retreat. For some minutes, the two sides were so closely packed together that men could not even swing their swords. They glowered at each other as they tried to free their sword arms while their powerful horses pushed and snorted. Still, some men eventually broke free, and their heavy swords inflicted monstrous wounds. Had the British Light Brigade pursued the retreating Russians, a great victory might have been won, but its commander, the ludicrous James Thomas Brudenell, Lord Cardigan, mistakenly believed himself under orders not to do so.

Soon after, Cardigan did receive an order to lead the Light Brigade in a charge that took it down a valley directly into the fire of a mass of Russian artillery while more Russian batteries fired into the horsemen from heights on each side of the valley. Tennyson made "The Charge of the Light Brigade" familiar to most English-speaking schoolchildren from then on, but despite the magnificent valor of the British cavalry, the suicidal charge accomplished little except to convince the Russians—and the French as well—that the British were quite mad.

The carnage would have been even worse had it not been for a gallant charge by French cavalry that destroyed some of the Russian artillery. Earlier in the day, thousands of Russian cavalrymen had charged toward the kilted and tartaned 93rd Highland Regiment, who, after promising General Colin Campbell to die where they stood rather than retreat, resolutely stood firing into the Russian ranks. The Russians shied away, then retreated. One surviving Russian officer later said that the men would have fought on but their horses became uncontrollable under the Scottish rifle fire, much of which went high or the Russians would have suffered even more. *The Times* correspondent, W. H. "Billy" Russell, was so impressed by the Highlanders that he described them as "the thin red streak." It was not until 1872 that this phrase was changed to the now-famous "thin red line."[31]

It may be true, as Soviet historians later insisted, that the battle of Balaclava was only a reconnaissance in force, not an all-out attack. If so, it was a large and bloody reconnaissance, and it failed to provide the Russians with the information they sought: On the next day, they carried out another, smaller reconnaissance attack against the rugged, ravine-cut terrain around Inkerman Heights, also on the British right flank. This probe set the stage for the largest and most deadly battle of the war. Menshikov had been reinforced again, this time by over 22,000 men who had returned from the "Principalities" under the command of Prince Mikhayl Dmitreyevich Gorchakov. Menshikov proposed to attack the thinly held British lines along the allied right flank with 35,000 men while Gorchakov would wait in close reserve ready to exploit any opening that appeared among the British, who were outnumbered by over six to one. It would be several hours before the French infantry could march to their relief, if they could do so at all.

The attack began at dawn November 5, in such heavy fog that the Russians fell upon the startled British before the British could see them. An entire day of brutal hand-to-hand combat followed, over which no senior officer had any control whatever. Junior officers and sergeants gathered small numbers of men who fought with bayonets, swung rifles like clubs, and when they ran out of ammunition, threw rocks. After the battle, dead men lay with their faces battered into jelly by rifle butts, the faces of those bayoneted contorted in great agony. The relentless Russian attacks had torn many huge holes in the completely unfortified British lines, but a sergeant or lieutenant would always rally a few men to rush into the gap. A British lieutenant, seen holding off several Russians with his sword, was later found dead with nine major wounds in his body. Soon after, when a British sergeant saw the 41st Regiment's "colour" (battle flag) go down, he grabbed it, but a Russian seized the other end and a deadly tug of war followed until another British soldier bayoneted the Russian.[32] Occasionally a lost battalion would appear out of the fog and mist to fire a killing volley before once again disappearing from view.

The Russians fought savagely, howling and screaming all the while, but they lacked the initiative shown time and again by the British. When fast-moving and hard-fighting French troops arrived in mid-afternoon, the battle was won. The French role proved crucial, as time and again they charged Russian forces just as it appeared they would win a decisive victory. As told by Zouave Colonel de Wimpffen, two Zouave battalions, one made up of Algerians and former African slaves, attacked. Led by six "enormous Africans" de Wimpffen's men threw themselves at the Russians in horrific hand-to-hand combat. The colonel's horse had been shot out from under him, and his men feared him killed. When they found him alive, one African said, "You are a wizard, God protects you." "Yes, my children [the standard affectionate term used by a senior French officer to his men], I am a person with supernatural power because I love you." One of the Africans kissed the colonel's hand, saying that God willing, it would always be so.[33]

Throughout the long day, Gorchakov's 22,000 men inexplicably made no move to advance. To be sure, poor visibility and the rocky ravines and steep cliffs of the battlefield made cavalry scouting ineffective, but had Gorchakov thrown his men against the British at any place along the line in the morning, he would certainly have broken through. Whether the French could have moved east rapidly enough and with sufficient strength to contain him is not at all certain. Perhaps their late-arriving infantry and cavalry would have defeated him, but he very likely would have decimated the British before they arrived. When the battle ended, Menshikov had lost over 12,000 men; Gorchakov had lost only 15 men to stray cannon fire. The British had lost over 2,500, and the French less than half that number. The British Guards regiments had borne the greatest casualties, losing 40 percent of their numbers, most of them in face-to-face combat as the tall guardsmen, made to seem even taller by their black bearskin busbies, clashed with the smaller, flat-hatted Russians, whom the British called "muffin-caps."[34] It was as heroic a battle as British troops have ever fought.

Soon after the battle of Inkerman, winter began suddenly with freezing rain and hurricane-force winds that demolished the allied camps and sank twenty-one major ships, many of them filled with essential supplies. The weather that followed was the coldest in memory. The Russians in Sevastopol were relatively well fed and housed, having adequate winter clothing, but those camped outside the city suffered dreadfully. The French were warmly clothed, well tented, and relatively well fed, but the British, who had no winter clothing, their tents in tatters, were so poorly provisioned that horses and men alike froze to death, some starved, and nearly all fell ill. In addition to deadly typhus and dysentery, cholera swept through the British ranks killing or debilitating so many that some entire regiments could muster only a handful of men fit for duty. Had the Russians attacked in earnest that winter, the decimated British lines could not possibly have held. But there was no attack. Except for small-scale but deadly raids, the winter passed without battle, and by the following spring, British reinforcements had arrived, equipped with by then unnecessary winter clothing and provisions galore. From this point on, the British forces grew in strength, and their health improved enormously. For the French, the opposite took place. Their once-impressive supplies and health deteriorated gravely.

Shortly after the allied landing near Sevastopol, the Turkish commander, Omer Pasha, with 20,000 Turkish troops and a few hundred French marines, landed some sixty miles north at Yevpatoria, a town of 26,000 people, many large windmills, and a substantial Jewish cemetery.[35] The mayor of Yevpatoria insisted that the troops be quarantined for a week before entering his town, but needless to say, the allies ignored him. The presence of this force greatly worried the Russians because it posed the threat of marching northeast to cut the Crimea's narrow land bridge to Russia and potentially starving Menshikov's army into submission. In February 1855, during the record cold of that winter, a Russian army attacked Yevpatoria, but the Turkish defenders, aided by a number of British and French officers, drove the Russians away, causing them heavy losses. Soon after hearing the news of this defeat, Tsar Nicholas I died—of despair many said. His son, Alexander II, chose to continue the war.

From that point on, the Russians attempted little offensive action, but their artillery dueled the allies in the heaviest exchanges of shell fire the world had ever seen. The French took the lead in continuously bombarding Sevastopol and tunneling ever closer to its fortifications. The British and French also launched several attacks against the now formidable fortress but were beaten back again and again with heavy losses. In August 1855, the pressure on Sevastopol had grown so great that the Russian commander was ordered by St. Petersburg to take the offensive. Knowing that an attack would be folly, he delayed as long as he could before finally ordering 25,000 Russians to attack the French and 17,500 newly arrived Sardinians. After a full day of fighting, the Russians were forced to withdraw, leaving over 8,000 dead and wounded on the battlefield. The French lost just under 1,500 and the Sardinians only 250.[36]

Earlier, a combined French, British, and Turkish expedition had destroyed the largely undefended eastern Crimean city of Kerch, devastating a number of palaces owned by Russian nobles, and disrupting Russian supply routes to Sevastopol. This and other campaigns away from Sevastopol have been regarded by many historians as sideshows of the main war effort to capture that city, but one of these unsung actions may have been the most crucial of the war.[37] A joint British and French fleet carrying some 10,000 soldiers and marines moved into the Baltic at the very start of the war. After some largely unsuccessful bombardments of coastal ports in Russia and Finland and the capture of an unfinished fort, Russia's great naval base at Kronstadt outside St. Petersburg became the target of largely ineffectual shelling.[38] Little damage was done, but Tsar Nicholas I had become so alarmed by the threat to his capital that he stationed 300,000 of his best troops, including his Guards regiments, in this region, where they remained throughout the war. Because the British and French steam-powered warships proved so superior to the Russian sailing ships, Russia's navy could do nothing to intervene. Because of the threat of Austrian belligerency and Polish insurrection, another 300,000 Russian troops remained in that region, too. Had any significant number of these more than one-half million men been available in the Crimea, they could have made a decisive difference.

After a series of failed assaults on Sevastopol later in 1855, during one of which young and poorly trained British troops broke under fire, the French finally captured a key fortress, and the Russians skillfully evacuated the city. The French assault was not without a terrible price. In addition to some 9,000 soldiers who fell in the assault, the French lost 5 generals, 8 colonels, and 823 other officers. Soon after, the starving Turkish garrison of the fortress of Kars surrendered. A large Russian force had besieged a smaller Turkish army led by a handful of British officers at Kars, a hastily fortified city in the mountains of eastern Turkey. Near-starvation finally forced the Turks to surrender, but they had fought, according to a British captain, "almost like fiends; I never saw such desperate recklessness of life."[39] In one attempt to take Kars, the Russians lost over 10,000 men. The Turks' role in this war has seldom been adequately acknowledged by the French or the British, who had made it *their* war.

The fall of Sevastopol ended the major fighting. For the warring countries and world opinion, Sevastopol was the key to victory; soon after its surrender, Austrian threats to enter the conflict, probably to be joined by Sweden and perhaps Norway, led Russia to negotiate, and peace followed.[40] Just as the belligerents had aimlessly meandered into the war, now they drifted toward peace. After long discussions, a French-, British-, and Austrian-dominated peace conference in Paris produced a treaty in March 1856. The Black Sea became demilitarized, Russian dominance in eastern Europe would end, and all the European powers guaranteed the independence and integrity of the Ottoman Empire.[41] Turkey was left deeply in debt to France and Britain, but the peace treaty meant having twenty years of breathing room before another war with Russia began the final collapse of the Ottoman Empire.[42]

Russia gained an advantage in the Caucasus and the Far East, but Russia's defeat—as the peace treaty was seen in Russia and everywhere else—freed Europe from the specter of Russian expansion. As a result, the Austro-Hungarian Empire grew in strength, and both Germany and Italy were unified. In Russia, the recognition by the tsar and many nobles that a serf-dominated economy was too inefficient to compete with the West led to radical reform. Because the ignorant and apathetic serfs neither could nor would adapt their ways to the needs of modern agriculture and industry, the tsar chose to emancipate them in a search for modernization.[43] Despite the misery of French troops as the war dragged on, France emerged from the conflict as the leading power in Europe, and Britain still ruled the seas as well as the world's greatest empire.

Few accounts of the Crimean War mention the involvement of the United States, but American interest in the war was intense. Major newspapers throughout the country carried hundreds of articles about the generals involved, the details of the battles, and the war's diplomatic implications for the United States. Following the spirit of the Monroe Doctrine, the Pierce administration was openly expansionist, extending its influence as far south as possible. Public opinion was strongly favorable as this editorial in the *Philadelphia Public Ledger*, shortly after Pierce's inauguration, makes all too plain: "America is bounded on the East by sunrise, West by sunset, North by the Arctic Expedition, and South as far as we darn please."[44] America's aggressive trade policies, especially in South America, and her disputes about fishing rights off Canada had created tension with Britain, as had her attempts to purchase Cuba. Fueled by the animosity of nearly 2 million Irish immigrants driven overseas by famine in Ireland, as well as by fears that France and Britain would intervene to weaken U.S. influence in Central America, newspapers in the United States began to take Russia's side. America's war of expansion against Mexico a few years earlier had so troubled the French and other European governments that they had criticized U.S. aggression, hardening American attitudes toward them as well.

As soon as the Crimean War broke out, the legendary American colonel Sam Colt traveled to Moscow to sell his "Colt" revolvers and rifles; he was followed by other arms merchants. Fifteen American mechanics also arrived to help with Russian railroad development. The U.S. minister to Russia, Thomas Seymour, such an admirer of Tsar Nicholas I that he declared him to be "perfectly irresistible," openly championed the Russian cause.[45] Others seemed to agree. Thirty American surgeons (twenty of whom had been trained in Paris) volunteered to go to Sevastopol, where they were welcomed enthusiastically; half of them would die of disease before the war ended. Three hundred Kentucky riflemen actually asked U.S. government permission to fight for Russia in the Crimea, but despite Seymour's urgings, permission was not granted.[46] Russia expressed its gratitude in many ways, including approval of the annexation of Hawaii by the United States and support for the Union during the American Civil War. Perhaps most important, Russia first leased, then later sold, Alaska to the United States rather than risk its seizure by Britain.[47] And in 1856, the United States played on Japanese fears of a military takeover by either Russia or Britain to convince Japan to extend favored trade status to America and to accept U.S. "tutelage."[48]

As the Crimean War wore on, the British Government complained in ever more strident terms about U.S. military aid to Russia. British attempts to recruit Americans as mercenaries added to the tension. So intense did the hostility become that James Buchanan, U.S. minister to Great Britain, accused Britain of preparing for war against America. In return, Britain sent large naval forces to the West Indies and troops to Bermuda and Canada, and war fever in Britain became so heated near the conclusion of the Crimean War that British officers serving in the trenches outside Sevastopol heard repeated rumors of war with the United States.[49] Britain cooled down the crisis, and conflict was averted. America benefited from its Crimean War diplomacy, but despite popular fascination with its battles, as described in the press, the American Civil War would prove that little had been learned about the nature of modern combat.

This brief introduction to the background of the war, its causes and consequences, and the major events of the conflict itself cannot hope to bring to life the men and women who took part in these events, nor can it explain what they actually experienced. But this overview is necessary to set the stage for what follows. This was a time of great heroism, ghastly brutality, and hideous suffering—all taking place in an era when the search for glory in war was commonplace. No one today can hope fully to recapture the experiences of these very different kinds of people as they marched, camped, played, hungered, fought, suffered, sacrificed, endured, sometimes triumphed, and often died. Using their own words as often as possible, I describe how their inept leaders failed them again and again; how they were ravaged by cold, hunger, and disease; how women and children became unseen heroes; how the universally despised Turks fought their own war; and, finally, why so many fought so bravely. To better explain these people, I will compare their experiences with those of Northerners and Southerners during the American Civil War, which erupted only five years after the Crimean War ended. First, let us meet the five armies that took part in this tragic Victorian drama as well as those that fought for and against the American Union.

# 2

# THE ARMIES

## *Men Ready for War?*

THE TURKISH-LED OTTOMAN EMPIRE that Britain and France decided to defend in 1853 reflected little more than a faded image of its former grandeur, but it still had direct rule or great influence over such cities as Algiers, Baghdad, Belgrade, Bucharest, Cairo, Damascus, Jerusalem, and Sophia. Athens had been part of the empire until 1830. Although the Sublime Porte, as the Ottoman Empire's seat of government in Constantinople was grandly known, had only tenuous control over some parts of its domain (most of Greece was now independent, and Hungary was under Austrian dominion), the empire still included portions of what is now the Ukraine, Georgia, Armenia, and southern Russia in addition to territory that eventually became modern nations such as Aden, Albania, Bulgaria, Cyprus, Egypt, Iraq, Israel, Jordan, Kuwait, Lebanon, Libya, Romania, Sudan, Tunisia, Turkey, and Yemen, as well as the currently embattled states that made up the former Yugoslavia. It also contained six of the seven so-called wonders of the world. The devoutly Muslim Turkish rulers of the empire protected many Jews and 13 million Christians, although as second-class citizens. At its zenith in the middle of the sixteenth century, the Ottoman capital, Constantinople (now Istanbul), was the largest city in Europe, with 700,000 inhabitants from all over the empire. It was also the wealthiest city in Europe, and many foreigners thought it the most beautiful.

In some parts of the Ottoman Empire, ethnic Turkish troops maintained order with brutal severity, whereas in others, local forces kept order with little influence from Constantinople. Some areas, like Kurdistan, seldom acknowledged Turkish rule at all. Despite the Sublime Porte's weak hold over much of the empire, wagons and ships carried tribute to the theoretically all-powerful sultan from all reaches of his dominion and in every form imaginable: money, rare gems, precious minerals, hides, furs, wild animals, succulent fruits, coffee, spices, tobacco, leather gloves, and weapons. As this cornucopia of riches arrived in Constantinople, the sultan and his senior government officials redistributed it to a host of pashas, beys, emirs, imams, and powerful landowners, especially the grand vizier, the head of the Porte and second in power only to the sultan. These riches paid for the mosques and minarets whose blue domes shone brilliantly on the city's seven hills and for the increasing number of palaces that lined the shore along the Sea of Marmora. Huge sums of money also created colleges, libraries, hospitals, and hundreds of elegant public baths. The city's thousands of shops sold everything available in the West and some things that were not, such as toys, animals, and children to be used for men's sexual pleasure.

Constantinople boasted magnificent stands of dark green cypresses and fruit trees as well as grand parks and gardens tastefully planted with roses and tulips. The city's clean streets hosted what appeared to visitors to be all the peoples of the world: Jews, Greeks, Arabs, Bulgarians, African slaves, Armenians, Poles, Egyptians, Hungarians, Tatars on horseback, and many Turks, including a wealthy pasha whose tame lion followed him about the streets of Constantinople like a pet dog. The city imported snow in vast amounts during the winter so that it could be stored in cool cellars to chill the sherbet that the Turks so loved all year round. In the 1520s, Sultan Suleiman I, called the Magnificent, abstemious by later standards, ate sumptuous fifty-course dinners on jewel-encrusted silver plates prepared by a dozen chefs in five large kitchens and served by 200 attendants. He drank his wine from a goblet cut from a single piece of turquoise. The sultans who succeeded Suleiman turned eating into an even greater parody of gluttony, making the culinary practices of European monarchs appear dietetic by comparison.[1]

This wealth and excess resulted from armed conquest by Turkish armies. From the late 1400s to the end of the seventeenth century, Turkish forces dominated their enemies in battle after battle. In 1524, when the Turks defeated the Hungarians, they massacred over 200,000 people and took 100,000 prisoners back to Constantinople.[2] Turkish cavalry, aided by their audacious Tatar allies, proved superior to anything that could be brought against them. Their hollow steel-tipped arrows could penetrate the best armor at 100 yards, and their muskets outranged those of their enemies. Turkish field artillery, pulled by racing camels rather than the plodding oxen used by the Turks' enemies, was the most mobile and powerful in the world, and Turkish siege guns were the world's largest. When the Turks took Constantinople in the mid-fifteenth century, they used cannons with a thirty-inch bore that fired a 1,600-pound ball. It took sixty oxen and 200 men to move a single cannon.[3] Turkish engineers became the best in the world at digging tunnels under enemy fortifications before blowing them up. The sturdy peasant infantry fought with religious zeal against the Christian infidels (and other Muslims, for that matter), and they had great loyalty to their leaders.

This was especially true of the Janissaries, an elite corps of men who formed the equivalent of an imperial guard. The corps consisted of promising Christian boys from conquered Balkan provinces, forcibly sent off to Muslim schools, where they were taught to forget their families and Christianity, to embrace Islam, to swear themselves celibate so that their only loyalty would be to the sultan, and to fight like devils. By the mid-1600s, over 50,000 Janissaries lived as homosexuals under absolute military discipline.[4] Like the Janissaries, ethnic Turks became renowned throughout Europe and the Middle East for their love of war. The fifteenth-century Greek document *Tractatus* said, "They come together for war as though they had been invited to a wedding."[5] But the Janissaries, in their magnificent white felt hats adorned by bird-of-paradise flowers, could outmarch and outfight any troops that dared to oppose them, even the Turks themselves.

Virtually every Turkish household in Constantinople, including those with only modest means, had at least one African slave to do its cleaning and cooking, and families with greater wealth purchased more slaves, including both men and women for their harems. The sultan's harem was a virtual city in itself. Enclosed by high walls, it could be entered only through a single passageway blocked by four locked iron and bronze doors, each one guarded at all times by armed African eunuchs who had the only keys. Inside these gates lay beautiful gardens, fountains, and pools surrounding luxurious apartments where some 300 concubines spent their lives. Usually captured as mere girls, each learned the arts of sensuality from the older women until the day might finally come when the sultan would select the young woman to join him in his royal apartment for a night of passion. Sultans often kept boys for homosexual pleasures, but there were many more female than male concubines. Most of these young women never visited the sultan, spending their lives instead in rollicking lesbian relationships.[6]

Blond and blue-eyed slave girls proved especially desirable and many were captured by Crimean Tatar horsemen, who regularly raided the Ukraine and the Caucasus. The descendants of the Mongol horsemen who burned and sacked Moscow in 1382 and 1571, these Tatars sometimes returned with 20,000 captives at a time. Many thousands of captive Russian men spent their lives chained to the oars of Turkish galleys; the Russian women became household servants or, if comely enough, concubines.

A concubine who bore the sultan a son could achieve great influence, although she might also suffer terrible loss if her son became involved in a losing battle over the succession. Eunuchs who had had their tongues cut out and their eardrums pierced to ensure confidentiality, strangled the losers of such battles with a silken cord.

The love of Sultan Suleiman the Magnificent for one of the Russian slave women planted seeds of discord and villainy that slowly eroded the power of the empire. A Georgian captive, red-haired and blue-eyed, so charmed the sultan that when she bore him a son nine months after their first amorous encounter, he not only married her but also astonished everyone by remaining utterly faithful to her for the rest of his life. She, however, coveted power for herself and her son, Selim. After intrigues that would have embarrassed Machiavelli, she succeeded in bringing her son to the throne, but her legacy of strangled opponents and broken promises so corrupted palace life that the empire would never be the same.

The first ten Ottoman sultans built an empire of perhaps 30 million people, speaking over twenty languages, by personally leading their armies to victory. They could be cruel, as their soldiers certainly demonstrated, but many were also gifted statesmen, poets, artists, architects, and scholars. With the death of Suleiman I in 1566, everything changed. To give her son, Selim, time to arrive in Constantinople from Asia Minor, Suleiman's Georgian wife had the physician who knew about his death strangled and then had Suleiman propped up, his eyes open, cheeks reddened, and hair dyed, while the business of the empire went on as before, his courtiers and servants keeping everyone else at a respectful distance.[7] When Selim arrived many days later to be installed as sultan, he immediately took to strong drink, despite the Koran, and because he was almost always drunk, de facto power soon passed to the grand vizier, who became a very able administrator.

Selim and the succeeding twenty-four sultans proved almost entirely incapable of ruling. They devoted themselves to alcohol, sex, food, and every form of self-indulgence, but after Suleiman's ill-starred marriage, no sultan ever again married. One sultan spent most of his days tossing gold coins to the fish in the Bosporus, and he was so enamored of fur that he covered the walls of his royal apartment with sable, perhaps the most expensive wallpaper in history. Attracted to very large women, he sent sleuths to find the most enormous woman in the entire empire. When they returned with an Armenian woman so immense she had to be carried in a cart, he was overjoyed. After he had gratified his sexual desires, something which must have required both ingenuity and caution, he gave her jewels and honors, eventually naming this gargantuan lady the governor-general of Damascus.[8]

The Ottoman Empire declined not solely as a result of the vice, indolence, and lack of interest of the sultans or the endless intrigues in the harems. Power was gradually usurped by newly wealthy bankers, merchants, and landowners—some of whom ignored the Porte altogether while making independent arrangements with foreign governments. Also, Turkey's small government, with only about 1,200 employees, did nothing for its citizens' health, welfare, education, or housing. It did not even maintain roads or bridges, and its great mineral wealth lay largely untapped. The government also became increasingly corrupt and inefficient.[9] Although officials stood exempt from taxation, the peasants paid heavy taxes; however, only about 3 percent of these tax revenues ever made it past greedy local landowners and government officials to reach the imperial treasury.[10] While European countries and Russia grew in economic and military strength, the Ottoman leaders allowed their empire to fall further behind. What is more, largely because of the widespread practice of abortion, the Turkish population declined. Internally, opposition to Ottoman rule grew so alarmingly that in 1831, an Albanian tobacco dealer who had taken the name of Mehmet Ali and become pasha of Egypt rebelled against Ottoman rule and even threatened to march on Constantinople. British intervention helped to defeat him.[11]

In 1839, two years after the coronation of Queen Victoria in Britain, Abdülmecid I became sultan at the age of sixteen. Because his mother, an uneducated country girl and former harem bath attendant, believed that drunkenness had caused his father's death and could threaten his life as well, she ordered that the royal stocks of liquor be destroyed. She had over 50,000 bottles of fine wine, champagne, and liquor smashed against city walls and all the sultan's decanters and glasses thrown into the Bosporus. To further ensure her son's abstinence from alcohol, she paraded lines of beautiful young concubines before him, urging him to concentrate his energies on them rather than the bottle. The frail young man did so with such enthusiasm that he became at least temporarily impotent. He then acquired a large new supply of fine liquor.[12]

Although Sultan Abdülmecid did remove the arbitrary power of pashas to execute anyone who offended them, he had no interest at all in the business of governing the empire and frankly found the daily doings of government bureaucrats annoying. To escape these tedious affairs of state, he decided to build himself a palace several miles away on the banks of the Bosporus. He gave his architect unlimited funds to carry out his order that the new palace must surpass all others on earth. The result was a half-mile-long marble terrace along the river with a throne room fifty yards long, made to seem even larger by the world's largest mirrors. It also contained the world's largest ballroom, featuring a four-ton chandelier, as well as 300 elegant rooms, including 25 magnificent salons. In all, fourteen tons of gold leaf went into this palace's decoration, much of it in the sultan's mother's immense bedroom. The sultan's bed was made of solid silver, and his bathtub and basin of transparent alabaster with silver water taps in the shape of swans, fed by hot water from a hidden copper boiler.[13] While stunned visitors from around the world gaped at the sultan's rococo marble monument to himself (and, some said, to bad taste) and luxuriated in the nightly feasting and entertainment, the empire declined ever further into apathy and weakness. The sultan himself spent many of his days doing nothing but smoking and eating raw cucumbers while a host of retainers watched intently for any sign that he might wish something.

Most of his ministers became equally indolent, but a few younger men attempted, largely in vain, to reform the empire's military and to curb corruption in government. Turkey had lost the Crimea to Russia in the war of 1774, and after five years of fighting from 1787 to 1792, Turkey's forces failed to reclaim the area. Beginning in 1794, the Turkish army had been reorganized along French and Russian lines. The Janissaries, who had by then become highly privileged but no longer efficiently warlike or politically reliable, resisted these changes until 1826, when Turkish artillery bombarded their barracks, killing over 10,000 men before the entire corps was disarmed and disbanded by ethnic Turkish troops.[14] During the following year, the Turks founded a modern military medical school, sending many students to Europe to learn the necessary skills. Despite this training and the creation of a military academy in 1834, when war broke out in 1853, many senior Turkish officers remained illiterate, and they detested better-educated junior officers.

These reforms were both well intended and rationally designed, but without enough money or dedicated officials to carry them out adequately, they had little effect. Not only had the sultan denuded the treasury to build his gigantic pleasure palace, but the government had also decided to debase the coinage to finance its budget deficit. The result was rampant inflation that caused the value of the Ottoman piastre to fall by almost 500 percent. Because most Turkish government officials lived on fixed salaries, their corrupt practices quickly took on a new urgency. The Turkish military found itself shortchanged by everyone, including its own officers, who pocketed every stray piastre they could. Among other things, they needed the money to bribe their superiors for promotions. Foreign observers unanimously declared all but a handful of Turkish officers worse than useless. Most of these men not only did nothing to lead their men but also often proved cowardly as well as corrupt, greedy, lazy, and ignorant. Quite commonly during the Crimean War, two or three junior officers from Britain, Hungary, or Poland would usurp

command over large Turkish forces, being obeyed enthusiastically
when seen to be brave, forceful, and knowledgeable about tactics.

Fortunately for the Turks, large numbers of foreign military officers offered their services to them. Hungarians, Italians, and Poles
who had fled their homelands after bloody repression by the Austrians and the Russians joined officers from the French, and especially
the British, armies in commanding Turkish units. Many were soldiers of fortune, but fine leaders nonetheless. An example was a
huge Italian who led his Turkish soldiers by waving his saber overhead after loudly letting it be known that he had earlier killed seven
Austrian "dogs" with it when Italy had fought for reunification a
few years earlier.[15] A few Americans volunteered as well, and two
distinguished themselves.

The Turkish commander in the Crimean War, Omer Pasha, a
Croatian-born, French-speaking former Austrian army lieutenant
named Michael Lattas, had converted to Islam and married a
wealthy, socially powerful Turkish heiress. His social connections
certainly did not hamper his career, but Omer Pasha achieved his position of command less through favoritism than as a result of his
ability. A medium-sized man of about fifty with graying hair, he rode
well, planned prudently, and led by example. Omer Pasha usually
dressed very plainly, but on ceremonial occasions, the extravagance
of his appearance baffled description. He wore so much gold braid
that none of the cloth on his uniform was visible. His fez sported a
solid gold badge, and his stirrups were gold as well. The hilt of his
sword was covered by diamonds.[16] He also allowed himself a luxury
or two. He ate very well and traveled with his personal brass band
of German musicians, which frequently played selections from
Verdi's new opera, *Il Trovatore*.[17] He was also rarely without a fair-
sized harem, which he kept in a large tent and always well guarded
by African eunuchs.[18] For most of the war, he led capably, if cautiously, but his last campaign proved tragically inept.

The only thing uniform about 220,000 men in the ragtag Turkish
army was their red-felt fezzes, adopted from conquered Moroccan
soldiers centuries earlier.[19] The army consisted primarily of infantry,
organized into regiments whose quality varied tremendously. Ethnic
Turks from Anatolia were physically powerful, loyal men, as hardy
and brave as any troops anywhere. To be sure, most of them carried
short-ranged smoothbore muskets rather than the recently invented

*Omer Pasha (1806–1871). A Croatian convert to Islam,*
*Omer Pasha was commander of the Turkish army.*
*(Photo courtesy of the National Army Museum)*

long-range rifles then used by most European armies, but even those who had been conscripted by force, as many peasants were, fought bravely when well led. Even the best Turkish regiments had little, if any, transport and virtually no commissariat. As a result, they lived off the land when they could and often went hungry.

*A Turkish officer and soldiers in dress uniforms.*
*(Photo courtesy of the National Army Museum)*

A British observer who accompanied the Turkish army throughout its campaign against the Russians in Romania during the opening stages of the war was suitably impressed:

> A Turk is every inch a soldier; eats whatever is given him, obeys without a murmur, works like a horse, marches till he drops, draws his own water, cuts his own wood. . . . The fact is, that the Turks have all the leading military virtues in a greater degree, I firmly believe, than any people in the world; and if officered as they ought to be, and armed as they ought to be, might once again make Europe tremble.[20]

However, many "Turkish" units were made up of Armenians, Tunisians, Romanians, Egyptians (including many Africans from the

Sudan), and other conquered minorities who hated the Turks and looked for the first opportunity to desert. When caught, deserters were savagely flogged on the soles of their feet, then on their buttocks and, if they were still alive, on their bellies. Most men died half-way through this ordeal and only one man was known to have lived through all of it.[21] Others tried to avoid conscription by cutting off their trigger fingers or blinding one eye; they were taken anyway and used in noncombat roles.[22] However, many ethnic Turks pleaded for a chance to fight the infidel Russians, volunteering by the thousands when the war began. Cries of *jihad* (holy war) rose in many parts of Turkey.[23]

Only a few contingents from conquered areas wore smart uniforms. The African-Egyptian troops from the Sudan wore white trousers and bright green jackets. They did not march very well, but they were clean, at least initially. But European observers complained about the dingy, dark blue uniforms of most Turkish troops, their slouching posture, and their conspicuous lack of activity. Unlike off-duty Russian, French, or British soldiers—always singing, laughing, or playing tricks on one another—the Turks seemingly did little but sit and smoke or sleep. Sometimes they played dominoes, but they seldom sang, and even when they sang about their victories in battle, they did so in a minor key that made their voices seem harsh and monotonous to Europeans.[24] Like the pashas who led them, Turkish soldiers often startled their European allies by walking hand in hand, but unlike their leaders, almost all of whom devoted themselves to debauchery, many seemed touchingly innocent. A British observer in Constantinople wrote about the sight of two Turkish soldiers, hand in hand, staring in undisguised horror at a naked doll in a store window.[25]

Turkish cavalry, although paid more regularly than the infantry, in combat proved similarly uneven in quality. Some well-equipped regular army cavalry units, well led by a Pole named Skender Bey, fought with valor and discipline, but they were few in number. Other cavalry units proved almost useless, with their small, old horses; short, dull sabers; nonfunctioning carbines; clumsy lances; tattered saddles; ragged uniforms; and rusty spurs—all this before they had done any campaigning. They had recently adopted the Prussian style of riding, sitting bolt upright with their toes barely touching their stirrups, but they had yet to master it or Prussian cav-

*Turkish irregular cavalry known as Bashi-Bazouks.*
*(Photo courtesy of the National Army Museum)*

alry tactics.[26] Even less effective as a military force was the Turkish irregular cavalry, the notorious Bashi-Bazouks (meaning "spoiled head" in Turkish, because they possessed no military discipline at all). Recruited in time of need by local leaders, this murderous rabble of Kurds, Albanians, Arabs, Africans, and various kinds of brigands came to the war zone in groups of 20 to 100, wearing an astonishing array of robes, sashes, feathers, and other finery, no two men looking alike. When they galloped, great streamers of brightly colored cloth floated behind them like a dazzling rainbow-hued cloud. A few of these bands were led by dignified, gallant men, but for the most part, they were bandits led by even worse criminals, in one case by a scandalously unveiled woman named Kara Fatima, who struck onlookers as being utterly ferocious. Although seventy years old, she carried a saber and two pistols.

Aged from sixteen to well over sixty, the Bashi-Bazouks sported all sorts of weapons, including bamboo spears, and sometimes played kettledrums as they marched. A French officer who described them as "hideously dirty" wrote that "they had truly a vile air that inspired all in the army to a profound distaste. Everyone knew that they had assassinated one of their leaders, a young (French) officer of the first armored division, and this only so as to rob him, and after having noticed that they had forgotten a coat, they dug up the cadaver to get hold of this last piece of clothing."[27] Like their Russian counterparts, the Cossacks, the Bashi-Bazouks were superb horsemen, but they would not fight against regular cavalry, nor would they attack anything more formidable than stragglers. They were unreliable as scouts, and their major contribution consisted of terrorizing enemy civilians, whom they readily robbed and raped. In spite of the Bashi-Bazouks' appalling reputation, the French and British each attempted to train some 4,000 of them to serve under military discipline. Predictably, the attempts failed miserably. Those who did not desert ignored their European officers and looted as they pleased. During their first action against a Cossack patrol, they rode away, leaving a French officer alone to be killed. The French soon disbanded them and finally drove them away by force.[28] The British followed suit.

The newly established, largely European-trained Turkish medical corps actually proved surprisingly effective. Turkish doctors seldom possessed the training of their European counterparts, but many were skilled, devoted to their patients, and eager to learn. Turkish military hospitals were surprisingly well equipped, if not always sanitary, some of them better than the hospitals provided for British and Russian sick and wounded. At the start of the war, the British sent sixteen qualified surgeons and numerous dressers to assist the Turks. Omer Pasha expressed his personal gratitude, but the Turkish government could never quite manage to acknowledge their existence.[29] Once the best in the world, many Turkish military engineers still proved competent, and the once awesome Turkish artillery continued to be outstanding. Equipped largely with modern British cannon, Turkish gunners were more than a match for the Russian artillery, itself consistently superior to that of both the British and the French. The Turks had some rifled cannon capable of firing explosive shells for 4,000 yards that could kill over a wide radius.[30]

The Turkish navy had six battleships in the Black Sea but could not begin to match the Russians in numbers of ships or range of guns, and because they had only a few of the newly developed steam-driven ships, they sailed at the mercy of the wind.

The Russians detested the Turks before the war began and learned to hate them still more as the war went on. The allies had no use for the Turks when the war began and soon branded them despicable cowards, treating them with contempt. In reality, with one widely publicized exception to be described later, Turkish troops fought with uncommon courage and skill.

## The British

The British Royal Navy stood well above all others in the world, its superb seamanship displayed almost everywhere that ships sailed. It had many more warships than any other navy, with longer-ranged guns, and many of its new battleships were powered by steam. Although they would sail the Baltic and the Black Seas throughout the coming war, they would not be challenged by Russia's sail-powered ships, but the British army would be challenged as perhaps never before. Referred to by all concerned as the "English army," it looked and fought almost exactly as it had forty years earlier at Waterloo. Most of its infantry regiments wore the same tight-fitting scarlet tunics with white leather cross-belts, although a few wore green, and the Scottish Highland regiments wore kilts. The scarlet tunics of the guards were topped by their tall black bearskin busbies, while other regiments wore a variety of tall leather helmets. The men wore tight leather collars called *stocks* that kept their heads erect but very nearly choked them. Some cavalry units wore brass helmets, and others wore tall leather shakos. They all wore dark blue trouser overalls except for Lord Cardigan's 11th Hussars, whose cherry-colored overalls were conspicuous in the charge of the Light Brigade. The 11th Hussars, at least three of them former African slaves from the West Indies, called themselves "cherubims" because of these trousers, but other regiments called them "cherry bums."[31] The artillery wore blue. All soldiers had only one uniform to be worn on parade and in battle, in summer heat and freezing cold. This was not the only lack of foresight by the British army. Despite the changed face of war, it had made no organizational changes for forty years.

Outside India, Britain maintained a small army of only 100,000 men, and many of these were stationed in other colonies. Unlike all the other armies in this war, Britain's used only volunteers. Except for a few criminals and vagrants sentenced to military service by

*Officers and men of the British 3rd Regiment (the "Buffs").*
*(Photo courtesy of the National Army Museum)*

magistrates—about 1 percent of the total—men were tempted to enlist by smooth-talking recruiting sergeants. Called "turning the green ones red," recruiting involved using cash bonuses, trickery, lies, and getting men drunk to obtain new soldiers.[32] Recruiting was difficult in the early 1850s because agriculture and industry were booming and both paid far better wages than the army's wage of a shilling a day. A few years earlier, however, poverty had driven many farm workers to enlist, and these large, powerful, placid men were a recruiter's ideal. The term of enlistment was ten years in the infantry and twelve in the cavalry.

Smaller and rougher men from the cities enlisted, too, and they proved anything but docile. Most came from the depths of poverty and depravity. One new private recruited during these deeply religious times not only had never set foot in a church but had never even heard of Jesus Christ.[33] Almost all English and Scottish recruits signed up because they were out of work, hungry, and cold. During the potato famine of 1845, Irish recruits had flocked to the colors,

*Officers and men of the 13th Light Dragoons, survivors of the charge of the Light Brigade. (Photo courtesy of the National Army Museum)*

and Irishmen made up fully one-third of the soldiers sent to the Crimea to serve in the "English" army. Some regiments were all or nearly all Irish, such as the Connaught Rangers, known as the "yellow" regiment because of the yellow facings on their jackets, not because of cowardice. In addition, 41 percent of the Royal Welch Regiment and 37 percent of an English regiment, the 95th Derbyshire, were Irish, along with 30 percent of its officers.[34] Half the British killed in the war's first large battle came from Ireland.[35] Some Scottish Highland regiments had so few Scottish recruits that they had to enlist Irish and English soldiers, but the 93rd Highlanders, who achieved fame in the war as "the thin red line," were so thoroughly Scottish that four Gaelic-speaking corporals had to be assigned as interpreters so that English officers could communicate with them.[36] Despite the recruiters' best tricks, recruits remained in such limited supply at the start of the Crimean War that the British government hired mercenaries from Germany, Switzerland, Sardinia, and even the United States. Thousands of foreign mercenaries enrolled, and many actually trained in England, but they became so disliked by the public that the government sent them home before they saw battle.[37]

The army that initially went to war was only 30,000 men strong, but they were veterans with an average age of twenty-six and seven years' service. They were large men, six feet in height being quite commonplace. A sergeant who stood five feet nine inches referred to himself as "short," and men in the Guards regiments averaged six feet.[38] Most officers stood even taller. Captain Dunn, who would became known for his courage in this war, was six feet three inches tall, and Colonel Thomas Egerton of the 77th Regiment stood a remarkable six feet eight inches. Lieutenant Graham of the Engineers not only stood six feet four inches, as did many other men, but had such strength that when his horse once became frenzied, he dismounted, grabbed it by the nose and forelock, and threw it to the ground as his companions looked on in amazement.[39] Not until later in the century, when much of the population moved to cities in search of work and severe malnutrition followed, did poor Britons become so physically stunted that the army recruited smaller and smaller men. By 1900, the army took recruits as short as five feet three inches. It was just as well that British soldiers in 1854 were so large and strong because their seventy- to eighty-pound packs would have been too much for smaller men, and they were often called upon to fight hand to hand with Russians who were almost as large as they were.

British officers were almost all "gentlemen," educated privately by tutors or, more often, at elite public schools like Eton, where they learned to play team sports, rule the lower classes, and exercise "muscular Christianity," as one leading educator of the time put it. One-third came from titled or landed families, and the rest from gentleman's professions—the clergy, the bar, and, most often, military service families. Most Guards and cavalry officers were wealthy and often members of the peerage, but many infantry officers of line regiments had such limited means that they had difficulty purchasing their initial commissions or later promotions. The seemingly archaic practice of selling commissions to the wealthy denied leadership roles to many men of talent, but it ensured, as intended, that Britain's officers would have the most to lose in any revolution aimed at the aristocracy. The practice of gentlemen purchasing their commissions, and selling them when they felt like leaving the service, did not apply to the Royal Artillery or the Royal Engineers, which needed men with technical training, not blue blood. Many of these men had quite modest incomes.

Some lazy and less than warlike officers served in the army, as the then young officer Garnet Wolseley (later Field Marshal Viscount Wolseley and head of the British army) noted with disgust, and those in the infantry and cavalry typically had little military training except in drill. Most officers ignored the study of maps, topography, and tactics. There was no armywide standard, no military academy to speak of (only six students studied at Sandhurst in 1854!), no exams, and, frankly, little interest in the profession of war. The artillery school at Woolwich was better attended but still in its infancy. French officers regarded British officers as amateurs, and when British officers arrived in the Crimea with their hunting rifles and horses, civilian clothing, bathtubs, and dozens of cartloads of other unwarlike paraphernalia, the French looked on in amazement. As an example, His Royal Highness the Duke of Cambridge arrived in civilian clothes with a superb French cook and seventeen wagons full of personal baggage.[40]

In time of peace, many officers spent little time with their regiments, leaving drilling and other routine duties to their sergeants. And drilling is what soldiers did. There was little time spent in target practice and less in tactical maneuvers. Instead, time was spent in barracks, polishing brass, whitening leather belts, and shining boots, and spare time was devoted to sleeping in cramped, unventilated quarters or, more often, at the regimental "wet canteen," where the men got drunk as rapidly as possible and, when they could afford it, visited the many prostitutes readily available near all military installations. Soldiers were quick to use their fists, broken bottles, and other handy weapons when their drunkenness led to brawls, as often happened. A surprising number of officers looked on their men with kindness and fatherly understanding, but many still thought of them as the lowest form of human life, animal-like creatures who required the harshest kinds of discipline if they were to be controlled. Flogging was still commonplace, but in 1852, the largest number of strokes that could be ordered had been reduced to forty-five. Only a few years earlier, 2,000 strokes had been ordered, and a few men had been flogged to death.[41] There was no shortage of harsh discipline, nor of close order drill followed by more drill.

In battle, as on parade, Britain's veteran soldiers proved to have unbreakable discipline. Their officers called them "solid." When the Turkish minister of war first saw them, he exclaimed, "They are the finest men I ever saw, and they hold their heads up well; but they will all run away; they cannot fight like Turks."[42] He could hardly have been more wrong. These veterans would not break on defense, and they would advance, unhurriedly but steadily, into enemy fire. Unlike the French and Russians, who screamed and shouted with animal-like sounds, they usually advanced in silence. A standard command was "Be steady, keep silent, fire low."[43] Men like these had stood against Napoléon's Imperial Guards and had advanced so suicidally against massed American guns at New Orleans that the American riflemen, many not long removed from Britain themselves, had tears in their eyes as they shot down one after another.

The musket these men had used against Napoléon, and that some still carried at the start of this war, was their beloved "Brown Bess," a brown-stocked, twelve-pound, .753-caliber flintlock with an effective range of only about 100 yards (a lucky shot might kill at a greater distance). Although difficult to aim, the musket shot a huge bullet, which was half again the size of a .50-caliber machine-gun bullet of today and smashed large bones, destroying vital organs as its soft lead expanded on impact. Most regiments, however, were equipped with the 1852 model American-manufactured Enfield rifle, an improved version of France's famous Minié rifle, which had revolutionized warfare. Lighter and more rugged than the Minié rifle, the Enfield's still large .577-caliber bullet could kill at 1,600 yards and was dead accurate at 800 yards. At 300 yards, a good marksman could hit a bull's-eye that was only six inches across. The smooth-barreled muskets used by the French and British in the Peninsular War that led up to Waterloo had been so inaccurate that they scored only 1 hit for every 459 shots fired. In the Crimea, however, 1 in every 16 rifle bullets found a human target, many of them at ranges of half a mile and more. Although the new rifles still had to be loaded at the muzzle with a percussion cap and bullet put in place by a ramrod while the soldier stood upright, it could be loaded twice as fast as a musket, and the bullets it fired had such velocity that a single bullet could, and sometimes actually did, kill four men marching in a column.[44]

The cavalry was armed with carbines, steel-tipped lances, sabers, and newly issued Colt revolvers, seldom used because of their very short range and the difficulty men had in cocking them after each shot without losing their grip on their horses' reins. Also, in the heat of battle, many men forgot that they even had these new weapons. The cavalry mounts were large, well-trained English horses, probably the best in the world, and officers and men alike were superb horsemen. Although they had seldom contributed much to British victories, cavalrymen fancied themselves far superior to the infantry. Most of the senior officers were wealthy aristocrats, and all officers affected an air of immense superiority. Wearing corsets to produce wasplike waists, they affected an elegant boredom, yawning ostentatiously, perpetually smoking expensive cigars, and pronouncing *r* as *w,* turning *very* into *vewwy, horrid* into *howwid,* their speech a cartoonist's delight. A cartoon in *Punch* had one cavalry officer asking another, "I say, old Fellah—Do you think it pwobable the infantwy will accompany us to Sevastopol?"[45]

The Royal Horse Artillery relied on six-pounder cannons, quite effective against infantry, but the heavier British siege guns were usually outranged by those of their French allies and their Russian opponents, who could fire thirty-two- and sixty-eight-pound explosive shells for several miles. The British had a few rifled cannon of even longer range, but they had little effect during the Crimean War, largely because no one thought to provide enough shells for them.[46] British officers and men alike assured themselves that theirs was the finest army in the world. After all, they had defeated Napoléon (Prussia's help was seldom acknowledged). The only doubts they had concerned which regiment among them was the finest, an honor that virtually every regiment claimed for itself.

The British army was commanded by FitzRoy Somerset, Lord Raglan, a sixty-six-year-old general who had lost his right arm while serving as a staff officer at Waterloo but had never commanded troops in battle. A gentleman to the bone, Lord Raglan would need every bit of his gentility and tact to maintain relations with the often touchy French, not to mention his own senior officers, who respected him as a person but found him weak and indecisive as a leader. It did not help that he often referred to the enemy as the "French," a habit from his days at Waterloo, and one he was the first to laugh about. Emperor Napoléon III called him an "old lady," and some of his own generals dismissed him as a mere staff officer rather than a commander. Early in the war, Raglan was totally out of touch with his troops, rarely visiting them in their camps or trenches and making few efforts to ease their suffering. Some of his generals were even older than he was, and equally unacquainted with modern warfare. Others, such as his cavalry generals, proved both incompetent and ignorant. One of the few competent generals was his commander of artillery, a sixty-six-year-old named Strangways, who was killed by a Russian shell. Despite his name, his ways were less strange than those of his fellow senior commanders. Fortunately for the allied cause, almost all of Britain's regimental officers proved brave and dedicated men.

## The French

The British soon learned what most of the world's military men already recognized: The French army had become the best-equipped, best-trained, and best-supplied force in the world. After the Napoleonic wars, the French fought in several small European wars and since 1830 had been at war in Algeria. The French army's weapons and equipment were the best in the world. All of its infantry carried Minié rifles; its cavalry was exceptional, and its artillery outstanding. Its engineers, medical corps, and commissariat had all been modernized. Unlike British officers, French officers received training in the science of war at various military academies such as St.-Cyr-l'École, Saumur, and Metz, and throughout their careers, they underwent frequent training in map reading, tactics, fortification, and topography, followed by examinations that tested their knowledge. At least once a year, an inspector would spend a grueling two-week period with each regiment to assess the state of its training.[47]

Unlike British officers, few French officers came from noble families. Almost all came from such humble social origins that they had to live on their army pay, and promotion was so slow that a captain might spend ten years at that rank. As a result, unlike the British regiments, where all the officers ate their meals together, French regiments provided separate tables with different menus for each rank, reflecting the varied earning power of colonels, captains, and lieutenants, who paid for their own meal.[48] Britain's aristocratic officers could claim little popularity with the country's growing middle class; France's middle-class officers were equally unpopular with the French public because of their strong anticivilian attitudes. Officers' low salaries forced them to delay marriage for many years while they spent their leisure time drinking in brothels. They endured the scorn of rich civilians, whom they in turn loathed and referred to as "Jews." Despite their low social class backgrounds, they wore their honor on their sleeves, and dueling was common.

French soldiers were conscripted for a six-year term of service by lottery, the price of buying oneself out of military service being about twice the annual income of a laborer. By choice, a wealthy count served as a corporal throughout the Crimean War, something that would have been unthinkable in the British or Russian armies.[49] Instead of the endless drill and brutal punishment used to instill discipline in British soldiers, French conscripts received education about the meaning of morale and military spirit. There was no flogging. Instead, there were various schools, programs, and activities that taught them principles of hygiene, history, and, above all, the spirit of *élan*—the dashing initiative that the French army so prided itself on. Insisting that individualism was fundamental to French national character, the army made great efforts to emphasize individual initiative as a tactic and to develop the physical skills necessary to carry out rapid actions. Soldiers learned to fence, swim, and even dance to improve their footwork, but most of all, gymnastics was emphasized to give men the ability to scale mountains or fortifications and successfully to engage an enemy in hand-to-hand combat. By 1853, the French had twenty battalions of chasseurs, elite riflemen trained in gymnastics. Vigorously trained in long-distance running, with a high knee action, they could cover twelve kilometers in ninety minutes, moving almost as fast as the cavalry.[50] Unlike the British, who preferred unquestioning obedience to orders, the French fostered what they referred to as "inner discipline," born of a soldier's own willingness to do anything necessary for victory.

Off duty, French soldiers were much given to drunkenness, and in an average year, 20 percent of them had at least one venereal disease. But ordinarily, they had little opportunity to be off duty because they regularly sweated in public works projects that required hard physical labor, or they responded to natural disasters. When they were not building roads or saving flood victims, their training focused on the attack—*audacious, relentless,* and *irresistible* were the words they used to describe themselves. French officers believed that their soldiers would lose their morale when not moving, and so, unlike the slow-moving British, they rushed to the attack, fearing that the only alternative for their men would be retreat. The French thought of themselves as a veteran army, but as foreign observers pointed out, entire French divisions had seen no action, and those that had fought had done so against Algerian natives, not the Russian army.[51] In fact, even the most elite French troops, the veteran Zouaves, had never before been under artillery fire. French officers wore all-blue uniforms that looked very much like those worn by the Union army in the American Civil War, but their soldiers wore blue tunics and red trousers and hats.

France's best infantry was its Zouaves, named after the Algerian mountain tribesmen they had once fought and selected for fine physique and courage. General George B. McClellan, soon to command the Union army in the American Civil War, had recently observed Russian and European troops on maneuvers. He declared the Zouaves the best infantry in Europe.[52] Some Zouave regiments had been raised in Algeria from among former African slaves, but most Zouaves were of French origin, although some were volunteers from other European countries. These full-bearded, deeply tanned men wore baggy red trousers, blue jackets, and long, red, floppy headgear that resembled nightcaps. As they marched to battle in the Crimea, some of them took along pet monkeys riding on top of their packs, and others carried pet birds in cages.[53] Even the British acknowledged the superb courage and skill of the Zouaves during the Crimean War.

Although France's generals had no experience of a large war against a formidable European army, most had had extensive combat experience in Algeria, and unlike the British officers, they had studied the profession of war. Even so, not everyone in the French government respected them. One former minister said, "There is not one I would hire as a clerk. There is neither sense nor honesty in the whole gang."[54] Still, the first French commander in the Crimean War, Marshal Leroy de St.-Arnaud was colorful, to say the least. When he first inspected his troops, he gushed, "What enthusiasm, what impulsiveness, what graceful bearing, high-spirited and confident."[55] Terminally ill when the war began, he died before his generalship could be assessed. Forty-five-year-old François C. Canrobert, with long flowing hair and perpetual pinkeye, replaced him. A cautious general, greatly concerned with the welfare of his troops, Canrobert devoted himself to their well-being, typically opening each address to them in the Crimea by saying, "Children, your sufferings are almost over."[56] Nicknamed "Bob Can't" by the British for his perpetual inaction, Canrobert was replaced by General Aimable Jean-Jacques Pélissier.

Pélissier was a squat, paunchy Norman with legs so short he could barely ride a horse. His short-cropped white hair led to his nickname of "tin-head."[57] This son of a sergeant so often shouted obscenities that a waiter once hit him in the face with an omelette, a story widely told in the army. A ruthless commander who had killed Algerians without mercy, Pélissier coldly ordered tens of thousands of French soldiers to their death in futile attacks against Sevastopol. It was Pélissier who first popularized the saying that one cannot make an omelette without breaking some eggs. He was France's only general with the courage to ignore the constant meddling of Emperor Napoléon III, whose heavy German accent made him seem even more officious than he actually was. No military genius, this Napoléon insisted on sending 4,000 ancient metal breastplates to his army in the Crimea. Embarrassed French officers tried to hide them from the amused British.[58] Strangely, Pélissier became a close friend of the gentle Raglan, and when the British general died, Pélissier sat by his deathbed for over an hour, sobbing "like a baby."[59]

The French navy was no match for Britain's fleets, but it was more modern and better led than Russia's navy. It saw only limited action in the Crimean War, but it performed well.

## The Russians

Russia's navy had almost 100,000 men, some 37,000 of them at Sevastopol. But because virtually no Russian ships had converted to steam, Russia could not confront the allies at sea with any hope of success. However, the Russians possessed the world's largest and, many believed, best army. The tsar thought it invincible, and it duly impressed the many European observers who saw it on parade or during summer maneuvers. Its regulars included fifty-nine regiments of cavalry, each of 1,000 men, led by the splendidly uniformed cuirassiers with their polished steel breastplates and helmets, huge swords, and massive horses. The infantry was splendidly uniformed, too, and its men marched with such precision that even jaded European military men were impressed. Each toe was pointed at exactly the same angle, and the backs were so straight that men would (and sometimes did) carry a full glass of water on top of their flat-topped helmets without spilling a drop, their often-performed manual-of-arms perfection to be seen and heard as thousands of muskets whirled, slapped, and clanged in perfect unison. Bright green artillery caissons pulled by three magnificently prancing horses were no less imposing as they sped by before men leaped down to bring the guns to bear on an imaginary enemy. Tsar Nicholas I referred to each parade of hundreds of thousands of his loyal soldiers as "the spectacle of the gods."[60]

Parades were one thing, war another. The regular army mustered about 700,000 men. Another 150,000 served as corps-of-the-interior troops and were used to police remote parts of the empire, not to fight in European wars. Cossack irregulars, more effective at intimidating unarmed dissidents than fighting enemy cavalry, counted for 250,000 more. Some 200,000 trained reserves existed, but most of these were older men with families who had no taste for another period of active service; the rest were new and untrained conscripts. What is more, some 200,000 men were tied down in unending combat against the Chechens and other Muslim mountain people in the Caucasus, and as we have seen, thanks to a continuing threat of attack in the Baltic by an Anglo-French invasion fleet, the tsar had rushed many of his best troops, including his tall, faithful Guards regiments, to the St. Petersburg area, where they sat out the war without firing a shot. Other troops had to be held in readiness in Poland to dampen Polish enthusiasm for another rebellion, or to ward off an attack by Austria. Thus, only some 150,000 men were left to face the Turks and their allies, and thanks to terrible roads and the absence of any railroads south of Moscow, the allies could actually bring troops and supplies to the Crimean war zone by sea much faster than the Russians could by land.

So there would be no great advantage in numbers to the Russians in this war, and except for their dazzling parade-ground performances, the Russian troops would prove to be sadly untrained for this war. Russian men typically saw their twenty-five-year conscription term in the army as a death sentence. Yet, each year, some 80,000 despairing men from all over the empire found themselves conscripted into the army by landowners, who usually chose the most useless or rebellious of their serfs; by village councils eager to be rid of local drunkards or troublemakers; or by conscription agents, who rounded up Poles, Jews, Latvians, Siberians, Ukrainians, or Kalmuks not able to hide in the swamps or forests, move to large cities and take on aliases, or buy their way out of service. Some mutilated themselves to escape duty.[61]

Fearing conscription even more than most of Russia's other minorities, Jews became especially adept at evading it. If not enough Jewish adults could be located, recruiters seized Jewish boys as young as eight and marched them away to military training schools. Many died on the road, but those who survived endured physical torture and near starvation until they accepted Christianity and baptism.[62] At the age of eighteen, they entered the army, where, like the other conscripts, they served for twenty-five years, if they lived that long.

Except for the Jews, few conscripts could read or write, and the army did nothing to educate them. A common saying by the officers was "The powers of reasoning are not expected in the ranks."[63] Soldiers endured endless drilling, polished their muskets or boots, or learned the manual of arms from screaming sergeants who never hesitated to punch anyone who misstepped, just as officers never hesitated to punch the sergeants. The brutal discipline included flogging and birching with a long rod, and in no other army were men so often punched or kicked.

The men learned discipline, to be sure, but little about war. Their old, short-ranged, smoothbore muskets were highly polished on the outside but often rusty inside, and many had other defects. Just before the Crimean War began, 1,400 of 1,991 muskets in one regiment proved to have significant defects,[64] not surprisingly because they were almost never fired during peacetime. As a result, Russian soldiers took twice as long as British soldiers to load their weapons.[65] Target practice was reserved for some 6,000 men in rifle regiments, who had newly issued long-range rifles like those of the allies. For the rest of the army, target practice was thought to be too expensive and actually unnecessary. Russian infantry was not expected to exchange aimed fire with an enemy; their only tactic was to advance, fire on command in perfect unison when close to the enemy (aiming was not required), and then charge with the bayonet. They learned nothing about skirmishing, taking cover, entrenching, defending themselves against cavalry, or any of the tactics then common in war. As one Russian officer put it, "Generally speaking, neither the soldiers nor the officers know their craft and are not taught anything in earnest. On our side, everyone is crazy only about proper marching and the correct pulling-on of a sock."[66]

That the infantry was a dumb mass to be flung at the enemy, to impale it on permanently fixed bayonets, remained an axiom in the Russian army, and few Russian officers took note that new weapons had condemned this tactic to bloody failure. The bayonet was no longer enough. Not only could artillery decimate the densely packed Russian columns while still a mile beyond bayonet range, but so could the new rifles used by the allies. This failure to adapt to modern warfare should come as no surprise because most Russian officers did not waste their time studying war, and the army's leaders abhorred change. Years of fighting a guerrilla war in the Caucasus had forced some Russian troops to adopt more flexible, small-unit tactics but these ideas had no effect on the 730 generals, most of them overage, who commanded Russia's troops in the field or served at imperial headquarters.

In Russia's diverse officer corps, about one officer in six came from high-ranking, wealthy noble families. These men had attended military schools, where they had learned French and German, mathematics, history, geography, engineering, and what was then known about science. Most had also been tutored at home. Urbane, artistic, sensitive, and chivalrous, they would have been at ease with aristocrats anywhere in Europe. Indeed, many had visited Europe's capitals and great houses. Most of them were brave and steadfast officers interested in improving the army and even in bettering the lives of the ignorant men who served in its ranks. For example, the Yamburg Uhlans, an elite cavalry regiment, had many well-educated nobles among its officers. These men played chess and the piano, read thought-provoking books from the regimental library, subscribed to magazines and newspapers, and sang in the local church choir. Most of them also rode brilliantly, excelled at swordsmanship, and usually avoided drunken debauchery.[67]

Unlike nobles like these, many of whom had sympathy and compassion for the men in the ranks, over 80 percent of Russia's officers were the semiliterate sons of petty nobles who had failed secondary school and entered the army as "Junkers," hoping to salvage a career. Junkers served in the ranks (although they roomed with officers and were treated very much like them) for six years before earning a commission. All officers had a soldier servant, and higher ranks had several (a colonel was entitled to six); all received free housing (a colonel could claim a seven-room house and a stable for five horses); and all received free medical care, as well as hay and oats for their horses. But pay was low, and Junker officers had expensive tastes in horses, food, drink, and women, if not good books.[68] To supplement their meager incomes (a colonel made only twice as much as a lieutenant), most freely stole the money the government provided to buy food, clothing, and even gunpowder for the troops. The practice was widespread and extreme. In 1853, the commanding officer of an elite cavalry regiment stole so much of the money meant to feed his men that many collapsed with scurvy and dropsy.[69] A favorite saying of hungry troops was "Make it sour, make it thick and make it more."[70] Few officers dared to deny a daily ration of vodka to their troops, as the men looked forward to it with a passion, but even some of this precious vodka was siphoned off for personal profit by the officers.[71] Partial protection came from the soldiers' artel, a communal group of about ten soldiers who shared what they had and protected one another as well as they could.[72]

Most of the Junker officers were as jealous of their peers and superiors as they were brutal to their subordinates. Obedience might be essential, but cooperation rarely took place. Some 7 percent of Russian officers were former sergeants promoted from the ranks. These men proved loyal to their superiors but typically were crude and brutal.[73] Senior officers often detested each other, as officers of Russian background often detested capable officers of German or Polish background, who were said to be ambitious, ruthless, and clannish. Despite plentiful intrigues and hostilities, there was little to relieve the grinding boredom of peacetime existence. With a few exceptions, most of the army's officers spent their peacetime lives playing cards, drinking, and visiting brothels.

All of these officers, good and bad, fell under the command of the tsar. Tsar Nicholas I did not take the field with his armies, but he did meddle in their command. Unfortunately, despite his lifelong obsession with military uniforms, drill, and parades, he cared little about weapons, tactics, or military modernization. Worse yet, he consistently displayed the worst possible judgment in choosing his generals. He gave overall command of his troops in the Crimea to seventy-year-old Prince Menshikov. Menshikov was well educated and witty, but he used his sharp tongue destructively. He spoke six European languages and lived a luxurious lifestyle but knew nothing about generalship. In the Crimean War, he bungled battle after battle while his cold, merciless approach to his subordinates led them to detest him.

When even the tsar could no longer stand Menshikov's failures, he replaced him with Prince M. D. Gorchakov, a French-speaking aristocrat who could barely make himself understood in Russian. Absentminded, if not quite feebleminded, and so nearsighted that he could not recognize faces at his own dinner table, he proved hopeless as a leader. Fortunately for Russia, three admirals and one engineering officer in Sevastopol proved to be superb and heroic leaders, and many Russian officers demonstrated enormous energy and courage. But others were inept and cowardly. Only in the Russian army did significant numbers of officers earn such hatred from their men that they were shot in the back as soon as combat began.[74]

Even more than Tsar Nicholas's infantry, his magnificent-looking cavalry was almost all for show. The fleet Turkish cavalry had run rings around it in a succession of wars, and in 1831, the dashing Polish cavalry had also embarrassed the much more numerous but slow-moving and poorly led Russians. Russian dragoons, who fought on foot after riding into battle, did reasonably well, but from horseback, the swords and lances of the vaunted Russian cavalry seldom did damage. Except for the huge horses of the cuirassiers, Russian cavalry mounts were noticeably smaller and lighter-boned than English or French horses, whereas their Russian riders weighed more than the French and almost as much as the British. In addition, Russian cavalry horses were forced to carry far more weight—in such things as food, kettles, overcoats, and large bundles of hay—than the allies' horses. As a result, the Russian cavalry moved so slowly that it often appeared to be ponderous. On the march, Russian cavalry regiments rarely marched more than ten kilometers a day, the horses periodically being led by dismounted riders, and all of the horses received at least one day of rest each week. These slow and tentative cavalry regiments did not do well in the Crimea.

Neither did the Cossacks, Russia's much publicized irregular cavalry. Originally freebooters and frontiersmen, the Cossacks had absorbed runaway serfs, Poles, Lithuanians, and others who moved on the fringes of Russia's settled areas, where they had helped to drive away the native peoples before settling down as farmers in the Ukraine, central Asia, and Siberia. Over time, the Cossacks developed their own system of military ranks; provided their own horses, uniforms, and equipment, except for government-provided carbines; and, in return for many benefits and social advantages, agreed to serve the tsar when called to active duty. In World War II, they fought with such gallantry that an entire division charged German tanks and machine guns until shot down virtually to the last man and last horse. In World War I, over 350,000 served, not infrequently with honor and courage, but in the war against Japan in 1904–1905, the Cossacks proved to be quite useless as scouts and only rarely willing to stand against Japanese fire.

During the years leading up to the Crimean War, Russian army officers had no use for the undisciplined Cossacks, whose idea of war consisted of making a profit and not having their horses shot or dying themselves, in return for a medal and the tsar's gratitude. To make matters worse, the Russians treated the Cossacks as servants and messengers, often cuffing them around and insulting them.[75] In the Crimea, the Cossacks retaliated with an indifferent performance. In this largely static war, their skills as scouts had little value, and they had no intention of crossing swords with the formidable British or French cavalry. Like the Bashi-Bazouks of the Turks, for the most part they devoted themselves to self-preservation, the search for plunder, and, now and then, rape.

Another area of Russian weakness was military medical care. Despite some gifted physicians like Nicholas I. Pirogov, the first person ever to use anesthesia during surgery with wounded troops, Russian military medicine stood well behind the none-too-high European standard. Between 1825 and 1850, 30,000 Russians died in combat, but at least 900,000 died of disease, and on the eve of the war in the Crimea, the peacetime death rate of Russian troops was twice that of other European armies. The practice of medicine in Russia was relatively inept, but more important, Russian hospitals were almost unimaginably corrupt. Doctors, orderlies, and apothecaries all stole medicine and food for personal profit, replacing effective drugs with cheap and useless substitutes, and nutritious food with the most inexpensive, low-protein rations available. Much of the responsibility for these conditions lay with Sir James Villiers, the chief inspector of the medical department of the Ministry of War. A Scot, who became the tsar's personal physician, Villiers completely neglected military medicine. That he could not speak Russian despite living in Russia for fifty years is suggestive of his lack of concern.[76] To his credit, Nicholas eventually recognized the depth of the problem and initiated some useful reforms, but the war in the Crimea came too soon for them to have much effect.

Despite these many deficiencies in the Russian army, it did have some notable strengths. Because Tsar Nicholas I had loved fortifications since boyhood, he gave special attention and support to his corps of engineers. Long an elite branch of the army, the engineers had officers who were well educated and often of wealthy noble birth; when called upon to erect defensive fortifications, build bridges, or devise means of destroying their enemies' fortifications, they had an excellent record. In the Crimea, the engineers' Colonel Todleben did such a superb job of fortifying the city of Sevastopol that he was proclaimed a hero internationally, an honor that came to few senior officers in any army during this war. The Russian engineers also had some technological advantages over the allies. The attempt to place mines under the Russian fortifications at Sevastopol was undertaken by the French, whose mines had to be detonated by conventional fuses that sometimes extinguished themselves. When Russian engineers dug tunnels under the French tunnels, to blow them up before they reached the Russian fortress, the Russian mines could be efficiently detonated electronically.

The Russian artillery was also impressive. The artillery officers, like those in the corps of engineers, were well-educated men dedicated to their profession. The Russians pioneered the use of rockets, in addition to that of horse-drawn artillery and heavy siege guns. During the early stages of the Crimean War, the Russian artillery was longer-ranged, more accurate, and better-managed than that of any of the allies, as even the British (seldom generous with praise for their enemies) usually admitted. At times, the Turkish artillery was even better than the Russian, something the British found even more impossible to admit.

During peacetime, because discipline was so brutally harsh, Russian troops often seemed morose. Occasional entertainment took place, and bands, jugglers, games, and much storytelling relieved some of the gloom. Even so, one officer wrote, "A Russian soldier is

perhaps the most unhappy being in the world." One soldier was ha-
bitually so grim-faced that his commander actually ordered 100
lashes to make him laugh. He did![77] But when Russian troops
marched off to war in the Crimea and away from the brutality of
camp life, observers were amazed by their high spirits. Despite heat,
dust, biting insects of all sorts, poor food, and too little water, they
laughed and joked as they marched day after day, heavily laden with
equipment and living mostly on the black bread they carried in
cylindrical bags that looked like bolsters and were actually used as
pillows at night. The Moscow Regiment covered 160 miles in only
five days, to arrive at the Alma River just in time for the battle. Like
most Russian troops on the march, they had sung much of the way.

And when the time came to fight, the Russians usually did so
bravely enough, but those who fought against them commented on
their blank and dazed expressions, and others on how similar they
all looked:

> Broad-shouldered, sinewy, nearly as tall as Englishmen, there was even
> a stereotyped and ugly uniformity of high cheek-bones, snub noses,
> elongated upper lips, cropped (heads) with colourless hair of the coars-
> est texture, thin wiry moustaches . . . fine, stout men but their faces are
> broad and flat and betoken great ignorance.[78]

They looked alike and they fought alike, tenaciously, with piercing
screams, and shouting "Hurrah!" Their faces often expressionless
even when they were drunk, as they very often were in battle, they
advanced against rifle and cannon fire that killed an average of 27
percent of those who went into battle. Why these degraded, neglected, and brutalized men fought so doggedly has intrigued military historians.

Pride in their regiment was one important reason, and so was
maintaining the respect of the fellow soldiers in their artel, as well as
the fear of punishment if they ran away. Perhaps a cynical Russian
officer also had part of the answer when he seriously declared that
they did not fear death because their miserable existence left them
with nothing to live for.[79] That may have been how some officers saw
it, but the role of religion was likely to have been much more important. These largely ethnic Russian serf-soldiers had been raised in the
Orthodox Church, where obedience to the tsar as God's anointed

ruler stood as divine doctrine, heaven being the reward for earthly devotion to the tsar's wishes. The troops knew that their tsar wished this war, and they believed that it was their duty to bring him victory. The hordes of priests who accompanied the troops wherever they went, even into battle, never let them forget their duty. The soldiers began every day on their knees in prayer, sometimes for half an hour or more, and whenever they passed a church, they crossed themselves. Just before the war's first battle in the Crimea, a Russian general gave each man of his regiment a cross to wear around his neck, saying, "Grenadiers, if God is with us, who is against us?" For him, and probably for his men, this belief was the ultimate in motivation. Ironically, General Prince Menshikov, the man whom the tsar had chosen to lead them in battle, was openly indifferent to religion.

## The Sardinians

The last troops to arrive in the Crimea were the best equipped and most admired. The 45,000-man army of the kingdom of Sardinia-Piedmont was the best among those of the still disunited kingdoms of Italy. It was so highly regarded that Britain, itself, very short of trained manpower, had earlier tried to recruit Sardinian volunteers to serve alongside its own troops. A few Sardinians served as volunteers with the French early in the war, and two Sardinian officers actually charged with the Light Brigade at Balaclava. One, Lieutenant Landrioni, was wounded and captured, dying in 1858; Major Crovone survived, living until 1872.[80]

The first major contingent of 5,000 Sardinian troops did not arrive until early May 1855, soon to be followed by 12,500 more men. They were led by General (later Marchese di) Alphose de la Marmora, a tall, handsome French- and English-speaking forty-year-old engineering officer whose energy, knowledge, and courtesy impressed everyone, including the stunning bride of General Lord Paget. This twenty-two-year-old blond woman, said to be one of the greatest beauties in all England, found Marmora and his officers "ravishing." The gallant general ordered his private band to play for Lady Paget every morning and evening on her yacht, the *Caradoc*. Lord Wolseley was not easily impressed, but he praised Marmora's knowledge of fortification and the martial spirit of his men.

The Sardinians' famous Bersaglieri riflemen wore light blue over-coats over blue turtleneck tunics with dark blue trousers tucked into polished black leather boots. They were distinguished by wide-brimmed black hats sporting black cock's feathers, which spilled from the top of the hats over the right side to the men's shoulders. All their wagons and gun carriages, including softly sprung ambulances, were of a light blue similar to that of the men's overcoats. Some of the troops from the Piedmont region wore uniforms that were all green, including the feathers. As the allies looked on, the clean-shaven Italians paraded by, led by a band playing operatic arias.

The Sardinians quickly set up a central camp that allied onlookers declared "beyond praise, ... every hat and tent decorated in perfect taste, even down to their theatre; and all sprung up like magic before they had been a week on the ground. The superb band played most afternoons outside Kamara church, a popular rendezvous, and was much in demand by the allies for social and state occasions."[81] Off duty, the men fished in the Chernaya River and listened to opera, but they soon began to fall ill with cholera. In less than a month, 200 had died, and the toll eventually reached 1,000. All observers agreed that they were a "very stunning looking lot of men," but no one was sure how well they could fight until the battle of the Chernaya, when their infantry and artillery both distinguished themselves, inflicting heavy losses on the Russians.[82] The Sardinians' role in the war was minor, but they made their presence felt. Not surprisingly, the British referred to them as "Sardines."

## The Americans

It will be helpful to compare the actions and experiences of the soldiers in these five armies with those of the men who fought on both sides in the American Civil War. That war began only five years after the Crimean War ended, it was fought with nearly identical weapons, and medical practice was still unable to deal effectively with either wounds or disease. In many respects, Americans' attempts to cope with the horrors of their civil war paralleled those of the men in the Crimea, but in some ways, their responses were different. For one thing, unlike the Crimean War armies, these Americans, whether Federals (usually called "Yanks" or "bluebellies" after their blue uniforms) or Confederates ("Rebs," "Johnnies," or "gray-backs"), were almost all volunteers. When the Civil War broke out, the U.S. Army numbered only 16,402 men, 1,100 of them officers.[83] Almost all of the officers were West Pointers, but the majority of the enlisted men had been born in Ireland.

With the exception of these few regular soldiers, most of whom spent the war years on the western frontier, hundreds of thousands of men who volunteered to defend either the Union or the Confederacy had had no previous military experience. Of the Union men who volunteered, 50 percent were farmers; 25 percent were foreign-born laborers, mostly German or Irish.[84] In all, some 200,000 men born in Germany served in the Federal army, along with 150,000 Irish. Some 50,000 Canadians, 45,000 Britons, numerous Scandinavians, and some Native Americans also served. During the war's later stages, 200,000 African-Americans also enlisted.[85] Although the Confederate states were more homogeneously American-born Anglo-Saxon than the North, many more men of foreign birth volunteered than is commonly believed. Alabama enlisted one regiment that was virtually all Irish and another composed almost all of Scots. There were Germans in the Confederate army, too, along with Mexicans, Poles, Dutch, Austrians, Canadians, and Native Americans, who sometimes scalped their Federal victims.[86] Boys as young as thirteen and men as old as seventy-three enlisted in both armies, but the great majority of soldiers in both armies were twenty to twenty-nine.[87]

Three hundred West Pointers cast their lot with the Confederacy, leaving eight hundred regular army officers to serve in the Union forces, but many thousands more than these were needed to serve as officers in both armies. With a few exceptions, newly raised regiments in the North and the South alike tried to fill this need by electing their officers. Each side benefited from the services of some professional officers, primarily from Britain or Germany, but at the start of the war, most officers on both sides had had no military experience and very little training, often none at all. The South allowed owners of twenty or more slaves to be deferred from military service, and a good many wealthy "aristocrats" stayed home as a result, but other wealthy men chose to serve in the ranks, believing such service to be more honorable than accepting an officer's commission. As a result, wealthy planters were often expected to take orders from poor, sometimes nearly illiterate farmers who could not afford a single slave.

But most officers stood above their men, or at least tried to. A good many officers in both armies were cared for throughout their war years by civilian servants or slaves, who were called "servants" in the South.[88] As might be imagined, the camaraderie that officer election was intended to foster rapidly slipped away, even as discipline remained so lacking that foreign observers were shocked.[89] Camp life was often chaotic, and even rudimentary training ran into every kind of obstacle. For example, some men were so uneducated that they could not tell left from right. Sergeants would teach them to march by tying some hay to their left feet and straw to their right, then calling out, "Hayfoot, strawfoot."[90] On marches, men in both armies threw away anything they found too burdensome, including the pistols, large bowie knives, and bayonets all Southerners initially took to war. The practice was called "simmering down."[91] As late as 1863, at the battle of Gettysburg, General Robert E. Lee complained about the lack of discipline of his men.[92]

The appearance of these soldiers was as irregular as their discipline. Most Northern troops were issued blue uniforms with trousers sometimes light blue, sometimes dark blue. But some regiments wore gray, the Confederate color, well into 1862. Many Confederate troops originally wore gray uniforms, but some regiments turned out dressed as Zouaves, and others wore yellow, orange, and even blue.[93] The rigors of campaigning soon devastated these original uniforms. Confederate troops then stained homespun coats and trousers with a dye made from walnuts (because of the Union naval blockades, the only dye available to them), so that most of the men were uniformed in yellowish brown, or "butternut," as the color was called. Shoes wore out rapidly and soon were in such short supply that a great many men marched barefoot. As time went on, retreating Federal troops threw away or left behind most of the uniforms, boots, and brogans that the Confederate army needed. It was not long before almost all tents in Confederate camps, as well as many blankets, uniforms, and boots, were marked "U.S." So were most artillery pieces and rifles.

The only advance in weaponry since the Crimean War was the use of repeating rifles by some units of Union cavalry. First, Spencer carbines, holding seven bullets, were issued, and later, sixteen-shot

Henry carbines. They were greatly feared by Confederates, who thought them "unfair." They were not as long ranged as the Enfield or Springfield rifles used by the infantry, but their rapid rate of fire was put to excellent use by some small units of "mounted infantry," as they were called. Artillery was produced and used in huge numbers, but these cannons were no more effective than the ones used in the Crimean War.

Cavalry units on both sides carried out some effective raids, but for the most part, they contributed little to victory. Most Union cavalry units were wildly undisciplined early in the war, and some remained so. Some Confederate units were dashing and gallant, but others were plodding because, like the Russian cavalry horses, their horses were too heavily loaded.[94] Infantrymen in both armies detested the cavalrymen as vain, lazy, and useless dandies. In a famous order, a Union general offered a reward for any one of his men who brought in the body of a dead cavalryman—blue or gray.[95]

As the war began, Southerners expressed great hostility toward Northerners, in part because they were using force to maintain the Union, but also because they were "foreign rabble," the "scum of Europe," and, at best, "greasy mechanics."[96] The South still saw itself as a bastion of chivalry, a land of cavaliers, the inheritors of England's noble traditions. They loved Tennyson's "The Charge of the Light Brigade," and they doted on Sir Walter Scott's works, filled with sentimental nostalgia about chivalry and the grandeur of the aristocracy, to such an extent that Mark Twain accused Scott of causing the war.[97] For their part, the Northerners thought of most Southerners as dirty, ignorant, and lazy. As the war began, men and women on both sides were intensely patriotic, their hostility expressed ferociously. But as the war went on, many men on both sides came to respect men on the other side and even to feel a sympathetic kinship with them. Women were slower to feel sympathy. When the war broke out, British-born Sir Henry Morton Stanley was living in Arkansas. At the age of twenty, he joined an Arkansas regiment and fought bravely at Shiloh, one of the bloodiest battles of the war. Captured, he was released after he offered to fight for the North. He did so, bravely again, before returning to Britain and beginning his career as perhaps history's most famous explorer of Africa (it was he who found David Livingstone). It is unlikely that his Confederate comrades would have forgiven his change of sides if they had known of it.[98]

So much has been written about the generals of these two armies that little needs to be said here. Ulysses S. Grant and William T. Sherman succeeded by accepting casualties as unavoidable and turning war into attrition and "hell." Lee was accorded the mantle of greatness for his achievements in leading the Army of Northern Virginia. Field Marshal Viscount Wolseley, who fought in the Crimea and later became the commander of the British army, visited the Confederacy during the Civil War. He called Lee the greatest soldier of his age and "the most perfect man I ever met."[99] But he found ample fault with others, and so have most historians. Many were every bit as inept as the generals who blundered in the Crimea.

Like the Crimean War, the American Civil War subjected men to close combat, but it also exposed them to month after month of trench warfare, marked by bloody raids, well-aimed sniper fire, and bombardment by heavy artillery shells. Men fought and died alone on guard duty and in small groups in the fog and smoke of battle, as well as in large formations of troops and horses. They also endured painful extremes of cold and heat and the daily torment of lice, fleas, flies, mosquitoes, and rats. They were often hungry (more than a few men in the Crimea actually starved). Fearing that they would be next, those in the Crimea who survived had to watch their comrades die in agonizing filth, as dysentery and cholera wracked their bodies with cramps and uncontrollably emptied their intestines. Most also endured the absence of women and the fear that their loved ones would die before they could return. They lived with the undeniable evidence that many of their leaders were inept and that they were completely at the mercy of blundering generals and government officials. How men responded to such fears, privations, and suffering is the concern of this book, not the details of the battles in which they fought.

# 3

# THE GENERALS

## *Butchered Leadership*

THROUGHOUT HISTORY, MANY ARMIES have suffered needlessly because of their commanders' blunders, but few can have suffered any more than four of the five armies that fought in the Crimean War. With the exception of the Sardinians, examples of appallingly bad, even criminally negligent leadership occurred so often during this needless war that only a few can be discussed here. These few amply illustrate the problems that inept leadership can create in time of war.

One of the most horrendous examples of truly mindless negligence in military history was the utter failure of the British Ministry of War to provide at the outset of the war the food, matériel, surgeons, medical supplies, and transport necessary for its army to survive, much less defeat the enemy. Field Marshal Viscount Wolseley, who as a young officer arrived in the Crimea just in time to experience the unspeakable horrors of the winter of 1854–1855, later wrote that the Ministry of War was "criminal."[1] The full impact of its dereliction of duty was not felt until that terrible winter set in, but it was clear to the French as well as the British at the war's very beginning that something was terribly wrong. Even as the two armies sailed up the lovely, fjordlike blue Bosporus, eagerly watching dolphins leap high out of the water while scores of eagles soared overhead, the French noted that their ships were being constantly visited by British officers asking for such staples as tea and sugar, which the British ships inexplicably could not provide them. A British officer referred to this lack of planning as "infamous," noting that officers as well as men went without tea and bread.[2] The British also seemed to have forgotten how to transport horses. Poorly harnessed, many injured themselves and had to be destroyed; others died from the heat of the ships' boilers.

The lack of foresight of the British was obvious during their disorganized encampment in Gallipoli, but it became even more alarming after they moved to Varna. The countryside around Varna was lovely, with wood copses and rolling green hills watched over by storks, hawks, and falcons. At first, British troops delightedly picked wild strawberries and cherries, swam in the sea, hunted wild boar, and fished in the lakes and streams. Some regiments, like the 55th, had a splendid time: They organized games, the officers shared beer with their men, and all but a handful escaped disease. But most were not so well led or so lucky. The city of Varna and its outskirts were far more filthy and insect-ridden than anything that even Gallipoli could offer, and French regiments, like their British counterparts, soon suffered from these horrors.

In addition to open sewers and cesspools, dead dogs, cats, and horses, and all manner of rotting garbage lying everywhere on the unpaved streets, immense numbers of voracious mosquitoes, fleas, ants, and centipedes plagued men and horses alike. So many flies swarmed about that one officer tried to blow them up with gunpowder. When that tactic failed, he lit a smoky fire in his tent, but nothing prevented flies from covering his hands and face and tormenting his eyes. When British soldiers collapsed in heat of more than 90 degrees Fahrenheit after drinking cheap Turkish brandy in an attempt to ward off cholera (as they did in very large numbers), they lay pitifully in the burning sun, their sweat-soaked bodies literally black with flies. The horses were driven wild by them, too. No one in Varna could have then believed it, but the flies would be even more numerous and aggressive in the Crimea during the summer of 1855. The only thing that could drive away the flies proved to be a plague of locusts so dense that officers actually hacked away at them with their swords, killing thousands. Fly and mosquito nets existed in 1854, and so did insect-repellent powders, but neither the British nor the French armies were provided them.

The greatest threat to the allies' health came from Varna's feces-contaminated water supply, a breeding ground for cholera. Dreaded for centuries before it struck during the allies' stay at Varna, it was known as *Asiatic cholera* because it had killed so many in India. It had also become a scourge in many of the overcrowded, unsanitary cities of Europe. In 1848, cholera killed some 70,000 people in Britain and hundreds of thousands in Russia. The entire population of St. Petersburg fled in an attempt to escape its ravages, and before the epidemic ended, 660,000 Russians had been buried.[3] In 1854, before the fighting began in the Crimea, cholera struck again, this time ravaging London—little wonder, as London, like many other cities at that time, funneled much of its sewage into its main source of drinking water, the River Thames. The river stank so vilely that during the summer, Members of Parliament working at Westminster, on the bank of the Thames, complained bitterly and sometimes refused to meet at all.[4] That cholera was caused by *Vibrio cholorae* bacteria in feces-contaminated water was not discovered until 1883, well after it had caused many more deaths throughout the world, including in New Orleans and elsewhere in the United States (although it was not a major cause of death during the Civil War). However, a British doctor, John Snow, working in the cholera-wracked slums of London in 1854, showed that boiling drinking water could prevent the disease. He discussed his discovery as widely as he could before British troops sailed for Turkey and even published a book about it early in 1855, but the British Ministry of War predictably took no heed, and neither did most British doctors. Thomas Buzzard, a young army surgeon who had worked with Snow before sailing to Turkey, personally tried to convince British army doctors in the Crimea to order the boiling of drinking water. They scoffed in disbelief, and many died of cholera along with the troops.[5] Buzzard boiled his own drinking water and remained well.

Cholera struck seemingly healthy people with no warning, often killing in only four to five hours. Usually beginning with profuse vomiting, it was followed by copious diarrhea. In addition, victims suffered cramps of the muscles and bowels so severe that many screamed continuously as they vomited and defecated uncontrollably. When the pains began, some victims who knew about the disease blew their brains out.[6] As the cholera progressed, the pain usually, but not always, subsided, and the victims sank into a near coma, their eyes sunk into their sockets, until death from hypotensive shock finally took place.[7] Little enough imagination will be required to understand how painful and degrading this hideous disease was for its victims or how doctors and nurses suffered as they attempted to help dozens or even hundreds of victims in the death throes of cholera. By the time the two armies left Varna for the Crimea, 7,000 allied soldiers had died, most of them from cholera, and 12,000 to 15,000 more were in the hospital, many to die later. The allied generals had been warned repeatedly to camp elsewhere because Varna was a notoriously unhealthy place, but they chose to ignore the warning.

The same generals ignored another obvious danger. The ramshackle wooden buildings in Varna posed a clear fire hazard, yet inexplicably, neither the French nor the British took any steps to protect against possible fire the essential supplies that flooded into the city. None of the wooden structures near allied warehouses were pulled down, no water was stored nearby, and no guards were posted on fire watch, so when a fire broke out in a French wine canteen, it quickly blazed out of control. The gunpowder magazines barely escaped destruction when the wind shifted, but the fire raged for days.

> Upwards of 700 private houses, and three mosques, with about 100 spirit canteens, and 200 or 300 storehouses belonging to the allies, with all their contents, were completely destroyed. In one Turkish military storehouse were 30,000 gallons of oil, 150 tons of soap, 400 tons of sugar, and nearly 100,000 lbs. of coffee and rice. Not a (penny's) worth of all these were saved. The injury to the French was most serious. In one large storehouse they lost nearly 10,000 uniforms, 19,000 pairs of shoes, and 3,000 blankets, with a large quantity of pack-saddles and trenching tools. In another, an immense store of accoutrements, such as muskets, sabres, dragoon-saddles, shakos, knapsacks, infantry swords, and side belts were entirely destroyed. The English also suffered heavily. All their magazines of biscuit, barley, sugar, coffee, tea, soap, &c. were consumed.[8]

Other decisions that Britain's leaders made, or more often failed to make, were similarly disastrous, such as the decision in early September 1854 to move the allied armies, including 7,000 Turks, from Varna to the Crimea. Lord Raglan and his staff once again failed to distinguish themselves. First, Lord Raglan chose profoundly nearsighted General Sir George Brown to scout the Crimean coast for an appropriate landing place. It should have been no surprise that the places he chose were useless, but not until the allied invasion force actually arrived was this discovered. While better landing sites were being located, horses were once again dying and men were suffering needlessly. Some British troops were at sea for seventeen days with only salt pork and biscuit to eat.[9]

Furthermore, while the French took along their small pup tents, and the Turks took their elegant bell-shaped tents, the British stored their tents so deeply under other cargo that their army was without any protection during its first night ashore, when a cold rain poured incessantly. A few men tried to lie down in the mud, but most spent the entire night standing and shivering. Their immune systems cannot have benefited from the ordeal. This rain was not heavy enough to create a muddy impasse or to send the Alma River into flood. (Exactly one year later, drenching rains did in fact create a sea of mud that the allied forces could not have advanced through, and if they had somehow managed to reach the river, they could not have crossed the raging torrent it had become.) Needless to say, the allied generals had no knowledge of the local climate when they planned their invasion. For once, they were lucky, at least on this score. But they also had no idea what the terrain was like, how the civilians might react to them, or how many Russian troops were waiting for them.

As the well-equipped French, followed by the Turks, moved south along the coast toward the Alma, the British took up the left flank, marching slowly in great heat. Short of shipboard space, Raglan had left 5,200 horses in Varna, expecting to find many horses and carts in the Crimea to use as transportation. He was shocked to discover that none were to be had. Almost all the horses left behind, including the officers' thoroughbreds, starved.[10] Raglan and his staff also expected to find freshwater streams, and again, they were wrong.[11] After a few hours, so many men had collapsed and so much equipment had been tossed away that regiments bringing up the rear could barely pass through. When the troops finally reached a small stream, the men's thirst was so terrible that regiment after regiment hurled itself into the now muddy water, completely ignoring the officers' orders to remain in ranks. The same thing happened repeatedly on both sides in the American Civil War, but those were undisciplined troops, not Guardsmen. That night, the British army slept almost within earshot of the Russians at the Alma. Raglan ordered no one to scout the enemy's position.

Marshal St.-Arnaud and his staff, on the other hand, had already determined that the Russian left flank was unguarded, and they planned to storm it early the next morning. However, the British did not break camp until 10 A.M., four hours later than Raglan had ordered, and it was not until midday that the French scaled the unguarded heights on the left of Menshikov's army. Although in range of Russian artillery, Raglan ordered his men to lie down at 1:30 while he awaited word of St.-Arnaud's attack. It did not come until 3 P.M., when a frantic French staff officer rode up to blurt out, "Nous sommes massacrés!" This was an immense overstatement, as the French had taken no more than a few hundred casualties, but the French line regiments, unlike Zouaves, had refused to advance against Russian cannon fire, so the attack had bogged down.

Raglan immediately issued orders for his army to advance, but several commanders misunderstood what was wanted. They were to march straight ahead across the river and up the heights into the Russian position. Instead, weak-eyed General Sir George Brown sent his men off in the wrong direction. Even so, British troops bravely carried the day. After ordering his 900 cavalrymen not to advance, humiliating them as they all said, Raglan took up a position atop an exposed hill on the extreme right flank of the Russian line, wearing a blue frock coat and a white shirt and cravat. Exposing himself to Russian fire astride his thoroughbred chestnut, Ronald, he ordered up some small guns and bombarded the Russians, causing them quickly to limber up their guns and withdraw. He was in no position to direct the battle, something he left to lower-ranking officers, but the battle was over by 3:40.

St.-Arnaud took full credit for the victory, declaring delightedly that compared to the British, "My soldiers run; theirs walk."[12] In reality, the battle had been won by British courage and Russian bungling, but the campaign itself may very well have been lost by what St.-Arnaud decided when he and Raglan met a short time later. Raglan urged immediate pursuit, asking St.-Arnaud to provide infantry, to be joined by British cavalry and artillery. Raglan explained that his own infantry was too exhausted to pursue and neglected to mention (perhaps he did not know) that 7,000 of his men had not been engaged at all. St.-Arnaud quickly declined, saying that his artillery was out of ammunition, that and his infantry could not advance without their packs, and that these had been left in camp.[13] He did not tell Raglan that 12,000 of his men and almost all of the Turks had not yet fired a shot.

Several Russian officers later said that their demoralized troops could not have resisted an allied pursuit, not even a small one, but there was none. The fault lay with both allied commanders and with neither one. Neither man possessed any intelligence about the strength of the Russian forces or their fighting ability. They had no coordinated plan beyond marching forward, held no reserve to exploit Russian weakness, and had too few cavalry to pursue the enemy effectively if it should retreat. It was the first of many examples to come of the failings of allied joint command. The next morning, St.-Arnaud was ready to advance, but Raglan now declined because he had many more wounded to attend to than did the French. Shortly after the battle, he had spent an hour with wounded officers and men, an experience that left him greatly moved.

Britain's generals also made the remarkable decision to leave behind at Varna all their hospital wagons, stretchers, pack animals, and bedding and most regimental medicine chests, with their bandages, splints, morphia, and chloroform.[14] After the battle of Alma, nearly 1,000 British wounded (and an equal number of wounded Russians) lay in bitter cold for two nights and blazing sun for two days, without water, because the British had provided no medical organization for tending to them. The surviving wounded were finally reached by sailors and marines from ships offshore, who fashioned crude stretchers out of hammocks and oars, and some field ambulances were borrowed from the well-equipped French, who had only a few casualties. The wounded still had to be carried for three to four miles, in awful pain, to a makeshift field hospital, where harried surgeons amputated their limbs as the suffering men lay on the muddy ground, which was saturated with cow manure.[15] Eventually, the British found a door to serve as an operating table, but because there were no candles—also forgotten—surgery had to be discontinued at night. There were so few medical supplies that surgeons could do little more than amputate limbs or bandage wounds. Also, far too few surgeons were available to cope with the many British wounded. Aware of the shortage, thirty-one British navy surgeons volunteered to come ashore and help, but the army indignantly refused their offer.[16] For the army to accept help from the French was bad enough; from the navy, unthinkable. The failure of Raglan's staff to plan for the care of casualties is unfathomable.

The next horror was caused by Britain's failure to send even a single hospital ship with the expedition. As a result, wounded British soldiers had to be put in small boats and rowed through heavy surf before being put aboard an ordinary warship, where they lay on open decks, cared for by a handful of sailors and marines with no medical training. One ship that transported hundreds of men to hospitals in Gallipoli had exactly one bedpan and one urinal. When a wounded man's blanket became soaked with urine and feces, it was thrown overboard. When soldiers died from their wounds, or from the cholera that so often struck these weakened men, each body was tied in a blanket, with a cannonball tied as a weight around the ankles, and then dumped overboard without ceremony. Bodies frequently bobbed to the surface, where they remained, head and shoulders above water, until those that were within easy reach could be weighted more heavily and finally made to sink.

At this early stage of the war, the British troops suffered many more casualties than their French and Turkish allies, and their suffering had only begun. Yet, despite the obvious mistakes and unpreparedness of their leaders, the British rank and file rarely complained.[17] In contrast, during the American Civil War, both Federal and Confederate soldiers rarely stopped complaining. A good many British officers railed against the incompetence of their military planners, but for the most part, they kept their voices down, too. The men in the ranks carried on as before, hoping for water to drink, a little rum (or a lot), something to eat, and a dry place to sleep. Often, they had none of these. Neither did many Civil War soldiers, but they seldom resigned themselves to their suffering.

The sick and wounded in all the Crimean War armies suffered as few who live in an age of pain-controlling drugs can fully appreciate, but neither they nor more than a few of the men who tried to care for them complained about their lot. A few asked to have a mangled leg or arm taken off, and others begged that they not be, but there were few if any complaints about the medical unpreparedness that so brutally exaggerated their suffering. They moaned and screamed in pain, loudly and often, but they rarely openly questioned the competence of their military leaders or their doctors. Instead, there was quiet resignation and grim humor, especially among the battle-hardened Zouaves. On one occasion, as Zouaves dragged their dead comrades off by the heels to dump them in a common grave, one Zouave used a stray leg bone lying nearby to give one of the dead men the appearance of sexual arousal. The others laughed delightedly.[18]

There was much more about British bungling to come, along with bungling by their allies, but incompetent leadership was also common among the Russians. Their tsar, Nicholas I, was devoted to his sense of duty and his idea of honor. He had, for example, been notably faithful to his beloved wife, the German princess Alexandra, until late in life when, because of a heart condition, she was no longer permitted to have sexual relations. Only then did he take a mistress, the dazzling young Varvara Nelidova. By the standards of the day, this was remarkable steadfastness.[19] He also possessed an undeniable majesty and a great love of country. But the critical concerns for Russia were not how majestic this very tall, stern man could appear in public but whether he could effectively guide Russia's future, and about that, many questions remained. Not least of these was his decision to appoint Prince Alexander S. Menshikov, his former emissary to Turkey in the failed peace talks, to command the Russian forces in the Crimea. Nicholas was not the utter dunce Western historians usually make him out to be, but this appointment was a calamitous decision.

Menshikov had some military experience, having fought against Napoléon in 1812, and especially against the Turks. A striking part of this experience consisted of being castrated by a Turkish cannonball, an event that left him, not surprisingly one supposes, a good deal less than friendly toward the Turks, as he demonstrated so vividly during the peace talks.[20] He was a descendent of a favorite of Peter the Great and a popular figure at court, where his nimble tongue and quick, if acerbic, wit and courtly manners made him something of a celebrity. The tsar thought well of him, but at the time of his appointment to command, Menshikov was completely out of touch with contemporary military affairs (such as the range of the newfangled rifles the allies and some of his own troops had), fortification, and the use of artillery. Also, he was a sick man, plagued by a host of ailments, from gout, nosebleeds, headaches, toothaches, abscesses, and chronic cough to serious, recurring fevers.[21] He later said that he knew nothing about tactics and never thought of himself as a general.[22]

He certainly did not act like one. Instead of creating a staff of reliable officers, he did everything himself while exchanging jokes with a few cronies, whom he referred to as his "chancellery," meaning the court of a nobleman. He never inspected his troops or inquired about their training or welfare. He also ignored the tsar's order to fortify Sevastopol. What is more, when Prince Menshikov took command in the Crimea, he scoffed at the idea of an allied landing there. Only two days before the allied landings took place, he wrote to a subordinate that the "enemy could never dare" to land in the Crimea because it was too late in the year for an invasion.[23] When news of the allied landing reached Sevastopol less than forty-eight hours later, the city's theater, which had been showing Nicolai Gogol's *Inspector General,* emptied in panic, but Menshikov confidently announced that he would thrash the enemy. To do so, he decided that he needed a position that would not be under the guns of the allied fleet and that had good defensive features. He chose the heights south of the Alma River; it was the most defensible position north of Sevastopol, but hardly an inspired decision. If he had blockaded the three harbors south of Sevastopol and moved his army inland, where it would be in the allies' rear if they moved on the city, he could have created an enormous problem for them. To attack Sevastopol under such conditions would have been foolhardy, and the allies lacked the transport necessary to attack Menshikov miles inland. While they hesitated, as they would surely have done, Russian reinforcements could have been on the march. Instead, Menshikov chose the Alma River line, then bungled its defense.

The left flank of his position lay along a steep cliff cut by rocky ravines, but it was accessible from below by several paths and roads. Menshikov did not inspect the position himself. Instead, he accepted the opinion of a junior officer that it would be impossible for the allies to move up these ravines or bring artillery up these roads, and therefore, he did nothing to fortify the position or to block the roads. In fact, for six long days, except for one position in the center of his line, where he did protect some guns with earth barricades, he did nothing to entrench his troops or protect his guns, leaving his artillery in the open in front of his infantry, where his guns lay helplessly vulnerable to the allies' long-range rifles. Harking back to the Napoleonic war, he intended to defeat the allies with a massive bayonet charge.[24] He was unaware that the allies not only had greater firepower but also outnumbered his troops almost two to one.

The Russian regiments had marched north from Sevastopol in high spirits, led by many bands, singers, and buffoons (soldiers who "played the fool" to keep the troops jolly). They were joined by several civilians who, caught up in the enthusiasm, volunteered their services. The troops were beautifully uniformed in gray greatcoats worn over green or blue jackets and blue trousers with a narrow red stripe down the side. Their leather cross-belts were dazzlingly white. To the surprise of the allies, who by now were far from clean, everything they wore, including their white linen underpants, was scrupulously clean. Most of them wore a black leather helmet with a brass spike on the top and a handsome brass imperial eagle on the front, but some wore tall shakos and others flat, visorless forage caps. They carried large cowhide knapsacks on their backs, each of which contained two cotton shirts, two pairs of socks, a pair of warm mittens, an extra pair of trousers, and an extra pair of leather boots. Each man also carried an extra pair of leather soles for his boots, as well as sewing needles, awls, and thread. It is doubtful that any American regiment in the Civil War was ever this clean or well provided for. Almost every pack contained a well-used deck of playing cards, but no reading material. Every soldier also carried, slung over one shoulder, a haversack filled with coarse black rye bread and some very hard and tasteless biscuits. Each man carried his money in a small leather pouch tied around his leg just below the knee. A cleaner or better-looking set of soldiers would have been hard to find away from the parade ground, but their weapons remained mediocre at best. Russian artillery was very good, but almost all of the infantrymen had only inaccurate short-range muskets with bayonets that could be bent in a man's hands.[25]

The Russian soldiers superstitiously believed that Menshikov was "unlucky," but because they had been told that the allies would be pushovers, they exuded confidence. Although his troops were outnumbered, Menshikov was so certain of victory that he encouraged thirty grand young ladies of Sevastopol to join him in a grandstand he had built on the heights above the river, where, at a champagne picnic, they could watch the action unfold through pearl-handled

opera glasses.[26] He assured them that the battle would end in a decisive trouncing of the allies because, as he dismissively said to the
women and his officers, the British were fit to fight only "savages."[27]

The night before the battle, bands played marches while regimental choirs serenaded General Menshikov and sang religious songs.[28]
Men in one regiment went to bed complaining because they had just
learned that they would receive no vodka in the morning, asking,
"And how can we fight without it?" It seems that the regiment's
colonel, who like many others was always eager to pocket money
meant for the soldiers, had reasoned that because half the men
would be killed, it "would only be a waste to give them vodka."[29]

The morning before the battle, as the ladies from Sevastopol admired the allied fleet at anchor, its ships sporting multicolored identi-
fication lights, they were suddenly thrilled by the sight of several
thousand Russian cavalrymen cantering down the slope toward an
advancing party of French troops. Both sides exchanged shots, but
the only known victim was a nearsighted French colonel who rode
his horse into the Russian cavalry, mistaking them for his own men.
He proved to be a high-ranking count, who became highly indignant
when he was taken prisoner. Eyeglasses were worn by a few officers
at this time, but as we have already seen, many hopelessly nearsighted officers were so vain that they chose to do without them.[30]

The force that Menshikov arrayed on the heights consisted of
forty-two battalions of infantry averaging about 800 men each, sixteen squadrons of cavalry, eleven squadrons of Cossacks, and eighty-
four artillery pieces. He also had 600 formidable Congreve rockets,
which could have been deadly, but unaccountably, no one had remembered to bring their launching frames, so they were useless. Believing the cliffs on his left close to the sea unscalable, Menshikov
chose not to expose his troops to naval gunfire and positioned only a
few Cossacks there to give warning should the allies somehow
achieve the impossible and make their way up those heights. On the
morning of the allied attack, the day was so clear that the French, in
their baggy red pants, blue coats and red caps, and the British, in
their scarlet coats with white cross-belts, could be easily seen with
the naked eye. It was so still that the sound of allied drums, bugles,
and bagpipes and even the clink of metal and horses neighing was
clearly audible on the Alma heights almost three miles away. As the
allies formed their regiments to advance, the tableau resembled

nothing so much as a wealthy young Victorian boy's dream of playing with a great many shiny tin soldiers. On the allies' right were some Turks following the Zouaves in their enormously baggy trousers; short, open-buttoned jackets; and green turbans. These veterans of the Algerian wars were the most aggressive troops on the field, and they had had years of experience in mountain warfare in Algeria. Farther toward the center were the red and blue French infantry of the line, derisively called "toads" by the elite Zouaves, and on the allied left were the British, flanked by their cavalry, the only cavalry the allies had thus far transported to the Crimean peninsula.

Priests encouraged the waiting Russians by carrying holy banners, crosses, and images among them. As the priests visited one regiment after another, sprinkling holy water, the soldiers removed their caps and knelt, often clutching the metal amulet that each man wore around his neck.[31] Golden embroideries reflected the sunlight while solemn liturgical hymns rose above the sounds of men making ready for war. As the Russians watched, the allies' bands played, bagpipes skirled, men sang, steel bayonets sparkled in the sun, and, to the surprise of the Russians, when the allies advanced—crushing lavender-smelling herbs under their boots and scattering hundreds of snakes, some of them eight feet long and as thick as a man's arm—they did so in long lines, not in closely packed, deep columns as the Russians expected.[32] Russian artillery tactics called for the firing of solid shot to tear dense enemy columns apart, but the allies, advancing in lines, merely sidestepped the balls and let them bound to the rear, playfully chased by a British officer's greyhound and a Maltese terrier named Toby.[33] The people most in danger from these potentially lethal missiles were the army wives who trudged along some distance behind their husbands for fear of losing touch with them forever. They carried such huge bundles on their backs that they resembled pack mules.

The Russians were surprised by just about everything that happened next—amazed that the French, led by Zouaves shouting, "Moscow," attacked so rapidly and that the British moved so sedately, never picking up their pace despite severe losses. As the allies advanced, the Cossacks set a village full of stacked straw on fire to blind the British, but the wind shifted, instead blowing acrid smoke into the eyes of the Russians, who for some time lost all sight of the British advance. When Russian soldiers began to fall to British rifle bullets while the enemy was still almost a mile away, they were shocked and frightened. Some knelt to pray for deliverance, and others became noticeably shaky.[34] Most vulnerable were the exposed artillerymen, who, without protective earthworks, fell before they could load and fire their guns. Those who survived soon ran out of ammunition because Menshikov had mysteriously left most of it far to the rear.

That Menshikov and his senior commanders were stunned by the range and accuracy of allied rifle fire was truly inexplicable: Menshikov's army had a rifle battalion of its own, entirely equipped with new long-ranged rifles, and another 1,700 rifles had been distributed in small numbers to sharpshooters in the other battalions. Somehow, two-thirds of these powerful new weapons were never fired at all, and the others quickly ran out of ammunition. Despite what should have been firsthand knowledge of these revolutionary new weapons, Menshikov's men used tactics that went right back to 1812.

Menshikov's other crucial blunder was leaving his left flank open, guarded only by the notoriously unreliable Cossacks. True to their past exploits, the Zouaves not only made their way up the cliffs but also brought their artillery with them. Instead of raising the alarm, the Cossacks rode away, allowing the French gunners to begin a devastating fire on troops commanded by one of the most useless officers in any army, Lieutenant General V. I. Kiryakov, said by a contemporary Russian historian to be "utterly ignorant, totally devoid of any military ability and rarely in a completely sober state."[35] Menshikov's so-called chancellery was so inept that it often lost track of entire regiments, and there was no communication among commanders. As his aides, Menshikov preferred inexperienced young princes to experienced officers. When young Prince Bariatinsky, Menshikov's aide-de-camp, rode west to find Kiryakov, he discovered that the general was presiding over a champagne party and seemed much the worse for it.

Bariatinsky, a junior naval officer with no experience of ground combat, pointed out the French artillery, causing General Kiryakov to respond inanely that he could "see the French but did not fear them."[36] This did not seem like an altogether appropriate answer to the young prince, nor to the men of the Minsk Regiment now being cut down by French fire. Kiryakov finally did manage to order his men to fire at what he thought was the French cavalry. They proved to be the Kiev Hussars, and their commander had to be physically restrained from taking his sword to Kiryakov.[37] Whether by the order of a regimental officer or by Kiryakov himself is not known, but the Minsk Regiment then fell back. At the very least, Kiryakov did nothing to stop this retreat, which began to roll up the entire left of the Russian defensive line, much of it falling back without firing a shot.

Some time later, General Kiryakov was found huddled in a hollow behind the front, without his horse and with no one to command.[38] He was not the only cowardly Russian officer, nor was he the only one who was drunk. Several officers cowered behind their horses when the firing began. After the battle, a dead-drunk artillery captain, found lying in a wagon, offered his British captors a swig on the bottle of champagne he had in his hand, but to their great regret, it was already empty.[39] Still, many Russian officers and men fought well, and some fought with reckless bravery. For example, sixty-year-old General Kaganov was wounded in the hip while personally leading an attack, but he refused to surrender his sword until he was bayoneted in the stomach by a British soldier. As he lay dying, he said of the British Guards who had just broken the Russian center, "With troops like these, you can beat anything." He also said that he admired the "savages without trousers," meaning the kilted Highlanders.[40]

The unopposed French continued to fire on retreating Russians, suffering few casualties in return, but in the center, the Russians still held firm. The British waded the shoulder-deep Alma, most men stopping to drink, and several of them drowning before they could scramble up the steep opposite embankment, in some places fifteen feet high, under heavy fire.[41] They took many casualties and on one part of the field were driven back before fresh troops came up and eventually sent the Russians reeling back as a disorganized mob.

Like Russian generals in the war against Japan that took place fifty years later, those at Alma had little desire to cooperate, and Menshikov's orders were too vague to force them to take corrective action before it was too late. He also did nothing to stiffen his men's resolve, leading one wounded Russian officer to curse at him in disgust.[42] The retreat that followed was orderly on the part of a few regiments, but it was a panicky, pell-mell rout of most, who ran when they mistook Cossacks for allied cavalry. As the demoralized, confused soldiers, led by equally uncertain officers, made their way back from the Alma, all the while expecting to be destroyed by the allies, they left a litter of equipment and wounded men behind. Some officers tried to stem the tide, even cutting some of their own men down with their swords, but most joined the runaway mob.

When Menshikov left the field, he impulsively ordered a young aide to tell Tsar Nicholas what had happened. After seven days of hard riding, this exhausted and excitable junior officer described the battle to the tsar in such uncomplimentary terms that the distraught tsar was convinced his beloved troops were cowards led by idiots. Nicholas took to his bed, where he languished without eating for several days. When he finally recovered his spirits enough to speak, he did not order Menshikov to be relieved of his command as most Russian officers had hoped. The old prince continued to lead his army without the least sign of military zeal or skill. To anyone who would listen, he blamed his defeat on the cowardice of his soldiers.

Fortunately for the Russians, the senior allied military commanders did not see eye to eye. For one thing, it was not clear who was in command, Britain's Lord Raglan or France's Marshal St.-Arnaud. The former was inexperienced and ineffectual as a military leader, and the latter, if a somewhat better general, was suffering painfully from stomach cancer and was only a few days away from death due to cholera.

After years of service in Algeria, St.-Arnaud had established himself as a gallant general with good military judgment, but as a young man, he had appeared to be anything but a future marshal. Bored by garrison life, he spent a dozen years in pursuit of adventure and debauchery. Then, after several years of mercenary military service, he went to London to teach fencing. When there was no money to be had in this profession, he became a dance instructor, then a marker at a billiard table, an actor, a singer, a poet, and a violin player. He left London just ahead of a horde of bill collectors, but he had mastered English, if not the art of making a living, and his skills as a musician and singer made him popular after he was reinstated in the army. He became a competent general, supported by professional staff officers, but he died shortly after the battle on the Alma, cared for at the end by his young wife, who had followed him to the Crimea aboard a French warship.[43]

Raglan entered the army at the age of only fifteen, when his commission was purchased for him. He served as one of Wellington's aides-de-camp at Waterloo, where he was severely wounded in the right arm. After the arm had been amputated without anesthesia, the surgeon prepared to toss it away, but Raglan coolly demanded that it be given back because the hand had a ring on "it" that his wife had given him. In the years that followed, Raglan continued to do staff work for Lord Wellington, becoming what a British colonel called a "good red-tapist" but "no general."[44] His forte was carrying out Wellington's wishes, not making his own decisions, and before the Crimea, he had never commanded troops in battle. His greatest strengths were his kind nature, gentlemanly tact, imperturbable amiability, and fluent French. Even so, when the French at the battle of the Alma played their bugles incessantly before attacking, he complained about their "infernal too-too-tooing," saying that it was "all they ever do."[45] Nevertheless, it is likely that no other British general could have held the Anglo-French alliance together.

Almost all of Raglan's officers were old for active campaigning, and some were old by any standard. Raglan himself was sixty-six; General Sir George Brown (known to the men of his division as "old imbecile bully" and hated by his fellow officers) was a roly-poly sixty-five; General Sir George De Lacy Evans, wounded at the battle of New Orleans in 1812, was seventy; and Raglan's chief engineer, Sir John Fox Burgoyne (known to fellow officers as a "nincompoop" and a "shocking old dolt"), was seventy-two.[46] (Burgoyne was the illegitimate son of Susan Caulfield, a popular singer, and General Lord John "Gentleman Johnny" Burgoyne, who had surrendered to the Americans at Saratoga in a crucial British defeat during the American War for Independence.) Brown and Burgoyne were also dangerously nearsighted for any active military campaign. Brown, in fact, had myopically strayed so close to some Cossacks at the Alma that other British troops were barely able to prevent his capture.

Although his field commanders were old, Raglan surrounded himself with aristocratic young staff officers who, while pleasant enough, knew nothing about war. For example, five of his nephews were on his headquarters staff. St.-Arnaud, on the other hand, had an experienced staff familiar with small-scale war, but he was often in such pain that no decisions could be made. Still, before attacking Menshikov at the Alma River, he pulled himself together long enough to urge Raglan to march around the Russian right flank and attack them from the rear. Raglan decided that he had too few men to turn the Russians' flank, so he chose the only other alternative, ordering his troops to attack the Russians' center, the strongest part of their line and the only place where they had placed their artillery behind heavy earthworks. The attack could easily have failed, but thanks to the valor of his troops and no small amount of Russian ineptitude, it succeeded.

After the firing stopped on the heights above Alma, an eerie silence spread over the battlefield. Close to 10,000 dead and wounded men lay there, many of them with hideous wounds, but not until later, when the men were no longer in shock, did the moans and screams begin, rising to a crescendo by nightfall, then slowly diminishing as many men died. Their corpses shocked even veterans—brains scooped out as if by a shovel, bodies torn in every way imaginable, headless torsos still quivering. One British officer was struck by the sight of a man's head completely severed from his body, a smile frozen on his face.[47] No Russian doctors had stayed behind to tend wounded Russians, so Raglan left a doctor from the 44th Regiment to care for them. This doctor did what he could but soon died of cholera.

The original plan agreed upon by the British and the French governments called for the allies to storm Sevastopol from the north, and to destroy its docks and sink the Russian fleet before reembarking. The French and the British moved cautiously toward the city, whose northern defenses centered on a large, star-shaped stone fort. Despite this fort and the guns of Russian ships in the adjacent harbor, it was obvious to many allied officers that the northern approaches to the city were weakly held, far more so than the Alma River line had been. Still, some hard fighting probably would have been required to enter the city from this direction, and after their shaky performance on the Alma, the French were unwilling to ask their troops to storm such a fortification.[48] Raglan's chief engineer, the seventy-two-year old Burgoyne, was little respected by his fellow officers, but this wizened veteran nonetheless had Raglan's ear. He pointed out that the southern approaches to Sevastopol were almost completely open and that, moreover, there were good harbors to supply the allied armies to the south of the city. He assured Raglan that the city would fall in two days to an attack from that direction.

Before the allied landing, the city of Sevastopol held some 43,500 people, about 7,000 of them civilians. Many of these were the wives and children of officers and men in the Russian army and navy; others were shopkeepers, waitresses, singers, actresses, and, in no small number, prostitutes. The area around Sevastopol had been occupied by the Greeks as early as 500 B.C. and, after a tumultuous history, had been annexed in 1783 by Catherine the Great, who had ordered that it be transformed into a naval base and fortress. She gave the place the Greek name of Sevastopol, the "majestic city." The city was built on the south bank of a bay that was four miles long and half a mile wide. The roadstead rarely froze, and its calm, shoal-free waters provided one of the finest harbors in the world. A number of smaller bays branched off to the south. One of these, known as South Bay, separated the old town of Sevastopol from a cluster of naval barracks, warehouses, and new suburbs to the east.

The main town to the west of South Bay occupied a regular grid pattern, with numerous squares, and two paved boulevards that featured shops, restaurants, theaters, an opera house, and hotels. There were seven Russian Orthodox churches, as well as a Lutheran and a Catholic church, a synagogue, and a mosque. There was a museum, too, a library, numerous large granite barracks, and government buildings. There were also 2,145 private residences, some of them elegant. The bay itself was ringed by arsenals, warehouses, workshops, admiralty buildings, and dry docks. Several bridges and ferries connected the northern suburbs to the southern parts of the city. This northern area included factories producing small arms ammunition, biscuits, and other provisions for the navy. In addition to wells within the city, water was piped in by aqueduct from nearby springs and the Chernaya River. The seaward approaches were guarded by numerous formidable forts, mounting nearly 400 large guns. Admiral V. K. Kornilov's squadron of warships added 230 guns, and Admiral P. S. Nakimov's ships added another 300 guns to the defenses.[49] Although Sevastopol was poorly defended against land attack, the fact that the city was cut in two by a four-and-a-half-mile-long bay made any land attack difficult.

The Russians in Sevastopol spent the summer of 1854 in nonstop revelry. Officers in full-dress uniform attended endless balls with their ladies in elegant gowns. Children often dressed elegantly, too. Count Tolstoy recalled the sight of a young girl in a pretty pink dress trying to avoid getting her shoes muddy.[50] Men and women promenaded along the two main boulevards, in the squares, and along the paths shaded by white azaleas, where single men and women did their best to dress attractively and meet one another.[51] Theaters, music halls, and restaurants with bands and chanteuses provided almost nonstop entertainment, while shops run by Greeks, Italians, Jews, and Armenians did a lively business. Street vendors sold rolls and glasses of a spicy lime drink. Houses of prostitution did their usual flourishing trade with drunken sailors and soldiers, while officers found comfort (and the same venereal diseases) in the embrace of the higher class of prostitute that typically worked in hotel rooms or private residences.[52] At the center of Sevastopol's busy social life stood Schneider's Hotel, with its large restaurant, its bar, and some vacant rooms upstairs. Officers gathered there every day and night to eat, drink, gamble at card games, boast about their bravery, and complain about the ignorance, apathy, and slovenliness of their soldiers and sailors.

As already noted, when news of the allied landings first spread in the city, civilians rushed about in patriotic fervor. The entire city milled around in the streets all night after first hearing news of the allied invasion. Even nearby farmers of Scottish and English ancestry joined in the Russian cause. One of these was an English engineer named Upton who had helped to design Sevastopol's forts. Another was named Mackenzie, and a general in the Russian army was also of Scottish ancestry.

Raglan led the French around Sevastopol to the east, leaving his flank invitingly open to Russian attack, but Menshikov had been too badly beaten at the Alma River to react to the opportunity. British commanders gleefully captured many Russian wagons full of riches, including Menshikov's elegant field kitchen and one of his carriages containing letters from the tsar, 50,000 French francs, ladies' underclothes, and pornographic French novels.[53] The allies also pillaged several elegant estates they encountered on the way, stealing everything of value and destroying everything they couldn't carry.

While the Russians in Sevastopol wondered when the French and the British would march into their nearly defenseless city, the allies were more concerned about securing harbors in their rear (the British at Balaclava to the south, and the French at two larger harbors farther to the west) than about taking Sevastopol. Just before leaving Varna for the Crimea, Sir George Brown had asked Lord Raglan what he knew about the Crimea. Raglan's answer was that "he had no information whatever."[54] As early as June 29, 1854, the

British Cabinet had ordered Raglan to take Sevastopol, but despite the availability of many reliable people who knew the Crimea well, Raglan inexcusably made no attempts to educate himself.[55] Somehow, he did not even become aware that a British naval officer had carefully sketched the defenses of Sevastopol in January 1854, while delivering a warning to Admiral Kornilov that British ships were entering the Black Sea.[56]

As the British and French armies slowly bypassed Sevastopol to approach it from the south, the city itself fell into chaos. While the allies admired the city's beautiful green copper domes, wounded Russian soldiers from the Alma River battle straggled into Sevastopol, looking for medical assistance that would not come for weeks in some instances. Most of Menshikov's troops attempted to reorganize themselves to the east of the city. So few potentially effective forces remained in the city itself—only ten understrength battalions, or about 6,000 men—that Sevastopol's defense had to be largely turned over to some 10,000 sailors from the Russian fleet. These 16,000 poorly armed men would have to face over 60,000 allied troops. The sailors began the slow process of removing guns from their ships to be emplaced around the city, and they managed to sink six of their ships to block the harbor's entrance. But for days, these men added little to the defense of the city because, thanks to a large supply of liquor, they made themselves gloriously drunk and ran through the streets shouting that Menshikov had sold the city to the English.[57] The Russian soldiers called Menshikov "Prince Judas"; the sailors preferred "Prince Anathema."[58]

The gallant and industrious Russian admiral V. K. Kornilov finally destroyed enough liquor to sober up most of his sailors, put 7,000 convicts to work, and urged many civilians to pitch in as well. They were faced with the daunting task of building fortifications with only broken shovels, crude baskets, and their bare hands to transform tons of dirt into obstacles that would thwart the approaching allies. When the allies reached Sevastopol on September 24, most of the city's inhabitants, including the governor and the police, fled in panic. By Menshikov's order, Russian troops forced them back into the city, but the motley garrison could have done little at that time to stop a determined attack.

The city's vulnerability was not lost on the first British general who brought his troops close to Sevastopol, its many white-walled and green-roofed buildings gleaming in the sun. Sir George Cathcart was so excited by the prospects of an early victory that he rushed an aide to Raglan with this note:

> "They are working at two or three redoubts, but the place is only enclosed by a thing like a low park wall, not in good repair. I am sure I could walk into it, with scarcely the loss of a man, at night, or an hour before day break . . . we could leave our packs, and run into it even in open day, only risking a few shots whilst we passed the redoubt. We see people walking about the streets in great consternation."[59]

It is unlikely that Cathcart could have walked in quite as easily as all this, but a strong assault by the British, even without French support, would almost certainly have led to an easy victory, as Russian officers afterward readily admitted. But Lord Raglan was not one to seize the day. Instead, he consulted the new French commander, General Robert Canrobert, who had replaced St.-Arnaud a few days earlier. Canrobert had earned a reputation for brave and intelligent leadership in Algeria, but no one, including Canrobert himself, had ever imagined him as the commander of an army. Suddenly faced with the task of succeeding St.-Arnaud, he froze. Unwilling to risk an assault, Canrobert (earning his nickname of "Bob Can't") told Raglan he could not trust his troops to attack a "fortress" across open ground, and he insisted on waiting for his siege guns to batter the city down before attempting any assault. Burgoyne now changed his mind. His nearsighted view of the city now convinced him that it would cost 500 lives to take Sevastopol, something he declared to be "utterly unjustifiable."[60] He apparently was oblivious that the British had lost close to 3,000 at the Alma.

Under orders not to act independently of the French, Raglan politely acquiesced and agreed to a siege. When General Cathcart, who still insisted that the city would fall almost without bloodshed, heard the news, he rushed to Raglan to say, "Land the siege train! But, my dear Lord Raglan, what the devil is there to knock down?"[61] Not only did the allies not attack, but they also waited an interminable twenty-seven days before firing a single cannon shot at the busy defenders. Granted this heaven-sent reprieve, a tall thirty-seven-year-old Russian engineering officer named Franz E.I. Todleben, who came from a family of Prussian ancestry in Latvia, achieved wonders in designing a series of fortifications, seeing to it that they were built by convicts, women, and children working in shifts around the clock, then continually modifying the forts to meet French and British threats. In addition to large forts (or "redoubts," as they were called), he built scores of shell-proof smaller forts that held half a dozen beds, tables, and lamps and had polished floors as well. There was usually ample food and wine, all blessed by an icon of the holy virgin hanging on the wall.[62]

Colonel Todleben was creative, tireless, and brave, as were the three Russian admirals—Kornilov, Nakimov, and Istomin—who organized sailors not only into effective gun crews, for which the sailors had been trained, but to fight as infantry as well, for which they had not. Some army reinforcements arrived, too, led by four battalions of Cossack infantry trained in the Caucasus mountains to fight as sharpshooters. Armed with long-range rifles, they communicated the location of their targets by animal cries—of wolves, jackals, dogs, and even cats—to confuse the allies.[63] When the French and British finally felt ready to bombard the city, and perhaps to assault it, Sevastopol was very nearly impregnable. It would hold out for another year.

Battles tend to be messy, unpredictable affairs, but few could doubt that a British attack launched a day or two after General Cathcart first saw the weak Russian defenses would have succeeded with minimal cost compared to the losses that followed. If Russia's best regiments could not stand against a British charge at Alma, it is almost certain that the disorganized and undisciplined motley of armed men in Sevastopol could not have thrown back a numerically superior force of British and French infantry. No one can know what effect the early capture of Sevastopol would have had on the course of the war. It is possible that the tsar would have negotiated a peace settlement, ending the war. Even if he had renewed his efforts, he had few available reinforcements to turn to. Although they might have had some limited successes in menacing British supply lines to Balaclava (which might have been abandoned), or to the two western French ports nearer to Sevastopol, it is difficult to imagine a scenario in which the Russians could have attacked the city successfully. Once quartered in the city, the allied soldiers would not have suffered such terrible losses during the winter of 1854–1855. Generals often make horrific mistakes, and the failure to attack Sevastopol when the allies first arrived was certainly one, but the French were even more at fault than the British.

The next calamity was entirely of Britain's making. The famous "charge of the Light Brigade" is still celebrated for the astonishing bravery of the British cavalry, and justly so. But it was also one of the more spectacular blunders in the history of war. Many were to blame: Lord Raglan, a young captain named Lewis Edward Nolan, and Lord Lucan, the commander of the Heavy Brigade. But the central figure in the tragedy was Lord Cardigan, one of the least likable men ever to command British troops. For reasons that are still difficult to understand, Raglan placed Cardigan in command of the Light Brigade under the direct command of Lord Lucan. The two earls were brothers-in-law who hated each other so intensely that *The Times* correspondent, W. H. ("Billy") Russell, wrote that the government that had made this choice was "guilty of treason to the Army."[64] Almost everyone agreed except Raglan, who, despite open conflict between the two earls, did nothing to put the matter right.

At fifty-four, Lord Lucan was a tall, slender, bald-headed, loud-mouthed, and unpopular martinet. Consensus in the army was that he was "invincibly stupid," but it is more accurate to say that he lacked the ability to distinguish what was important from what was not.[65] The tall, thin, blond, and aristocratically handsome Cardigan was also a martinet who imposed discipline capriciously and was stupid—even more stupid than Lucan. A cavalry officer summed up the two men this way: "As to Lord Cardigan, he has as much brains as my boot, and is only equally in want of intellect by his relation Lord 'Look-on.' [So named because of his inaction at the Alma, where his cavalry stood by while Russian cavalry jeered at them.] Without mincing words, two bigger fools could not be picked out of the British Army to take command."[66] Both men had monstrous tempers, and Cardigan's was often wholly unrestrained. As colonel of the cherry-trousered 11th Hussars, he railed against his junior officers, court-martialed them for no reason, fought duels, and threatened to fight others with his expensive hair-trigger dueling pistol. He also seduced other men's wives with no sense of concern—once, fully aware that a spy hired by a cuckolded lord was watching—and then bought himself out of trouble. He became so notorious that he was even booed and hissed in public.[67]

Rather than suffer the inconvenience of a boring sea voyage to Turkey, Lord Cardigan sent his magnificent yacht on ahead and traversed France by land with some other senior officers, accompanied by servants, grooms, riding horses, and tons of baggage in dozens of wagons. After hosting a lavish dinner in Paris, he was received by Emperor Napoléon III and Empress Eugènie. Once he had arrived in Constantinople, he let it be known that he was not under Lucan's orders, although neither Lucan nor Raglan understood any such thing. Cardigan's first brush with action came at Varna, where he was ordered to scout north to locate the Russians. He was to take two squadrons of cavalry with three days' rations and, as soon as possible, "ascertain the movements of the enemy."[68] Instead of a quick scout, Cardigan took seventeen days to discover that the Russians were nowhere to be seen, something the Turks already knew perfectly well but were never asked. While his men barely survived on their three days' rations of salt meat and biscuits, and their horses broke down, the Seventh Earl of Cardigan was the only man to sleep under canvas—on a spring sofa bed that he insisted on having carried along![69] When the patrol finally limped back to Varna, the men leading their broken horses on foot, it was found that only 80 of their 200 horses were fit for duty. An equal number of horses had died. The patrol proved an example of brutal incompetence, and Cardigan followed it by having his men drilled every day from 4 A.M. to 9 A.M., usually while he slept. It is no surprise that his men detested him.[70] The chief critic of this abuse of cavalry, as he saw it, was Captain Nolan, a tall, handsome, blond cavalryman, who had achieved a sparkling reputation as a swordsman and horseman and had written two books about the training and use of cavalry. As if to prove Nolan right, a few days later a patrol of twelve men rode out and quickly obtained all the information Cardigan had missed.[71]

Lord Lucan's achievements at Varna were only slightly less ludicrous. When he first attempted to drill his cavalry, he used commands that had been in vogue when he last commanded cavalry— seventeen years earlier. The result was total confusion because these commands had long since been replaced. Rather than learn new commands, Lucan insisted that his troops learn the old ones, something they never managed to do because even their officers were ignorant of the old drill.[72] Finally, Lucan's officers asked Lord George Paget, an acquaintance and peer of Lucan, to talk to him about the impasse. Lucan listened and "graciously" agreed to change to the new commands.[73] He also quarreled with Lord Cardigan and alienated the otherwise genial Lord Raglan, who would rebuke him in front of his men during the confused march from the Alma to the south of Sevastopol.

Soon after the Light Brigade arrived south of Sevastopol, Lord Cardigan complained to Lord Raglan that he was ill. No doubt he was, as he was chronically afflicted with piles, painful urination, and bronchitis. Now he pleaded exhaustion. Ever the patrician, Raglan allowed Cardigan to live aboard his yacht, the *Dryad*, in his elegantly furnished cabin with filtered running water, his French chef, and many cases of champagne. Captain Nolan called him the "noble yachtsman," and the label stuck. Lord Cardigan's routine called for him to rise late, eat well, and then canter the nine miles from his mooring to his troops, arriving around 11 A.M.

It was at just this hour that he arrived during the Russian attack at Balaclava. The battle took place on a day so beautifully clear that many observers on both sides could see the drama unfolding. From his vantage point on a hill, Raglan saw the Russians preparing to haul away some captured British guns, and he ordered Lucan to attack to save the guns. The order, hastily written by an aide in pencil, read, "Lord Raglan wishes the cavalry to advance rapidly to the front, and try to prevent the enemy carrying away the guns. Troop of horse artillery may accompany. French cavalry is on your left. Immediate."[74]

Instead of asking one of his own aides to deliver the message, Raglan gave the order to none other than Captain Nolan, the dashing cavalryman who regarded Cardigan and Lucan as the two greatest fools in the entire history of the British army.[75] Perhaps Raglan chose Nolan because he was one of the finest riders in all Europe, and he happened to be nearby, but he was hardly someone to be entrusted with such a dangerously vague order, to be delivered to a general he loathed, something Raglan must have known. Dramatic to a fault, the scarlet-and-gold-uniformed Nolan leapt onto his tiger-skin saddle and galloped away to find Lord Lucan. Lucan read the order with amazement. The only guns he could see from his position in a valley were the main line of dozens of Russian artillery pieces, which were stretched across that valley about a mile and a half away. The guns Raglan referred to were to his right, just out of sight.

Lucan denounced the order as absurd. Clearly irritated, Nolan reminded the general that the order called for an "immediate" attack. Lord Lucan recalled saying to Nolan, "Attack, Sir! Attack what? What guns, sir?" Expressing the disrespect he obviously felt, Nolan grandly waved his hand in the general direction of the valley and said contemptuously, "There, my lord, is your enemy! There are your guns!"[76]

Furious, but stupidly obedient, Lucan sent Nolan with the order to Cardigan, who was so horrified by what seemed like suicide that he sent his aide to Lucan asking for clarification. Lucan actually deigned to ride the short distance to Cardigan, who saluted him with his sword. Cardigan pointed out to Lucan that he was being ordered to attack a battery of artillery that was protected on each flank by more artillery and riflemen: "There must be some mistake. I shall never be able to bring a single man back." Lord Lucan responded, "I cannot help that. It is Lord Raglan's positive order that the Light Brigade attacks immediately."[77] With these abrupt words, Lucan rode away. As Cardigan prepared his more than 600 horsemen (the exact number is in dispute) to ride into the "Valley of Death," as Tennyson immortalized it, Nolan rode up and sneeringly wondered if Cardigan and his men were afraid to face the Russians. Already stung by the accusations of his own officers that he should have supported Lucan's Heavy Brigade in their fight a short time earlier, Cardigan exploded, saying that if he lived through the attack, he would have Nolan court-martialed.

Cardigan did live through the attack, resolutely leading his men into the Russian guns and beyond. He returned unhurt largely because Russian Prince Radziwill, who had met him in London, recognized him and ordered the Cossacks to try to take him alive rather than kill him. Nolan, however, was the first to die, screaming in agony as a shell splinter hit him in the chest. Others fell soon after, as exploding shells, grapeshot, and rifle fire tore into their ranks. The four battalions of Russian cavalry that rode out to meet the charging British horsemen panicked and rode back behind their artillery, but not before the Russian gunners had managed to kill some by mistake. To the amazement of the Russians, who could not believe that any cavalry would be insane enough to charge directly into the muzzles of their cannon, some British horsemen survived, and these sabered the Russian gunners, briefly taking possession of the

entire line of guns. They also scattered much larger numbers of
Russian cavalrymen who had no enthusiasm for combat with what
they thought of as "madmen." When more Russians arrived, the
195 survivors of the Light Brigade made their way back to the safety
of the British guns and the French cavalry that had come to their aid.
One who survived was an officer's pet, a wire-haired terrier named
Jeremy that had run all way to the Russian guns and back with only
a scratch. He lived to return to England.[78] So did a boyish officer
named Denzil Chamberlayne, whose horse was killed under him.
Refusing to lose the valuable saddle, he calmly uncinched it and carried it back on foot. For some reason, the Russian cavalry ignored
him.[79] But some Cossack artillerymen did not, firing the artillery
guns at him and other British troopers despite the presence on the
field of Russian cavalrymen, many of whom were accidentally
killed.[80]

The entire battle took only twenty minutes, and the numbers
killed and missing were modest when one considers, as a British surgeon observed, that three times that many men would soon die every
week of disease and that those in authority would "think nothing of
it."[81] Still, this example of British bravery amazed all who witnessed
it. As a French general said of the charge, "It is magnificent but it is
not war." British bravery will be examined in a subsequent chapter,
but this decision to charge represented arrant stupidity. As is so often the case in military disasters, many were to blame. Even Nolan,
who was most obviously at fault, may have tried to change the direction of the attack from the Russian battery to the guns on the causeway heights to the right of the "valley of death" just before he was
killed. Lucan could have, and probably should have, arrested Nolan
for his impertinence, and he certainly should have sent an aide back
to Raglan asking for clarification. And at the very start, Raglan
should have specified the location of the "guns" as being on the
causeway heights. The odious Cardigan was least to blame. As a
military subordinate, he had no choice but to carry out Lucan's order, and he did so with great bravery. After his return, Raglan be-
rated him for the madcap charge, but when Cardigan explained that
he had had a direct order from Lucan, Raglan blamed Lucan, and
Lucan never forgave him. When Lucan was soon after recalled to
Britain, most of his fellow officers believed that Raglan had unfairly
singled him out for blame.[82]

After the charge, Cardigan comforted some wounded men, especially his bugler, and then thanked the French cavalry commander before collapsing in exhaustion. He would soon return to England, where he criticized others for the disaster and boasted about his own bravery. Some of Cardigan's former troopers now admired him, and a few asked for and received favors. Many of his former officers continued to detest him but when he died at seventy-one, eight of these men nonetheless volunteered to carry his coffin. Lucan was relieved of duty, but after returning to England, he became colonel of the Life Guards and was eventually promoted to the rank of field marshal.[83] He lived to be eighty-six years old.

There were many other examples of wrongheaded leadership throughout the war. It is usually overlooked that the battle of Balaclava, in which the Light Brigade made history, was a Russian attack against the British lines along the allies' right flank. At this time, General Burgoyne, Raglan's chief engineering officer, had done nothing to prepare defensive positions, even though virtually every junior officer had pleaded with him to do so.[84] Half a century later, Viscount Wolseley, a young officer at the time, wrote, "In all the history of modern war, I do not know of another instance of such culpable neglect on the part of divisional commanders of all the well-known and long established precautions that should be taken by troops in the field against surprise."[85]

For his part, Menshikov chose to attack two weeks before the arrival of two full divisions that he knew were on the way to reinforce him. Properly deployed, these additional men might have meant a Russian victory. Of course, proper deployment by Menshikov could hardly be taken for granted. When these men were used in the attack on Inkerman Heights a few weeks later, many were sent in the wrong direction, while Prince Gorchakov's corps of over 20,000 men stood idly by throughout the entire battle. And had Burgoyne not refused to do anything to fortify the Inkerman Heights, as so many officers had implored him to do, or had Raglan intervened, knowing how vulnerable the British lines were, the Russians would never have attacked at all.[86] Later, during an attack on Sevastopol, Raglan watched while a French attack was decimated by Russian fire; 3,500 men fell before the slaughter ended. Although there was not the slightest chance of success, Lord Raglan felt honor-bound to order British troops forward. Over 1,500 British men fell, to no purpose except to show solidarity with the French. Wolseley, wounded in the assault, called the plan of attack "idiotic."[87]

And from February into April, Emperor Napoléon III secretly took command of the French forces, refusing to allow them to attack Sevastopol before he had perfected his plan to land a large French army north of Sevastopol to fight the Russians in the open. Nothing came of his impractical idea, but his insistence that Sevastopol not be attacked for close to three months angered the French troops, many of whom began to curse their officers, and it embittered the British, who believed Canrobert responsible.[88] Raglan wanted to attack but did not have enough men to do so on his own, nor was he free to act on his own.

There are many other examples of inept leadership during this war, such as Tsar Alexander's insistence during the summer of 1855 that the now beleaguered and outnumbered Russian troops attack the French and Sardinian troops occupying a ridge overlooking the Chernaya River. The attack cost the Russians 8,000 men, 11 generals, and a morale-crushing defeat. But few things the commanders in the field did can match the failure of the various governments to provide enough food, clothing, transportation, and medical care to keep their armies alive during the appalling winter of 1854–1855 or the deadly summer of 1855.

# 4

# THE "REAL" WAR

## Cold, Hunger, and Disease

LONG BEFORE THE RUSSIAN WINTER ravaged Napoléon's invading army in 1812, Russians joked about January and February being their best generals. Even though the Crimean winters were the mildest in Russia, after the battle at Inkerman the Russians once again looked forward to the coming of winter to save Sevastopol from the expected allied onslaught. They were not disappointed. The winter of 1854–1855 proved to be the coldest European winter on record. In London, from mid-January to the end of February, the Thames froze so solidly that heavy carriages crossed it routinely, and even though some sunny, mild days occurred during the Crimean winter, these only created a sea of knee-deep mud.[1] On several days, the temperature fell to near zero, and strong winds made the cold unbearable for scantily dressed men. The snow was so deep during several days in January that men could scarcely walk through it.[2]

The night of November 13, 1854, only a few days after the carnage at Inkerman, was warm and clear, but shortly after a vivid crimson sunrise, a pelting rain began followed by winds that rapidly grew to hurricane force. It would prove to be the worst storm ever recorded in the area. Within minutes, the French and British camps were devastated as tents collapsed before flying through the air like huge bats, followed by drums, barrels, boxes, hats, clothing, blankets, tables, chairs, and almost everything else in the camp, much of it disintegrating as it crashed onto rocks. The men tried to save what they could but often found themselves unable to stand against the icy winds. Horses turned their backs to the wind, trying to stay on their feet by leaning back into the gale. Even pots, cauldrons, harnesses, bales of hay, and brass instruments sailed into the air. One British officer compared the bouncing barrels to cricket balls and described heavy wagons being thrown through the air, dragging heavy bullocks after them as if they were "mere kittens."[3]

Hospital tents flew away, leaving patients lying in pools of icy water, as the storm began to lash the exposed allied positions with first sleet, then heavy snow. It became so cold that several men on outpost duty died of exposure.[4] French hospital buildings collapsed, killing several patients, and elsewhere, both horses and men fell into ravines, where some drowned in flash floods. General Canrobert's tent flew away with all the others; nevertheless, the French commander went among his soldiers to do what he could to cheer them.[5] Neither Lord Raglan nor any of his staff, safe in their comfortable stone farmhouse, ventured out to comfort their men.

As terrible as the destruction was on land, the ships offshore suffered far worse. Even the eighty-four-gun Russian battleship *Gabriel* sank in Sevastopol's harbor. Many French, Turkish, and British ships lost their masts and rudders; others were driven ashore onto the rocky coastline. Smaller ships burst open like matchboxes, and large ones, including steamers, crashed onto rocks and sank instantly. The HMS *Resolute* went down with 900 tons of gunpowder and millions of cartridges, while the *Prince*, one of Britain's finest ships, which had arrived only the day before, went under with tons of food and 40,000 sets of desperately needed winter clothing; only 12 of the crew of 150 survived. A score of other ships crashed into one another before sinking, losing their entire crews, and eight others suffered severe damage. *Henri Quatre*, perhaps the most impressive ship in the French navy, also sank with all its stores, as did several lesser ships. The loss in supplies proved irreparable, especially the loss of hay for the horses and winter clothing for the men. Over 1,000 men drowned, among them Briton Richard Nicklin, the first government photographer sent to the Crimea. He was aboard HMS *Rip Van Winkle*.[6] A British officer's wife, who watched the disaster from a ship that managed to survive, described the British ships as "all adrift, all breaking and grinding each other to pieces."[7]

The day after the hurricane, Lord Raglan dispatched a staff officer to Constantinople with orders to replace everything that had been lost, but it was fully six weeks before vital supplies arrived. In the meantime, the French were well dressed for the cold that followed the hurricane, and most were quartered in wooden huts. They also had an efficient transport system, but even their well-organized troops would soon suffer serious shortages of food, fuel, and hay. The Turks dug themselves warm, dry underground shelters, but by prior agreement, they were dependent on the British for food, clothing, and other supplies, and it soon became apparent that the British supply system had broken down completely. Men's packs containing extra clothing, which had been left aboard ships before the battle at the Alma River, had never caught up with the troops, and newly arrived food and winter clothing had been lost in the hurricane.

The British soldiers did their best to stay warm by covering themselves with rags, bits of Russian greatcoats, canvas, hides of dead horses or mules, and blankets that their dead comrades had been buried in. So many graves had been dug up by desperate men that orders were issued not to bury men in blankets anymore. Freezing soldiers tried to make gloves out of socks, but their fingers remained so cold that they often could not load their rifles or fix their bayonets. When men returned to camp after hours of trench duty, they had to thaw their frozen beards over a fire before they could open their mouths.[8] To replace their boots, which had long since disintegrated, they made crude sandals out of the greatcoats and knapsacks that they had taken from the dead Russians who littered the ravines after the battle of Inkerman. Nevertheless, the loss of frostbitten toes and fingers was commonplace (many men had to go barefoot in the snow).[9] No weather during the American Civil War could match this hurricane, but men there also suffered greatly from frostbite. Many Confederate soldiers went without shoes, and so did a good many Federal troops. Bloody footprints in the snow were a reality.[10]

A British captain wrote that "the best-dressed" man in his battalion that winter was the only one to retain even a vestige of a scarlet jacket. His trousers were patched with "cloth taken from the clothes of dead Russians at the Battle of Inkerman, and he has had the good fortune to provide himself at the same shop, with a pair of Russian soldier's boots that come up to his knees."[11] Although the man's big toe stuck out of one of his boots, he was among the best shod. Offi-

*Soldiers of the British 68th Regiment (Durham Light Infantry) in winter dress. (Photo courtesy of the National Army Museum)*

cers were so ragged themselves that orders came to wear their swords so they could be distinguished from private soldiers. One British major, reduced to wearing French uniform trousers and a fez, was mistaken for a French barkeeper as a result. A British captain sported red Russian boots, a cap made from the tops of revolver holsters, a white cowhide coat embroidered on the back with multicolored silk flowers, and an old cloth tied around his head.[12]

Except for Raglan, his staff, and many other senior officers, British officers and men alike slept in tents, usually on the frozen ground. Few trees grew on the empty Crimean uplands, and these had already been cut down; despite fire from Russian snipers who tried to pick them off, the freezing men dug roots for fuel until there were no more. The hurricane that had smashed so many wooden ships left enough wood stacked up on the beach to warm much of the British army, but each stick of this wood was reserved for Lord Raglan's headquarters, where a gigantic pile accumulated: "All that Lord Raglan was able to consume, of course, made no perceptible difference in the vast pile, which was at last set fire to, and burned for some days. And this, be it remembered, was while the troops died each night from cold."[13] A large number of prefabricated wooden huts eventually came to Balaclava but proved so heavy that only a few made it to a British regimental camp. The rest became walkways over the mud at Balaclava or were broken up for firewood.

So little food reached the British troops that the standard ration was salt pork and coffee beans, shipped while still green because roasted beans might spoil. With no firewood, the beans could not be roasted, and salt pork caused many men to suffer such painful diarrhea that they could eat it no longer. Sometimes, the men had nothing but a ration of four ounces of rum, twice a day. "Grog men" carried a keg of rum to the front on a stretcher, leading one wounded man carried away on a similar stretcher to say, "Good-bye, Jack! Here I goes, for all the world like a jolly old barrel of grog."[14] When there was no rum, as happened all too often, the men despaired.

In the American Civil War, neither Federal nor Confederate troops received a regular liquor ration, and food was often lacking as well. Both armies were often hungry, and doing without food for twenty-four hours was commonplace. Even when food was available, the men often considered it inedible. Hardtack was frequently too hard to eat, and desiccated vegetables were so detested that they were known as "desecrated" vegetables.

In the Crimea, the Turks received almost nothing to eat and were even closer to actual starvation than the cadaverous Britons. During the Civil War, horses and mules were often hungry, but few starved. After the Crimean hurricane, no feed for British horses reached the front, and no forage existed. Starving cavalry horses galloped frenziedly through the British camps, searching for the food of the equally hungry artillery horses.[15] They found nothing. Soon too weak to carry a rider, the pitiful animals attempted to stay alive by eating canvas covered with mud, old socks, blankets, saddles, and even one another's manes and tails.[16] One officer kept his horse alive only by feeding it bread he purchased from the French. When horses collapsed to die, as most of them did, French and Turkish soldiers tried to butcher the skeletal remains before the crows and vultures ate all the flesh. Vultures were not native to the Crimea, but now they were everywhere, and they grew so fat they could barely fly.[17]

The French imposed strict censorship, wanting the Russians, along with the rest of the world, to believe that all was well in their camps, but those few outsiders who had unguarded access to them reported that French suffering had soon become as terrible as that of the British and the Turks.[18] In February 1855, a French corporal complained to a British soldier that the French were even hungrier than the British, and that scurvy was even more widespread than it was among the British troops.[19] In that same month, French soldiers were so cold and ill clothed that they dressed themselves in the cast-off rags of the now well-dressed British.[20] Officially, General Canrobert admitted to losing 11,458 men to hunger, cold, and disease over the winter of 1854–1855. The actual number must have been much higher.

Showing what remarkably good leadership can accomplish, the 3,200-man British Naval Brigade, which served in the forward trenches, was spared most of this misery. The brigade had come ashore in September dragging their cannons and singing, their hair decorated with flowers and the leaves of vines, with fifes and fiddles playing gaily.[21] Throughout the winter, they received regular supplies of food, were issued warm clothing, and had ample supplies of quinine and lime juice. Even during December and January, they received fresh oranges and lemons.[22] They even drilled wells for clean water, and they practiced excellent sanitation. They were dependent on the army for food stacked up in huge piles at Balaclava, but unlike the army officers, who could not devise a plan to carry those supplies the seven to nine miles to the front lines, the navy officers managed to feed their men by organizing daily supply columns to Balaclava. Seizing the food they needed, they marched back, even the officers actually carrying a load, and the men pulling heavy loads on improvised wooden sleds.[23] Officers in the Royal Navy were trained to think ahead about supplies, but army officers were not. When the organization broke down and red tape proved insurmountable, army officers did not know how to proceed, so they often did nothing. The navy also built its own hospital, as well as a large, heated shed to dry clothes so that the men did not have to sleep in wet clothes, as the soldiers did. As a result of all these innovations, from October 1854 through August 1856, only forty-four men of the British Naval Brigade died of disease![24]

Every day and night, a considerable number of those soldiers still able to take up arms served in the forward trenches, sometimes for twenty-four hours at a time, with only three hours' sleep. With nothing to sustain them but rum and rock-hard biscuits, they stood or sat in icy mud. Those with enough strength tried to pound green coffee beans with a stone or a rifle butt, while others dug for roots to burn to roast the beans. Few roots were found. Some men froze to death at their posts, and others fell asleep, only to be bayoneted by Russian raiders. Despite warnings, troops burned charcoal in their tents, frequently dying of asphyxiation as a result. So did some officers. Colonel Sterling of the Highland Brigade wrote, "None but the people of the hardiest constitution can stand it; all the others are dead or dying. . . . I hear of men on their knees crying in pain."[25] Another British officer wrote, "The poor men are certainly suffering more than human nature can stand."[26] During January 1855, one British regiment could find only fourteen men fit enough to go to the trenches, and in what must have been unprecedented in the British army, the 63rd Infantry Regiment could not muster a single man. Amazing as it may seem, on January 21, the British could find only 290 men able to man a trench line over a mile in length.[27]

The Brigade of Guards, originally 3,000 strong and once the pride of the British army, could muster only 400 men by early February. When their new commander, Lord Rokelay, who replaced the Duke of Cambridge, inspected these ragged, gaunt survivors they were in such pitiable condition that he burst into tears in front of them.[28] It is perhaps just as well that Queen Victoria, who had been so proud of her Guardsmen as they marched past Buckingham Palace on their way to war, could not see them now.

Every morning, those men still alive heard the call "Bring out your dead," just as in the days of the Great Plague in London.[29] Some men who could take it no longer sat down, put a toe against the trigger of a rifle, and killed themselves. Others actually dropped dead while trying valiantly to stagger to the trenches one more time. One soldier fell dead as he tried to lurch from trench duty back to camp. An officer who tried to help him could do nothing. A British soldier with sixteen years of honorable service killed himself because he could no longer endure the cold.[30] Along with the cold, hunger, and exhaustion, diseases also became epidemic. Yet, at this stage of the war, only a few men deserted to the relative comfort of Sevastopol.

Throughout much of this terrible winter, Lord Raglan and his staff officers seldom ventured out of their warm quarters to see to the needs of their officers and men, who had rapidly ceased to be an army. By the start of January, 16,000 of Raglan's 30,000 men were in the hospital, and by the end of the month, 23,076 were listed as dead or "ineffective."[31] Dr. John Hall, a doctor stationed at Balaclava Hospital, now frequently wrote to Raglan and his quartermaster general, Estcourt, requesting that the staff order regiments to bury dead animals, clean up garbage, and dig better latrines. He was ignored.[32]

Amid this horror, a loyal but baffled colonel wrote, "At Headquarters they have every possible comfort, both for themselves and their horses; good beds, good stables, good fires and good dinners."[33] Another officer wrote that in addition to hoarding all the firewood, Raglan's staff received regular supplies of game, vegetables, and confectionery. Like Lord Cardigan's, Lord Raglan's meals were prepared by a French cook he employed. While Raglan and his staff were living in warmth and comfort, The Times' embittered correspondent, "Billy" Russell, lived miserably in a ramshackle house he shared with a number of Turkish soldiers, their horses, and some cattle. The only well nearby was polluted by the decaying body of a Tatar. Of the British troops, who suffered far more than he did, Russell wrote, "Not a soul seems to care for their comfort or even for their lives."[34]

Russell was not sharing in the luxuries of headquarters because some British officers scorned him as a "vulgar, low-born Irishman," and others were offended because his dispatches to The Times exposed the blunders of British leaders as well as "military secrets."[35] The burly, vain, sometimes pompous but always perceptive Russell was hardly a "low-born Irishman." His Protestant father was well born and had enough money to send his son William to Trinity College, Dublin. Although young Russell did not take a degree, he studied law and was admitted to the bar in London in 1850 at the age of thirty-one. His articles in The Times saved many lives by so galvanizing British public opinion against government apathy and incompetence that vital corrective measures were taken.

Russell very nearly played the same role during the American Civil War. Arriving in Charleston only days after the bombardment of Fort Sumter, which began the conflict, Russell toured the Confederate states, enjoying the sumptuous wining and dining that wealthy Southerners provided, but he had nothing sympathetic to say about slavery. He traveled north just in time to witness the Federal rout at Bull Run. His description of the Northern soldiers' lack of discipline and courage was criticized by newspapers throughout the North, and Russell was repeatedly denied a pass to visit the front ever again. But his article led to military reform in the North. Ostracized by Federal leaders, he returned to England and, in years to come, continued his activities as a war correspondent. Three years after the death of his first wife in 1867, he married a wealthy Italian countess. He was later knighted and lived until 1907, only a few days short of his eighty-eighth birthday.[36]

Following war correspondent Russell's trenchant criticisms of Raglan and his staff, on October 23, 1854, *The Times* published a scathing denunciation of his aristocratic officers' indifference to the suffering of the men. On that same day, however, Raglan wrote to the government expressing grave concern about his men's fate during the cold weather that was sure to come, emphasizing their exhaustion and the ravages of cholera. This apparent contradiction reflected Raglan's retiring personality. Like many aristocrats of his time (and later times, for that matter), he had no interest in music, art, science, or reading, something he rarely did, and almost never for pleasure. Like his peers, he loved hunting, riding, good food, and the pleasures of society, especially the company of beautiful women.[37] At the same time, he was painfully shy and was profoundly embarrassed by the cheers of his troops. On several occasions, when they cheered, he ignored them, creating the natural enough impression that he had no interest in what they thought. Actually, he was both embarrassed and aloof, often remarking that troops should neither cheer nor boo. And yet, his dispatches and private letters repeatedly expressed his concern for the welfare of the troops and the urgent need for supplies, warm clothing, housing, and improved medical care. In November, he began to ride among the troops more often and to visit the hospital at Balaclava. By February, he was seen everywhere and was a regular visitor to the sick and wounded. But until then, he had had no conception of the conditions under which his men were trying to live.[38] On December 13, for example, he wrote a scathing letter to a medical officer at Balaclava, complaining about the conditions for the wounded aboard a ship that had just sailed for Scutari. What Raglan did not realize was that this ship was no worse than scores of others that had preceded it.[39]

Still, he continued to be uneasy in the company of his soldiers. According to a well-born captain, one of Lord Raglan's first visits to the men under his command occurred just after Christmas:

> Lord Raglan yesterday saw a man in the regiment cutting some wood, and said to him, "Well, my man, I suppose you are pretty comfortable?" "Never so uncomfortable or so miserable in my life," says the man. "Well," says Lord Raglan, "you got a good dinner on Christmas Day, didn't you? All I got on Christmas Day was a pound of charcoal; that's all I got." Lord Raglan moved off and did not speak to any more soldiers on his visit.[40]

Most of his staff did not speak to any of the soldiers at all.

Raglan and his staff officers were not the only British officers who did not share the hardships of the soldiers. A good many lived in near luxury and knew nothing about men sleeping in icy mud, starving or freezing to death on sentry duty. By March, conditions had improved greatly for the British, but their soldiers could scarcely imagine how well some officers lived. For example, when Roger Fenton, the newly arrived photographer, dined with Guards officers, his dinner included gravy soup, fresh fish, fried liver and bacon, a shoulder of mutton, pancakes with quince preserves, cheese, stout, sherry, and cigars. His breakfast was hot chocolate, tongue, fish, toast, marmalade, and tea.[41] Neither Fenton nor the other photographers, James Robertson and the Frenchman Charles Langlois, focused their cameras on the misery of the ordinary soldiers. Unlike Matthew Brady, who shocked the world with his photos of mutilated and bloated bodies of men and horses during the American Civil War, they had been told what their superiors wanted to see, and they complied.[42] Before the war ended, all armies would impose strict censorship.

French officers, who routinely shared in the lives and suffering of their men, were contemptuous of the aristocratic British officers, who ignored their starving soldiers while using their own private funds to purchase food from civilian merchants at Balaclava and requesting wealthy relatives and friends to send them packages of delicacies. The French officers admired British bravery but said repeatedly that British officers knew nothing about managing an army in the field. Like many angry junior British officers who agreed with this accusation, the French attributed the suffering of the British troops directly to the selfishness of Raglan's elderly aristocratic staff, and some French officers even complained that if they had not had to feed and care for the British army, they would have taken Sevastopol long ago.[43] Viscount Wolseley, then a young officer shivering in the trenches with his starving men, accused the Ministry of War of nothing less than criminal conduct for its failure to supply the British army, and there can be no doubt that singular stupidity took place at this highest level of responsibility. But the problem was not just the failure of London to provide the necessary sea and land transport to arm, feed, and clothe its army; it was also the stunning indifference and incompetence of a host of officials in the war zone. First, except for Raglan himself, his inept staff seemingly neither knew nor cared about supplying the army. Aside from ensuring that delicacies reached headquarters in a timely manner, the mundane matters of supply were left to others, most notably Rear Admiral Edward Boxer, an elderly but energetic "blood-and-guts" commander who was fond of introducing himself as "bloody old Boxer." He had shown great gallantry in the past, but he was now in command of the transport service at Constantinople, a post for which he had absolutely no aptitude or interest.

An officer who was in Constantinople recovering from a wound wrote that it was said Boxer had "never done anything properly in his life."[44] He kept no records and knew nothing about the needs of the men or the supplies carried by the hundreds of ships that passed through Constantinople under his alleged authority. He did not even know where various ships were located. Captains who came to him asking for coal were told to go and look for it themselves.[45] Food supplies vitally needed at Balaclava piled up at Constantinople, where they rotted or were stolen. Ships steamed back and forth across the Black Sea and even across the Mediterranean without unloading any of their supplies, while empty ships took up space in Balaclava's small harbor. The body of one officer sent home by ship for burial was lost, never to be recovered.[46] As Rear Admiral Boxer's complete inability to keep track of his ships or their cargos became notorious, Lord Raglan wrote in despair, "As regards Admiral Boxer, I am powerless. No man can make him a man of arrangement."[47] Many men died as a result.

The situation at Balaclava quickly became equally chaotic. The supply officer there, Sir Thomas Hastings (known as "principal storekeeper") was at least as inept as Boxer. He, too, kept no records and, in fact, had only the vaguest of ideas about the contents of the thousands of bales, boxes, drums, and barrels stacked up in immense piles all around Balaclava. Perishable food rotted, warm clothing went unpacked, and cattle, sheep, and goats disappeared thanks to hordes of light-fingered Zouaves who lurked nearby, along with hundreds of unscrupulous traders who had by then arrived from all over the Ottoman Empire and much of Europe. Even Russian storekeepers set up shop in the booming little town of Kadikoi near Balaclava, determined to make a profit from sales to British officers.[48] That many British contractors were guilty of fraud and criminal neglect did not help matters. One large shipment of boots arrived, all for the left foot. Ten thousand pairs of socks arrived, all made for children. Overcoats arrived that were too small for any of the men to wear.[49] Equally shoddy uniforms, overcoats, and boots were sometimes produced by American contractors during the Civil War, and government cooperation, particularly in the South, was often nonexistent. For example, near the war's end, when General Lee's army was literally dressed in rags, warehouses in North Carolina held 92,000 complete sets of new uniforms. The Confederate states had insisted on their right to raise their own regiments and to supply them. North Carolina felt no need to clothe Lee's army, even though it was the only large Confederate force still in action.[50]

As goods of all kinds continued to arrive, only to become lost or stolen, Balaclava harbor turned into a cesspool in which dead horses and soldiers floated about next to every kind of garbage and filth, including the feces of thousands of soldiers and sailors. This disaster resulted most of all from the British army's medieval organization of its system of supply. In an attempt to cut costs, the responsibility for supplying the army went to civilians in two labyrinthine departments at the Treasury Ministry, which were strangled by petty regulations and seldom given to cooperating with each other. Civilians in the Purveyer's Office had the responsibility for purchasing the supplies thought necessary by the commissary general, who also had the duty of seeing to it that these essential items reached the troops in the field. The commissariat was staffed—or, more correctly, understaffed—by other civilians also not subject to military authority in either London or the Crimea. The crucial job of commissary general in the Crimea was given to a

long-retired former army officer in his late sixties named James
Filder. Filder had too few assistants, and those he had were almost
wholly inexperienced. In Filder's partial defense, Lord Raglan did
not tell him that the army would winter in the Crimea until November 7, just a week before the icy hurricane destroyed so many of the
supplies that Filder did have. The lack of a serviceable road from
Balaclava to the front was also a problem beyond his control. But
Filder turned a difficult situation into a disaster.

First, he grossly underestimated the number of transport animals
that would be needed in the Crimea, and in an effort to save money,
he ordered such inexpensive boots that the soles fell off after a week
of wear. But even more damaging than his incompetence was his astonishing inflexibility about petty regulations. In January, while
scurvy was rampant, entire shiploads of fresh vegetables were
thrown overboard because the consignment documents had not been
properly filled out.[51] Because the captain of a ship had an improperly
signed bill of lading, 150 tons of desperately needed vegetables remained aboard the ship until they rotted. When Filder refused to issue available vegetables to an officer to feed hungry troops because
regulations specified that they could not be issued in quantities of
less than two tons, Raglan wrote him a blistering letter. When absurd regulations continued to be treated as sacred, Raglan again
wrote, despairing, that "something really must be done."[52]

Filder had previously taken the position that it was not his responsibility to inform Lord Raglan of what supplies were available at
Balaclava. As a result, while British troops attempted to roast green
coffee beans without wood to burn, a ton and a half of tea sat un-
used at Balaclava. Filder also failed to inform Raglan that there were
large supplies of rice, potatoes, peas, and barley. For his part, Raglan
did not specifically inquire about the supplies of food available for
his starving men until January 1855.[53] Although a large supply of
firewood finally became available, and Raglan ordered that it be issued to the men, Filder refused this order for an entire month on the
grounds that British troops always collected their own firewood.
That no wood existed anywhere on the barren plateau was irrele-
vant to him.

Filder continually allowed many crucial supplies to remain in the
holds of ships in the harbor, where no one could reach them. He also
failed to mention the presence of 20,000 pounds of lime juice that ar-

rived at Balaclava in early December. The lime juice was not "discovered" until February, after many men had died of scurvy and many others had been hospitalized. At the height of the winter cold, 25,000 heavy rugs arrived. These would have been ideal as bedding material, but Filder issued only 800 of them because the regulations did not call for rugs. Similarly, although many of the badly needed greatcoats that finally arrived proved too small for any man to wear, 12,000 properly sized coats did land, but Filder refused to issue more than 3,000 of them because the regulations stipulated that a man could be issued a greatcoat only once in three years. Even though he had thousands of new blankets on hand he also refused to issue them to freezing men because the regulations did not call for blankets to be replaced. A British colonel had this to say about Filder: "I never in the whole course of my existence met so disagreeable a coxcomb and so utterly impracticable an official as this little viper."[54]

Filder's subordinates could be every bit as regulation-bound as he was. Newsman Russell of *The Times* reported the following episode.

The "Charity," an iron screw steamer was in harbour for the reception of sick British soldiers, who were under the charge of a British medical officer. That officer went on shore and made an application to the officer in charge of the Government stoves for two or three to put on board the ship to warm the men. "Three of my men," said he, "died last night from choleraic symptoms, brought on in their present state from the extreme cold of the ship; and I fear more will follow them from the same cause."

"Oh!" said the guardian of stoves, "you must make your requisition in due form, send it up to head-quarters, and get it signed properly, and returned, and then I will let you have the stoves."

"But my men may die meantime. It is my firm belief that there are men now in a dangerous state whom another night will certainly kill."

"I really can do nothing; I must have a requisition properly signed before I can give one of these stoves away."

"For God's sake, then, *lend* me some; I'll be responsible for their safety."

"I really can do nothing of the kind."

"But, consider, this requisition will take time to be filled up and signed, and meantime these poor fellows will go."

"I cannot help that."

"I'll be responsible for anything you do."

"Oh, no, that can't be done!"

The surgeon went off in sorrow and disgust. Such were the "rules" of the service in the hands of incapable and callous men.[55]

Filder's superior in London, the purveyor-in-chief, Sir Charles Trevelyan, an aged Peninsular War veteran who did not know what supplies he had on hand, sometimes lied about what he did know and commonly ignored legitimate orders for food or shirts for naked men in hospitals.[56] Trevelyan often ignored Filder's requisitions for long periods and sometimes did so altogether. He delayed action on Filder's urgent request for hay for eight months. By then, the horses were dead.[57] When he did authorize purchases, other officials created endless delays as they sought the cheapest prices, which inevitably meant inferior goods. Before the war began, the director general of the Army and Ordinance Medical Department, Dr. Andrew Smith, sent three doctors to the prospective war zone to determine the needs of troops should war break out. They recommended large supplies of winter clothing and bedding. The Secretary of State for War, the Duke of Newcastle, rejected the request.[58]

Even if Filder, Hastings, and the commissariat officers had known what supplies they had and had been willing to issue them, getting them to the front would have proved extraordinarily difficult. Balaclava lay some nine miles from the front lines, by an uphill road, and the road, at its best merely a dirt track, became almost totally impassable after heavy guns had been dragged up it in deep mud. The freeze had left ruts large enough for a man to fall into, and frequent warm spells had created rivers of mud. Even if the road could have been repaired (and it was not repaired until months later), far too few wagons, horses, camels, or mules existed to carry supplies. Everything had to be carried by British and Turkish soldiers who were so weak that they could hardly walk that far, much less carry any weight. And yet, Raglan never ordered that a supply depot be set up closer to his front lines.[59] What is more, even though he was authorized to hire Turkish laborers if need be, he did not use them to build a road. Not until the end of April 1855 did British civilian laborers complete a railroad from Balaclava to the front.[60] Soon after, the small town of Kadikoi, inland on the railroad, resembled an English county fair with everything imaginable for sale.[61]

The French, who did have wagons and mules and were much closer to their own harbors to the west, helped tremendously by carrying shells and food to the front for their allies. It was a comradely act, but also one of necessity. At this time early in war, in addition to delicious, fresh-baked white bread, French regiments had ample supplies of dried vegetables, which could be rehydrated by the addition of hot water. Unlike the American version of dried vegetables, these were edible. The British had neither, but they enjoyed any bread the French could spare.[62] Without French help, the British army might have ceased to exist. As it was, it could not possibly have repelled a serious Russian attack during the winter of 1854–1855.

More French help came from an unexpected source. Although the condition of the British army had improved greatly by then, in March 1855 Alexis Soyer, the master French chef of London's exclusive Reform Club, with perhaps the most famous kitchen in the city, offered to go to the Crimea at his own expense to teach the British army how to prepare more nutritious and flavorful meals. Alarmed and embarrassed by press reports of conditions in the war zone, the ultraconservative war office surprisingly agreed. The flamboyant, excitable Soyer was a comic opera version of a pudgy French fop, a pointed, waxed mustache sticking out for several inches on each side of his face. He seemed still more absurd because he rode everywhere on a small white pony, singing lustily, while his dignified mulatto secretary, who followed him like a shadow, tried vainly to keep up.[63] He gave the British much to chuckle about, but he also provided an invaluable service, and he was cheered by Lord Raglan and Florence Nightingale, as well as by thousands of British and French soldiers.

Soyer started with the two British hospitals near Scutari, then visited the general hospital at Balaclava, before going to individual regiments. Despite the usual inertia due to lack of supplies, transport, and skilled workers, he succeeded in using ordinary army rations to create meals so delicious that he managed to stop the ancient British army practice of boiling all food until it was a vitaminless mush. He also helped the French. Later, he distributed printed recipes for tasty dishes that he named "Camp Pot au Feu," "Stewed Salt Beef and Pork à la Omar Pasha," and "Cossack Plum Pudding."[64] Soyer not only improved the diets of the British but also designed a teapot that would keep tea for fifty men hot, and he invented a field stove that was such an improvement over the old model that it served as standard equipment in the British army for over 100 years; this stove was also admired by the French.[65] After falling desperately ill for three months in the Crimea, Soyer recovered enough to visit almost all regiments. On his return trip to England, he passed through Paris, where he was received by the emperor, and he received great acclaim in London. His health never recovered, however, and he died in August 1857.[66]

During the winter of 1854–1855, the Russians in Sevastopol had warm clothes, shelter, and far more food than the British. Heavy wooden carts filled with bread, flour, wood, ammunition, and corpses clogged the city's streets with their loudly squeaking wheels, while the hobnailed boots of soldiers clattered along the stone streets past huge piles of cannon balls, shells, and barrels of food. Now and then, a cart passed by filled with wounded soldiers or the bright pink coffin of an officer. Bands played incessantly, as white-gloved officers joined civilian officials crowding into dozens of restaurants that featured bad veal cutlets and sour Crimean wine. While off-duty soldiers played cards, smoked short pipes, and rolled cigarettes, off-duty officers complained about everything, and servants provided them meals of cheese, caviar and brandy, beet and cabbage soup, bread, mutton, Polish sausage, and rancid butter. For dessert, there were sweet cakes, cream, and glasses of tea, all washed down by brandy and vodka. When Florence Nightingale looked at the city through binoculars early in May 1855, she described it as "so beautiful, so unscathed, so gorgeous."[67] But as the months passed and the allied bombardment grew heavier, the life in the battered city changed to one of misery. Life in the Russian forts and trenches that lay outside the city had always been dreadful: Officers and men alike lived in mud up to their knees as they endured allied bombardment. Now, the city itself became hellish.

As the famed surgeon Nicholas I. Pirogov approached Sevastopol to do what he could for the wounded, he found

the whole road . . . crowded with transports of wounded men, guns and forage. Rain was pouring down as if from a pail, the sick, among them amputation cases, who lay two and three in a wagon, groaned and shivered from cold; and men and animals scarcely moved in mud up to the knee; dead animals lay at every step; out of deep pools protruded the swollen bodies of dead oxen, which burst with a crash; and at the same

time one heard the cries of the wounded, and the cawing of predatory
birds, flying down in whole flocks to their prey, and the shouts of tormented drivers, and the distant roar of the cannon of Sevastopol.[68]

Once inside the doomed city, Pirogov was to discover that the actual roar was far worse than he had imagined, and that death was
everywhere. There was still a semblance of civilized life in the city
away from the batteries and fortifications ringing its southern approaches, but inside these forts, death came regularly from well-
aimed rifle fire, by frequent raids from the French trenches, and from
huge shells. A young Russian officer wrote about it:

> Yes, I'll never forget that night. . . . I don't remember the previous
> bombardments to be the least bit like this one; this time, it was decid-
> edly hell. You could see that they were preparing for something extra-
> ordinary. . . . Believe me, my friends, that the hurricane was, compared
> to the bombardment, an easy time. . . . It is, after all, easier than
> watching, cold-bloodedly, how with one shell tens of people get killed.
> I will never forget the time when, during this bombardment, one of the
> gun-ports was wrecked; I, coming near, ordered the crew, of about ten
> men, to fix it quickly, so that in as short a time as possible the weapon
> could start functioning again; they started working, and I looked at
> their work for some time. Then I went to another gun, to see whether
> they were shooting well there; I took only a few steps away when I
> heard a scream; I looked backwards, and what do you think? The
> whole crew had been killed . . . by a shell. . . . That day I saw things
> that could easily make a man age thirty years.[69]

Although many of its men were warmly housed and reasonably
well fed in Sevastopol, the bulk of the Russian army was in the field
miles away, and these men suffered almost as much as the British.
Part of the problem was Prince Menshikov, who had even less interest in his men than Raglan's staff had in theirs. Menshikov had been
in command for five months before the allied landing and had never
bothered to determine anything about the health and well-being of
his troops. They were, as we have seen, very poorly fed by regimental officers who pocketed the money allocated to feed them. During
the bitter winter of 1854–1855, money for food continued to be
stolen, and bad weather held up resupply columns.

In Sevastopol, army and navy cooks prepared food in a central kitchen far from the defensive batteries south of the city. By the time huge tubs resembling gruel finally reached the men, the food was cold, and large cakes of pork fat were floating on top. Many men refused to eat the food, saying they would soon be killed anyway. They survived solely on the brandy issued in double portions every morning and evening.[70] Many very thin Russian soldiers captured at this time said that the army was starving. It was also dying of the same diseases that were killing the allies in such numbers. It is no wonder that there was no large-scale Russian attack that winter.

Watching comrades dying of wounds or disease and fearing for one's own fate became a ceaseless ordeal in this war. Seeing the mangled bodies of the dead and dying, helping with their burial, and listening to the screams of the wounded challenged the very sanity of men in all those armies. After one attack on Sevastopol, British bodies lay all day in the sun until their faces turned black, swelled horribly, and then burst. A battle-hardened British officer vomited repeatedly at the sight.[71] The same officer was moved to tears seeing French soldiers lying maimed but still wearing their medals, now covered with blood. Another was sickened by the sight of a Russian killed by French shelling: "Not a vestige of clothes remained on the body, from which the hair and features had also been burnt; the legs were doubled back, the chest torn open and shriveled, and the whole figure blasted into the appearance of an ape or monkey."[72]

The field of battle after the nine hours of hand-to-hand fighting at Inkerman was equally shocking to see:

Here and there small groups ... stood absorbed in pity round some prostrate foe to whom their kindness came too late, and who, shot either through the head or lungs, gasped out his existence in painful sobs, or terminated it in a horrible convulsion which it made your blood curdle to witness. There is nothing so awful as the spectacle of the bodies of those who have been struck down by round shot or shell. One poor fellow of the 95th had been struck by two round shots in the head and body. A shell afterwards burst on him and tore him to pieces, and it was only by the fragments of cloth, with the regimental buttons adhering, that you could tell that the rough bloody mass which lay in the road had ever been a human being. ... Some had their heads taken off at the neck, as if with an axe; others their legs gone from the hips;

others their arms, and others again who were hit in the chest or stomach, were literally as smashed as if they had been crushed in a machine. Across the path, side by side, lay five Guardsmen, who were all killed by one round shot as they advanced to charge the enemy. They lay on their faces in the same attitude, with their muskets tightly grasped in both hands, and all had the same grim, painful frown on their faces.[73]

But as one Russian officer said, being wounded often became worse than being killed outright. Many of those hit by cannonballs, shell fragments, or rifle bullets died quickly, but the ordeal of the wounded had just begun. After most battles, the Russians bayoneted allied wounded, some of whom survived to describe the agony they had experienced. More and more often, the outraged allies returned the atrocity. Those wounded men killed by enemy bayonets were later found with their faces contorted by expressions of pain and rage. Some wounded men lay untouched on the field of battle until help arrived, something that often did not happen for two days or even longer. They lay freezing at night and burning in the sun by day, covered by biting flies and fleas and tortured by thirst. When rescuers finally arrived and gave them a drink of water, rum, or vodka, the men were so grateful that they often cried. Sadly, it was also common for them to die immediately thereafter. Yet some men survived horrendous wounds. One British cavalryman received eleven lance wounds during the charge of the Light Brigade yet survived, and Sergeant Major Andrew Henry survived twelve bayonet wounds, including a stab to the chest so powerful that he later said it lifted him off his feet.[74] And a British lieutenant named Harkness was so hardy that he served until the end of the war without missing a day of duty due to illness.[75] So did a thirteen-year-old drummer boy in the Union army who served three years in the American Civil War.[76]

Those who survived long enough to be carried to a first-aid station usually lay in the mud there for hours, still tormented by thirst, insects, and their wounds until a surgeon arrived. Wounds went undressed until a harried surgeon determined whether a wounded limb needed to be amputated. Surgery during the early months of this war seldom consisted of more than the use of a large knife or saw to hack off a limb. The idea of contagion had been widespread for centuries, but there was still no clear understanding of sepsis, as this sketch of Russian surgeons in Sevastopol illustrates:

> Once I went into Schneider's Inn [Hotel]. Doctors from the main wound-dressing point ran in there in their oil-cloth aprons, with blood baked on them and dried-on pieces of flesh on their hands which, as if in gloves of dried blood, were shiny. Quickly they wolf down some chicken with those same hands, and, licking their bloody fingers, again hurried to their horrible work.[77]

American surgeons during the Civil War were equally unconcerned about sepsis, even though Ignaz Philipp Semmelweis had clearly shown in 1861 that washing hands could save lives. Stranger still, surgeons possessed potent antiseptics, such as iodine and potassium permanganate, but rarely used them.[78]

Even in the finest European hospitals, surgery in the 1850s was a primitive art at best. According to a modern medical historian, at that time hospital gangrene "assumed epidemic proportions, and sepsis was an inevitable consequence of operations."[79] Compound fractures were almost always treated by amputation, with a mortality rate of over 25 percent. During the endless process of healing, a tray was placed under the wound to collect what was referred to as the *laudable pus,* which was allowed to drip from the wound. Surgeons required not only "'the eye of an eagle, the strength of a giant, and the hand of a lady,' but also a degree of dexterity and agility with which few men are favoured."[80]

Surgery in field hospitals was even more primitive and deadly. Every army involved in the Crimean War used regimental surgeons to dress wounds and perform surgery in tents close to the field of battle. Wounded men lay on the ground while physicians examined them. With rare exceptions, these physicians lacked tourniquets, bullet forceps, ligatures, laudanum, and disinfectants. Although many surgeons had a variety of saws, knives, scalpels, pliers, cleavers, and probes, when confronted with hundreds of badly wounded men, they simply hacked off arms and legs with a large knife, while blood flew and limbs piled up in a welter of gore.[81] Some wounded men pleaded with surgeons not to amputate, and on a few occasions, the surgeons obliged. Some who lost an arm or a leg to the surgeons' knives were lastingly bitter. When the Russian grand dukes Michael and Nicholas visited a hospital in Sevastopol, hundreds of men whose limbs had been amputated implored that the grand dukes do something about their misery. Angered, Nicholas replied sternly, "Never mind, my father will reward you all!" "Yes," said one, "but he cannot return me my arm."[82]

But not everyone resisted the surgeon's knife. A French soldier with two broken legs sang a military refrain while a surgeon attended him.[83] A Russian wrote, "It is hard to imagine . . . the patience and calm with which many wounded survived their ordeals. One sailor, for example, was getting an arm amputated, and he asked the doctor to put the skin back neatly, without folds."[84] An Irish soldier who was wounded at the Alma complained that his leg "will never be any good." He asked to have it amputated, saying, "Shure, doctor dear, you threw away many a better leg at the Alma; I'll thank you to take it off."[85]

Add to this scene of unmitigated horror that anesthetics were not always used, that many of the wounded suffered from terrible dysentery, and that most of the surgeons were inexperienced young men who had received only twelve to eighteen months of training, had passed few or no exams, and had rarely before attempted an amputation.[86] Many Russian "surgeons" were mere students, not fully trained doctors. When one patient cried out as these surgeons began to cut into his leg without the use of anesthesia, a Russian surgeon punched him in the face.[87] On another occasion, Russian surgeons amputated a leg from each of four British prisoners while other British prisoners looked on. They used no chloroform; they simply sprinkled cold water on the men's faces. "It seemed a butcherly job, and certainly was a sickening sight; nor was any good purpose served, for each of the sufferers died immediately on the removal of the limb."[88]

The only anesthetic available was chloroform, discovered in 1846 and first used during warfare by Dr. Pirogov in 1847. The French used it in most of their surgeries, but the Russians and the British were less consistent. The Russians often lacked enough chloroform to use it widely, and the British were under orders not to do so by John Hall, the acerbic principal medical officer of the British army in the Crimea, because, as he put it, "However barbarous it may appear, the smart of the knife is a powerful stimulant, and it is much better to hear a man bawl lustily than to see him sink silently into the grave."[89] At least one French soldier agreed. He refused chloroform when his arm was cut off because he wanted to watch: "Truly, I wanted to see a little."[90] Most British doctors used chloroform despite Hall's orders, but because the methods of application were so crude, some patients were overdosed and died just as Hall had feared. Usually, though, they were brought back to consciousness by having their name shouted in their ear before being given a large drink of wine. Alcohol was thought to combat shock and was still routinely used for that purpose during the American Civil War. After surgery, patients lay in pain until they were transported to Scutari, near Constantinople, where what passed for hospital care awaited them.

In all the hospitals of this war, men suffered terribly from untreated wounds, and they suffered from the psychological pain of the loss of an arm or a leg just as they did from the physical "phantom limb" pain that often lasted for months after an amputation. But over 80 percent of the men who came to hospitals suffered from disease, not wounds. Surgery left many men too weak to carry out any duties, and the surgeon's knife, along with frostbite, killed thousands. But the deadliest killers were diseases, including pneumonia and tuberculosis. A far greater killer was febrile disease: typhus, typhoid, and malaria. The high fevers, dreadful aches, and skin eruptions of these victims were terrible to endure, and many more men died from these fevers than from all the previously mentioned disorders. But the greatest killer of all was diarrhea, in the form of either dysentery or cholera. Dysentery killed many thousands, and the prolonged suffering of these victims was as terrible for them to endure as it was for those who tried to help these feces-smeared men. Even more awful was cholera, which ravaged all armies in this war, although the five British regiments that had been serving in the Mediterranean were relatively free of it. They believed that they had been exposed to milder strains of the disease, which had given them immunity or "seasoned" them, as they said.[91]

No one then knew that cholera victims could be saved by fluid replacement, but without intravenous technology, this would have been very difficult even if it had been known about. A British medical report did recommend that patients be given as many fluids as possible, especially alcoholic ones, and that an enema of opium be administered, but in practice, there were no enemas, and the best treatment was thought to be wine or champagne, which did not replace enough fluid to be helpful.[92] Some victims also received opium in rum, but more received calomel, a harsh purgative that could hardly have helped. The stink of feces from many hospitals during this war was so powerful that it could be smelled from substantial distances away.

It was a common practice to try to relieve the pain of the cramps caused by cholera by rubbing, and as the following example illustrates, there were other creative attempts to deal with the scourge. A Russian officer came upon a soldier having convulsions from cholera:

> His blue limbs were horribly stretching out; the muscles on his feet were pulling together into balls, and the bones, it seems, were ready to bare themselves; around his mouth, there was foam; convulsions were winding him into an arc; this soldier was terrible. How could we help him? There were no residences around, at least we could give him something warm to drink, to warm him up. We started a bonfire nearby and gave him a double portion of anti-cholera drops. The first portion was thrown back up; we repeated the medicine, and, in the meantime, were rubbing him, as much as we could, with soldiers' overcoats. There was, it seemed no improvement. A few cadets, trying to catch up to the regiment, rode up "Gentlemen, take this man to the nearest village."
>
> "With great pleasure, but it doesn't look like he'll make it," answered one of them, looking at the sick man. Indeed, on the blackened face of the soldier there were hardly any signs of the fading life, but in his eyes there was still a prayer, perhaps for help, perhaps for something else! . . .
>
> "You know, I've heard of a real remedy for cholera!" almost screamed one of the cadets who had arrived.
>
> "What? Tell us quickly, for God's sake."
>
> "Rub him with nettle."
>
> "What do you think, gentlemen? It won't be any worse."
>
> "Why would it get worse?"
>
> "Let's try it."[93]

The young Russians threw themselves into the treatment. Tearing some nettle out of a ditch, they began to rub it on the sick man. Immediately, his body reddened as the fresh nettle produced burns on many parts of him, but the convulsions began to decrease. In a short time, the patient was much improved. After arriving in a village, where he was given a warm drink and put in a warm room, he improved greatly. However, the next day, along with the other sick men picked up along the road, he was placed in an open wagon and sent ahead to catch up with his regiment. The wretched horses could not catch the regiment by nightfall, and once again, a cold rain fell on the unprotected men. The cholera victim again sickened and soon died. Many cholera victims in all armies died with far less help.

The trip from the battlefield first-aid area to a regimental or divisional hospital was harrowing for all wounded, even the French and Sardinians, who had horse-drawn ambulances with springs. Turkish and British soldiers were tossed into unsprung bullock carts, where they were jostled in such pain that their screams and moans could be heard for long distances. It was no better for the Russians. Wounded were piled together in tents until wagons arrived to carry them away, "transported like calves to the slaughter; their heads banged against the carts, sun baked, they swallowed dust; their arms and legs hung over the side of the carts, and their overcoats were sometimes bloody from top to bottom."[94]

Sometimes the less badly wounded and the sick among the allies were put on horseback, where they swayed their way feebly to Balaclava and a waiting ship. When a Turk too weak to ride fell off the horse, his companion would squat by him, smoking his pipe and saying nothing until the man felt strong enough to climb back on the horse, and the ordeal would begin again. Some painfully wounded men were carried three or four jostling miles in a blanket held by four men, who frequently had to put down their charge and rest. French soldiers began to carry British wounded to Balaclava as well. At first, they were kind and gentle, but soon they wearied of the task and handled the victims roughly despite their screams of pain. A British officer's wife who saw several such incidents, wrote in despair, "Why can we not tend our own sick? Why are we so helpless and broken-down? Oh, England! England!"[95]

The Russians had several hospitals in Sevastopol, the French built a well-equipped hospital just behind their lines south of the city, and the Turks had hospitals close at hand, too, in Kars and Yevpatoria, but the British chose to transport most of their sick and wounded all the way back to Scutari, across the Bosporus from Constantinople, where the sultan had made available to them a huge former Turkish army barracks to serve as a hospital, along with a smaller, general hospital, a mile away. These places, especially the Barrack Hospital, would prove to be hell incarnate, and the trip to them was, if anything, even worse. The British navy had no ships in the Black Sea fitted out as hospital ships, so wounded men in great pain and sick men suffering from the explosive diarrhea and dreadful cramps of cholera had to be manhandled up ladders and onboard ordinary transports. Few of these ships had even a single surgeon onboard, and none had any nurses at all. Many civilian doctors had volunteered their services, but army regulations did not permit the use of civilians in a military capacity. As *The Times* of London put it, the army preferred "to let wounds fester and brave men die in excruciating agony than employ a sufficient medical staff."[96] Later, some civilian doctors were accepted, and about thirty served in Turkey and the Crimea.[97]

When cholera first struck, someone, apparently Dr. Hall, decided to put all the stricken men onboard a single ship, the *Kangaroo*. H.M.S. *Kangaroo* was able to accommodate, at best, 250 sick men, but before it sailed for Scutari, 1,500 men were piled onboard, so many that the crew could not move about at all and the captain had to signal that the ship was unmanageable. When an officer from another ship went onboard to assess the situation, "He found the decks covered with dead and dying men; he described the scene as being one of the most horrible he had ever witnessed."[98]

Later, over 400 sick and wounded men were regularly crowded into the stinking, unventilated holds of transport ships or were stretched out day and night on bare wooden decks covered with a single bloody and feces-soaked blanket. There were no medical supplies available and only one or two bedpans, with only a handful of army wives and a few invalid soldiers and sailors to serve as orderlies. The only food available was salt pork and biscuits; the only drinking water was placed out of reach of most of the sick and wounded men, and there were too few orderlies to help them drink. And so they lay in the heat of the day and the cold of the night, covered in feces; tormented by flies, fleas, lice, and maggots; their shoulders and buttocks rubbed raw by the heaving wooden decks. Ordinarily, the voyage to Scutari took only four or five days, but many of these charnel house ships filled with dead and dying men took two or even three weeks to get there. Numbers of the sick and wounded died before the voyage ended. On one ship, the *Caduceus*, 114 of

430 patients died; on another, the death toll was 47 of 177.[99] These voyages were so reminiscent of the horrors of the slave trade that the trips came to be referred to as the *middle passage*.[100]

When those wretched men who survived the voyage finally arrived at Scutari, they were carried by British invalids or "stupid, careless and unfeeling" Turkish soldiers and porters across a wooden landing platform that was in such bad repair it was difficult for the carriers to keep their feet.[101] Many patients were dropped, and some died. Turks then piled the survivors into rough wooden wagons that jolted them to the Barrack or General Hospital. One wounded British officer lying on a stretcher was so appalled by what he saw that he said, "Do cover my face for me."[102]

When these tormented men finally entered the hospital, the horror continued. The huge, dilapidated three-story building had been unoccupied for some time except by vermin. Rats, fleas, and flies covered everything. Even before the feces-covered men entered it, the place smelled foully from the sewers that lay beneath its wooden floors, so rotten they could not even be cleaned. The stone walls were covered with algae, and they oozed water, the roof and flooring so porous that rain showered all the way down to the bottom floor. Florence Nightingale later testified that the vermin were so numerous they "might, if they had unity of purpose, carry the four miles of bedding on their backs and march with them to the War Office."[103]

There were blankets, all of them filthy, but no beds. The men lay on the rotten floors or hard, flea-infested Turkish pads, packed so closely together that no one could walk between them. This proved not to be a great problem, however, because until November 4, the day before Inkerman, there were no nurses to care for them, and the few drunken orderlies either ignored the patients or stole from them. No medicine, bandages, morphia, soap, bedpans, brooms, plates, or cutlery existed either, and there was no kitchen and no laundry. Even water was scarce. Neither the patients, their clothes, nor their blankets were washed. It was not for some time that it was discovered that the only running water available was filtered through the rotting carcass of a dead horse.[104] Nightingale refused to believe in the existence of germs because she had spent three days caring for cholera victims in London and had not contracted the disease, but she did demand cleanliness, and conditions improved dramatically under her demanding regime.[105]

Dr. John Hall had at first insisted that the British hospitals had no deficiencies, and as late as January 1855, he fatuously told the Ministry of War, "The number of Surgeons, if we had no casualties, would be enough."[106] The surgeons he did have had no time for the sick, who lay unattended for days and even weeks. All their time was spent amputating limbs, with singular lack of success. Thirty-six of the first forty-four men who had a limb cut off died.[107] Conditions were even worse for captured Russians who were shockingly ignored and mistreated in a separate portion of Barrack Hospital.[108]

Conditions in the small British hospital at Balaclava, where some men were sent, were even worse. One of the first nurses to arrive there wrote that cases of frostbite were dreadful to see, as toes and fingers fell off when bandages were removed. Because some men's wounds had not been looked at or dressed for five weeks, they were covered with maggots. One nurse removed a quart of maggots from a single wound.[109]

Before the reforms of Florence Nightingale and various commissions sent out by the government had taken hold, many sick men entering the Barrack Hospital at Scutari pulled their filthy blankets over their heads and waited for death to come. Half of the men did not have long to wait. Each day at about 2 P.M., corpses were dragged out of the so-called hospital to waiting wagons, which carted them off to the cemetery. There, they were interred in layers in a large ten-foot-deep pit. When the fourteen-foot-square bottom of the pit was full of bodies, a little dirt was shoveled on top of them, and another layer of dead men was laid down. Many were buried anonymously. No records were kept of the fifty to sixty men who died each day. From the beginning of November 1854 to the end of February 1855, roughly 9,000 men died in the Barrack Hospital. The eight British regiments that served in the front lines around Sevastopol lost 73 percent of their men, a death rate that actually exceeded that of the Great Plague.[110] General Hospital, reserved for wounded men, not those with disease, was less appalling to look at, with fewer vermin and better treatment. In its large interior courtyard, it had a garden, where flowers grew. Now and then, each patient was given a rose. And although it has seldom been acknowledged, from the very start of the war the British naval hospital twelve miles away along the Bosporus was excellent in every respect, another example of naval forethought and organization.[111]

In January 1855, a convalescent hospital was established at Smyrna, on Turkey's Mediterranean coast. Staffed entirely by civilian surgeons and nurses, it treated about 2,000 patients, with an 8 percent mortality rate. Later, another civilian hospital was set up at Renkioi, 100 miles from Scutari on the southwest shore of the Dardanelles. It was particularly well designed and managed but was never fully utilized.[112] Thanks to the beneficence of Lady Stratford de Redcliffe, who donated large sums of money, British officers were treated at Haidar Pasha Hospital. It was cheerful, sunny, clean, and almost luxurious. Instead of salt pork, the officers' meals were prepared by a first-rate French cook.[113]

Dr. Hall was seemingly incapable of dealing with any of the medical disasters that tormented the British. As one historian concluded, he was "a worthy representative of a system in which ignorance, apathy and idiocy predominated."[114] Some of Hall's subordinates were able men, but they lived in constant fear of him. Hall's deputy, Duncan Menzies, who served as inspector of hospitals, proved even more incompetent than Hall. In December 1854, at the height of the horror at Scutari and the other hospitals, Menzies wrote that "our hospitals here are in first-rate order as regards cleanliness and comfort."[115] When asked what additional supplies he would like, he replied, "Nothing."[116] Menzies was later recalled and reprimanded, but inexplicably, Hall, who also invariably reported that all was well, was knighted. Florence Nightingale scornfully said that his *KCB* must have stood for "Knight of the Crimean Burial Ground." Stratford de Redcliffe, Britain's powerful ambassador to Turkey, who lived in a mansion with twenty-seven servants, simply ignored the disastrous situation altogether. Nightingale described him as "bad-tempered, heartless, pompous and lazy."[117]

The distance between most British officers and their men was so great that many referred to soldiers as "scum," "brutes," and "animals," and even those who respected their soldiers seldom visited them in the hospital. This was not an era when British officers, especially aristocratic ones, typically visited hospitalized soldiers. Lord Raglan eventually proved to be an exception. It is true that he made no visits to the hospital at Balaclava until harshly criticized by *The Times* for failing to do so. However, he eventually made numerous visits, seemed concerned about the patients, and made suggestions for improvements. The highest-ranking aristocrat in the British army also visited wounded men. His Royal Highness, the Duke of Cambridge, was the first cousin of Queen Victoria. A thirty-five-year-old lieutenant general, he was affable, good-natured, and well liked by the men under his command, especially the three Guards regiments that he commanded. His visits to soldiers at Barrack Hospital impressed and delighted Florence Nightingale. During one visit, he spotted a badly wounded Guards sergeant he knew. Swearing a loud oath, as he often did, he called the man by name and jokingly asked, "Aren't you dead yet?" The sergeant laughed delightedly.[118]

British regimental hospitals were at least as horrible as the larger hospitals at Balaclava and Scutari. One surgeon wrote that in his regimental tent hospital during the winter of 1854–1855, "There were no medicines, no medical comforts, no bedding. It was not uncommon for the only ration procurable for the sick to consist of rice and powdered biscuit boiled into a kind of soup."[119] In another regiment, an unqualified dresser acted as a surgeon. Most of the actual surgeons were caring, compassionate men who risked their lives treating the wounded under fire, but the pressures tolled heavily on them. Five doctors died of disease, and one medical officer wrote that "numbers of Doctors are going mad out here."[120] Dr. Pirogov, who commanded the Russian surgeons, wrote to his wife about the ordeal faced by his doctors:

> The doctors who came with me have worked so very hard. Every one of them has been sick, many have died right in front of my eyes ... Sokhranichev died, Giuliani died, Kade was dying but by some miracle survived, Petrov lost his legs, Dmitriev has become melancholic. Every single one has had typhoid, to a greater or lesser extent; I myself was sick for four weeks. If at least it all had a point, there would be reason to sacrifice, but this way no matter what you do, no matter how hard you try, everything stays the same. ... Goodbye, my dear, thank the Lord that you're a woman.[121]

The Turkish hospitals near Balaclava were as dreadful as those that failed to serve the British, but the Turkish hospitals in Kars and Yevpatoria were far better. The directors were British surgeons, but some Turkish doctors were efficient and conscientious.[122] In Kars, every patient had a bed, and the death rate was remarkably low.

Early in the war, French hospitals were impressive. Soon after the French took up positions south of Sevastopol, they put up a clean, well-equipped field hospital in the Crimea and staffed a larger one in Constantinople. British visitors familiar with the filth and chaos of their own hospitals were amazed at the cleanliness of the French hospitals. Patients had clean bedclothes and blankets, a bed, and bed stand; neatly uniformed French nurses, who were members of the Catholic order of Sisters of Charity, provided cheerful and efficient care. Until February 1855, when everything changed in French hospitals and throughout the French army, there was ample food, no vermin, and no stench.

A British visitor who had just been appalled by a visit to the British hospitals at Scutari wrote of the French hospital in Constantinople:

We found things here in far better condition than at Scutari; there was more cleanliness, comfort and attention; the beds were nicer and better arranged. The ventilation was excellent, and, as far as we could see or learn, there was no want of anything. The chief custody of some of the more dangerously wounded was confided to Sisters of Charity, of which an order (St. Vincent de Paul) is founded here. The courage, energy and patience of these excellent women are said to be beyond all praise.

At Scutari all was dull and silent. Grim and terrible would be almost still better words. Here I saw all was life and gaiety. These were my old friends the French soldiers, playing at dominoes by their bed-sides, and twisting paper cigarettes or disputing together, just as I have seen them anywhere else from Paris to Constantinople. . . . I liked also to listen to the agreeable manner in which the doctor spoke to them. "Mon garçon" or "mon brave" quite lit up when he came near. I could not help noticing it.[123]

Because of strict French censorship, it was not until after the war that the full extent of French casualties became known. During the terrible winter of 1854–1855, the French probably suffered fewer deaths from disease than the British or the Russians, although they suffered more acutely from scurvy, but in 1855–1856, they suffered terribly from typhus, a louse-borne disease that usually reaches epidemic proportions only under unhygienic conditions.[124] So many French soldiers died of disease in this period that the French death rate from disease reached 253.5 per 1,000— the highest known rate in history! The comparable Russian death rate was 161.3, and the British rate was only 119.3.[125] When typhus first appeared, in February 1855, disinfectants were used liberally, and it remains a mystery why the French were hit so much harder than their allies or the Russians.[126] However, the French were simply overwhelmed by over 50,000 patients during the winter of 1855–1856, sanitation became a serious problem, and poor diets led to scurvy. Even earlier, French troops had suffered dreadfully from disease. A newly arrived British civilian visitor to the battle area could not identify a strange humming sound coming from the French camp. On close investigation, he identified the noise as the entire French army coughing incessantly.[127]

While British hospitals had improved enormously by February 1855, those of the French had deteriorated badly. Beds and bedclothes went unchanged for several months, and when a patient died, "no matter of what disease, his bed was occupied by a fresh arrival."[128] There were far too few surgeons, no trained attendants, and few nurses. Reversing the conditions of the previous winter, the British now offered to help the beleaguered French with food, supplies, and medical aid, but except for some port wine, the French proudly refused British aid.[129] The French admitted to 24,000 deaths from disease during the first three months of 1856, but the true figure was probably over 40,000.[130] In addition to the 39 nurses who were known to have died, 80 French surgeons died, most of them from typhus.

But however dreadful the French and British hospitals were, Russian hospitals were typically even more horrendous. In October, soon after the battle at the Alma River, this account was recorded:

One day the surgeon of our regiment, Lebedieff, related to me that he had been to see the wounded of the battle of Alma lying in the naval hospital. This was soon after we entered the town, the second or third day; when, to his horror, he found the place full of wounded men who had never had their wounds dressed from the day of the Alma, except such dressings as they could make themselves by tearing up their own shirts. The moment he entered the room he was surrounded by a crowd of these miserable creatures, who had recognized him as a doctor, some of whom held out mutilated stumps of arms wrapped up in dirty rags, and crying out to him for assistance. The stench of the place was dreadful, and he learned that after they had arrived from the Alma they were all put into this hospital, where they had seen no one except the soldiers who gave them food, or carried out such of their comrades as death had relieved from their sufferings. Dr. Lebedieff, for the sake of humanity, attended to as many of them as he could, choosing the worst cases, and performed several amputations with such instruments as he could find in the hospital; but when he turned to go away, fatigued and disgusted with the authorities for letting these poor wretches rot in their wounds, there were so many whom he had not been able to attend that he could scarcely tear himself away, and then only with a promise to return. These unfortunate men were a fortnight without having their wounds dressed![131]

As Dr. Pirogov continually complained in letters to his wife, the conditions in Russian hospitals were slow to improve, and when they finally did, there was invariably a new influx of sick and wounded that overwhelmed the doctors and nurses. From April 1855, the Russians in Sevastopol averaged 600 casualties a day until the last month or so of the siege, when the figure rose to 2,000 or 3,000 each day. After the final assault that led to the Russians' retreat from Sevastopol, what the Allies found in the abandoned city sickened them:

The Russians lay inside the work in heaps, like carcasses in a butcher's cart; and the wounds,—the blood,—the sight exceeded all I had hitherto witnessed. . . . Of all the pictures of the horrors of war which have ever been presented to the world, the hospital of Sebastopol offered the most heartrending and revolting. Entering one of these doors, I beheld such a sight as few men, thank God, have ever witnessed: . . . the rotten and festering corpses of the soldiers, who were left to die in their extreme agony, untended, uncared for, packed as close as they could be stowed, . . . sopped and saturated with blood which oozed and trickled through upon the floor, mingling with the droppings of corruption. Many lay, yet alive, with maggots crawling about in their wounds. Many, nearly mad by the scene around them, or seeking escape from it in their extremist agony, had rolled away under the beds and glared out on the heartstricken spectator. Many, with legs and arms broken and twisted, the jagged splinters sticking through the raw flesh, implored aid, water, food, or pity, or, deprived of speech by the approach of death or by dreadful injuries in the head or trunk, pointed to the lethal spot. Many seemed bent alone on making their peace with Heaven. The attitudes of some were so hideously fantastic as to root one to the ground by a sort of dreadful fascination. The bodies of numbers of men were swollen and bloated to an incredible degree; and the features, distended to a gigantic size, with eyes protruding from the sockets and the blackened tongue lolling out of the mouth, compressed tightly by the teeth which had set upon it in the death-rattle, made one shudder and reel round.[132]

A British officer gave this report the same day:

Accustomed as I now am to the sight of human suffering in almost any shape, I confess I almost fainted on looking in at the door of the first room of these stores converted into hospitals. About fifty men lay on the ground before me, about ten still breathed. . . . I did not see one that looked as if he had died quietly and without great pain. They were almost all naked and had crawled about the room. Some had been dead for days, and their flesh was falling off them, some looked like negroes, so black, and almost all were swollen to an enormous size.[133]

In all, the Russians abandoned somewhat more than 2,000 of their wounded. Only 500 could be saved.[134]

Allied soldiers and civilians were also appalled by the scenes of death and destruction in the battered city. An officer's wife who rode about the city with Admiral Edmund Lyons recorded this reaction:

What is it? It cannot surely be—oh, horror!—a heap, a piled-up heap of human bodies in every stage of putrid decomposition, flung out into the street, and being carted away for burial. I think the sight of that foul heap of green and black, glazed and shrivelled flesh, I never shall be able to forget. To think that each individual portion of that corruption was once perhaps the life and world of some loving woman's heart—that human living hands had touched, and living lips had pressed with clinging and tender affection, forms which in a week could become so loathsome, so putrescent![135]

As these scenes of horror were being recorded, a French soldier was seen carrying a piano on his back; another had donned a priest's vestments. A British soldier led away a live pig, many allied soldiers wore ladies' bonnets, and a Russian soldier lay flat on his back, dead drunk.[136] Inside the city, allied troops also found a music book with a woman's name in it, a vase of flowers, a canary in a cage, a lock of blond hair, a microscope, tiny pink satin shoes, and a small print of *Mater Dolorosa*.[137] Among the Russian prisoners taken in the city was a handsome little boy wearing a tiny Cossack's uniform, as well as a fat soldier who danced drunkenly with a Zouave. The allies also found many abandoned cats and dogs and a one-eyed Russian woman who had been a cook for the Russian staff. She stayed to become a cook at British headquarters.

One of the most scathing criticisms of Britain's mismanagement of the war came from Karl Marx, then living in England but writing in the *New York Tribune*, January 22, 1855. Marx acknowledged that Lord Raglan was no great leader but insisted that he was not solely to blame. Naming everyone of consequence in the government as culpable and referring to the "pitiable helplessness of every British official," he concluded, "Never was the business of destroying an army done more efficiently than by these gentlemen."[138]

What Marx did not mention was the equally destructive mismanagement of the Russian army and the shocking decline of the French forces, which, though strongly reinforced, became almost hopelessly mismanaged over the same period that the British regained their strength and efficiency. The Sardinians were well managed throughout. The Turks were not, as we will see in Chapter 6. Six years later, Americans of the North and South alike would show the world once again that it was easier to put armies into the field than it was to supply them. Throughout the first year of the war, both sides were often hungry, shoeless, and without blankets.

The Confederate states had a limited productive capacity to feed, clothe, and arm their troops, and the Federal naval blockade made matters much worse. Even so, production was less a problem than distribution, because of a badly underdeveloped network of roads and railroads. The North had both ample productive capacities for everything an army might need and an extensive transportation system, but lack of coordinated planning, along with profiteering and corruption, led to painful shortages. Few senior military officers and government officials were as inefficient or bureaucratic as the British, but they often caused needless suffering among the troops. A Confederate private wrote, "A private Solger is looked upon by the big officers as no more than dogs."[139] A good many Northern officers commandeered choice food for their own use, leaving little for their troops. Other officers were simply incompetent. The calamitous failures of commanders in both armies are all too well documented, and lower-ranking officers were often just as inept. A Federal cavalry lieutenant described his colonel as a "lunk headed old fool . . . the old puke . . . a God damned fussy old pisspot utterly incompetent for the position he holds."[140] This same description would have fitted many officers in the Crimean War.

As bad as military leadership and government agencies were in the American Civil War, neither Northern nor Southern troops suffered as much as their Crimean counterparts. Neither typhus nor cholera achieved epidemic proportions during the Civil War, and there was no devastating hurricane to destroy vital supplies. Yet it is not the American armies that provide us with a model for military efficiency; it is the British Naval Brigade. Thanks to superior leadership, the Royal Navy's brigade of 3,200 men was spared almost all of the suffering undergone by the British, French, Russian, and Turkish armies, even though this naval brigade also served in the trenches throughout the bitter cold, the disease epidemic, and the supply fiasco at Balaclava.

# 5

# THEY ALSO SERVED

## *Women and Children*

WOMEN AND CHILDREN HAVE often been both victims of warfare and active participants in it. Vietnam is a well-known example, and in World War II, so was the Soviet Union, where nearly 1 million women went to war in uniform, flying combat aircraft, commanding tanks, and serving as frontline infantry.[1] Closer in time and conditions to the Crimean War, some 1,000 women served in combat, disguised as men, during the American Civil War.[2] A few even became officers. Early in the war, wives and daughters followed Confederate officers and soldiers to war, and so did entire families in the North. As camp life became more difficult and combat more frequent, most women and children returned home. But a few stayed on.[3] Women sometimes risked their lives searching for their wounded husbands, as Fanny Ricketts did when her husband, a Federal captain, was wounded and taken prisoner. After a harrowing ordeal, she found him near death in a Confederate prison hospital. He said, "I knew you would come."[4]

For centuries, women played a part in European armies as wives, mothers, sutlers, cooks, nurses, midwives, prostitutes, seamstresses, and especially laundresses. Women, children, and pet dogs became part of the baggage train of an army on campaign, and women sometimes fought alongside their men in disguise, as a few did in the Crimean War. In earlier wars, some young officers actually took their mothers with them, and some did so in this one. At least one

British officer's mother died of cholera at Varna. The Crimean War was the last one in which women accompanied a British army in any numbers.[5] Senior Turkish officers took some of their concubines with them to war, and Turkish soldiers sometimes had access to prostitutes, but Turkish wives stayed home, where they were not necessarily deprived of male company. Disguised by their veils, many well-to-do Turkish women had lovers whom they met in back rooms rented out for that purpose by Jewish shopkeepers. Much of the time, these henna-eyed young women, their fingernails painted red, could be seen lounging around on pillows, sipping lemonade, eating sweets, and sharing gossip.[6]

Except for the spouse of an occasional senior officer, Russian army officers' wives stayed home during this war, but the families of many Russian sailors, officials, and ordinary people lived in the war zone at Sevastopol, Kerch, Odessa, and other Russian cities that came under fire. Aside from a few senior officers, including Marshal St. Arnaud, who was accompanied by his young wife, the French left their women at home, except for their nurses and vivandières, smartly uniformed, often pretty young women who rode with the men selling cognac and other essentials.[7] They also went into battle with the troops to inspire them and to help care for the wounded. A few wives of British officers went to the Crimea, and so did substantial numbers of wives of British noncommissioned officers and privates. A good many female nurses were with the Russians, French, and British, just as boy buglers and drummers served with all these armies. These women and children were often heroic as they shared the danger and misery of the men, and for many of them, the experience of war proved to be even more dreadful than for the soldiers. The most is known about British army wives and nurses.

Having at least a few soldiers' wives around the barracks could be helpful to a regiment for their cleaning, sewing, and especially washing clothes. But large numbers of wives would prove difficult to house, their children could spread epidemic diseases like measles and mumps, and the wives and children could distract and slow down troops on campaign. For these reasons, commanding officers in the mid-nineteenth century seldom approved their soldiers' requests to marry, and junior officers most often remained single, some even celibate. Yet this was a time of long service for the troops, and most of them sought out prostitutes, who were never in short supply. In a

*A French vivandière in regulation dress.*
*(Photo courtesy of the National Army Museum)*

given year at that time, it was not uncommon for a British regiment
to have as many as 40 percent of its men admitted to the hospital for
the treatment of venereal disease.[8] The French had a similar record
of infection. When armies went to war, prostitutes would follow and
infect many men. Condoms were known but rarely used by troops.[9]

In 1851, 25 percent of British commissioned officers and 15 percent of noncommissioned officers and men were married. Women
married to commissioned officers lived as well as their aristocratic
and often wealthy husbands could afford, but the wives of soldiers,

like the soldiers themselves, often came from great poverty and could afford no separate living quarters. Most soldiers' wives lived in a corner of the men's barracks, separated from the soldiers only by a thin cloth curtain or a blanket slung from the ceiling. There was no privacy and little dignity in these unheated, unlighted hovels, where the only cooking possible was by boiling, and several families shared a single towel, a bar of soap, and a lone basin.[10] Yet in 1851, one in every five people living in unventilated British army barracks, stinking of stale bread and boiled meat, was a woman.[11] The death rate of these soldiers and their wives due to tuberculosis was five times that of the civilian population.[12]

Not everyone in Britain was indifferent to the plight of married soldiers. In 1852, after being told time and again by the Ministry of War that no funds were available to improve conditions in the barracks, an officer in the Brigade of Guards raised money from fellow officers and wealthy friends to acquire a large lodging house that provided fifty-four apartments of two rooms and a kitchen for a small monthly rent. These philanthropists also established a club where soldiers could read, play billiards, work as carpenters, and enjoy refreshments.[13] Unfortunately, this was a rare exception to the general pattern of miserable married life.

Of the 31,394 men sent to Turkey with the first British army—the Army of the East, as it was called—10 percent had legal wives, and almost as many lived with women outside marriage. These women had over 4,000 children. Regulations at that time allowed only four wives in each company (a company was usually 100 men) to go to Turkey at army expense—"on the strength," as it was known. This regulation would have permitted over 1,200 wives to go if each company filled its quota. There is no information about exactly how many did go, but it is most unlikely that 1,200 women embarked. It is also unknown how many children were born in the war zone. Children were not permitted to sail for Turkey, even though at this time, by the age of five or six, poor children like those of army parents swore constantly, smoked short pipes (*nose warmers,* as they were known), and drank as much beer and ale as they could get their hands on. Army wives with children had to remain in Britain.[14]

The British army made no provision for wives and children left behind. Unless a wife was attractive enough to support herself by prostitution (and not many were) or skillful enough with a needle to earn money as a seamstress, she and her children fell to the mercy of the local workhouse. A private in the Scots Fusilier Guards, Queen Victoria's favorite regiment, had to leave his pregnant wife and two children in England. When she learned of her fate, his wife miscarried, leaving the dead fetus in the street. The workhouse gave her one shilling and a loaf of bread, then turned her away. The queen gave her nothing.

Faced with destitution and possible starvation, several women tried to sneak aboard their husbands' ships, and at least one is known to have succeeded. Others pleaded, railed, cursed, sobbed, and fainted before giving in to their abandonment. Still others rushed past police barricades to cling to their men before they were physically torn away from the distraught husbands. A newspaper wrote, "The sight was a sickening one, and calculated to arouse the deepest sympathy of all who witnessed it."[15] The brokenhearted men marched aboard ships singing "The Girl I Left Behind Me," and "Oh, Susannah, Don't You Cry for Me," but some could not manage the bravado. One sergeant with fifteen years' service, forced to sail without his wife, slit his throat onboard ship.[16]

Although no one knew it at the time, the patriotic fervor that consumed Britain as the war broke out would lead to such an outpouring of philanthropic donations that many abandoned wives and children would suffer much less than ordinarily.[17] And most of those who went with their husbands fared far worse than anyone could have anticipated. Among the first women to suffer the effects of war in the Crimea were the Russian ladies whom Prince Menshikov invited to observe the battle of the Alma River. Instead of the glorious victory they had been promised, they saw death, dismembered bodies, and the panic of retreat before returning to Sevastopol as fast as their carriages or horses would take them. They left in such haste that British troops found all manner of feminine apparel left behind, including a petticoat, an item that led to much ribald speculation. A Russian officer saw one woman riding away from the battle on a badly limping three-legged horse, her face set in such anguish that he had no doubt she had seen her husband killed.[18]

Some 250,000 Tatars lived in the Crimea, and an unusually large number of widows and divorced women among them turned to prostitution.[19] These women were in much demand by allied and Russian troops, but so was any other attractive Tatar woman. No sooner had Lord Raglan promised the Tatar headmen that their families, farms, and livestock would be protected than he received the unwelcome news that Zouave soldiers, as well as some of his own men, had raped Tatar women. This was not an isolated incident, as the Zouaves, especially, were said to have often shown their appreciation of Tatar women in this "unorthodox" manner, as one British officer called it. The Zouaves, accustomed to living off the land, also stole Tatar sheep and cattle, while helping themselves to ripe fruit and vegetables, just as many of the advancing British troops did. The experiences of the Tatars during the war were not always negative; some fortunate ones grew wealthy by selling food to the allies.

Accompanying the allied advance toward the Alma River, and staying as close to their husbands as possible, came many British army wives, each one carrying her possessions in a large bundle on her back, pots and pans hanging from her belt as she trudged through the heat and dust, determined not to lose touch with the man she had followed to war. At least one wife did not lag behind her husband. Mrs. Wilding, the wife of an artillery corporal, actually helped him load his cannon during the battle of the Alma River; she was armed with a pistol and ready to use it.[20] Most of these women had been physically toughened by years of toil, often as washerwomen: Mrs. Wilding would make a large sum of money as a laundress before the war's end. These army wives had managed to survive their stay in Gallipoli and Varna by sleeping where they could, often in uncovered ditches, but this long march in great heat, with almost no water to drink, became an ordeal none of those who survived it would ever forget.

Some wives lost their husbands in the first battle of the war, at the Alma, and others lost theirs soon after, at Balaclava. Mrs. Longley watched the charge of the Light Brigade in horror, then waited agonizingly for her sergeant husband to return. When he did not, she set off on foot looking for him while Russian cannon fire still swept the valley. Although hit in the wrist, she refused to turn back. A lancer who had known her and Sergeant Longley helped with her search until they found his body. She wrapped her dead husband in a greatcoat and, with the help of the lancer, found enough wood to fashion a crude coffin, mostly made of boxes advertising Bass ale. Somehow, they dug a shallow grave and buried the body.[21] Another wife sat on the grave of her dead husband, shivering in the cold until she collapsed and also died.[22] A third woman lay on the wet, muddy floor of her dead husband's tent, covered by a single wet blanket, her fever so high that she had dried out the floor beneath her before she, too, died.[23] A destitute woman who sailed to Gallipoli with their child to meet her sergeant husband after the fighting began wrote to him that her life without him had been terrible but being with him again would make it all worthwhile. When the woman arrived at Barrack Hospital, a nurse had to tell her that her husband had died of cholera a few days before her arrival: "The women said nothing, but sat down suddenly as if turned to stone, and remained in that frozen attitude for several days. She neither ate, spoke nor wept, nor took any notice of the child. Her only movement was a convulsive sob that seemed almost to break her body."[24]

A few British wives managed to live in tents with their husbands and make themselves a respected part of the regiment. The pretty wife of Trooper Rogers of the 4th Dragoon Guards was so brave that the regiment's colonel recommended her for a medal. The wife of six-foot-four-and-a-half-inch Color Sergeant Major Pool Field Davis was also well respected. Anne Davis tried not to take her eyes off the "great Grenadier," as he was called, a task made easier by his size. Later in life, he would weigh over 400 pounds.[25] Also well respected was "Becky" Box, a large and powerful woman who spent her days searching the forward lines for wounded men, whom she carried to safety on her back. Elizabeth Evans refused to stay behind when her husband was ordered on picket duty 300 yards in front of the British lines. Slipping past the officers, who had forbidden her to join her husband, she shared this risky duty throughout the war and became much respected as a result.[26] Nell Butler bravely and skillfully worked as a nurse in the forward hospital tents and never flinched when shells fell nearby. She worked under all conditions, even when her frostbitten arm was bare to the bone. What is more, she invented a means to prevent the thread used to suture wounds from rotting.[27] These women and other army wives often served as nurses in hospitals near the trenches. Despite their ordeals, Mrs. Box lived to be eighty-three, Mrs. Evans to eighty-four.

American women in the Civil War served as bravely as these British wives. The wife of Colonel Ivan Turchin proved to be a remarkable heroine when Colonel Turchin, a former officer in the Russian Imperial Guard, fell seriously ill. She assumed command of his regiment, the 19th Illinois Infantry, and "her commands were obeyed with the utmost promptness." Throughout several battles, she was under heavy fire but displayed "the most perfect indifference to the shot and shell or the minié balls that fell around her. She seemed entirely devoid of fear."[28] Others, including some very pretty women, served bravely in battle even though they had no relationship to a soldier or officer.[29] Harriet Tubman, the escaped slave who did so much to help others find freedom in the North on the Underground Railroad, actually guided a corps of black Federal troops on several raids into the Confederacy. On one raid that she led, the black cavalrymen brought some 800 slaves to freedom in the North. On several other occasions, she passed through Confederate lines, later to return with important intelligence about their strength. Although often quite ill, Tubman lived well into her nineties.[30]

As brave as many British wives proved to be in the Crimea, most fared badly. After their husbands were killed or died of disease, many had to sleep in ditches, or in barely covered holes that they had dug. To his amazement, one member of Lord Raglan's staff discovered an army wife and her newborn daughter living in such a hole, covered only by a small piece of canvas. It was midwinter, the temperature was near freezing, and a bitter wind was threatening to tear away the flimsy canvas. Told about the woman, Lord Raglan visited her himself, startling her corporal husband speechless, then sent his personal physician to tend to her. He also provided her with hot meals from headquarters and sent her a rubber sleeping bag lined with flannel. The woman and her baby survived the winter.[31] Another woman was found by an officer's wife lying alone on the wet ground, where she had spent the last twelve days exposed to the winter rain and snow. Desperately sick with a high fever, she had only some moldy biscuits, a piece of salt pork, a little cheese, and a pot of rum to sustain her. Her soldier husband stayed with her when he was off duty, but because she was unpopular with the other women who camped nearby, no one else would help her.[32]

After large battles like Inkerman, British army wives could be seen walking all over the battlefield looking for the bodies of their husbands. Amid the grisly carnage, with torn bodies, disfigured faces, blood, intestines, and dismembered parts of men lying everywhere, these distraught women wandered about, lifting up heads to examine their faces. When a wife found her husband, she cradled his mangled body in her arms, often sobbing all night. Sometimes, the man's pet dog would join the grieving woman. In the morning, other women came to lead the sufferers back to relative safety. A young British princess, newly arrived in the Crimea, painted one such scene in watercolors; many copies of this picture of a grieving woman cradling the dead body of her husband were sold to aid a fund for the war widows.[33]

One wife had a much happier experience. The colonel of a British regiment pointed out to a visitor a Scottish soldier who amazed him with his capacity to gain weight while all the other soldiers grew thinner by the day. This was a very fat soldier, but a good one, who had won acclaim for saving a comrade from a Russian bayonet at Inkerman. A few days after this conversation, the soldier disappeared, leaving everyone aghast that so loyal a soldier would desert. Five days later, a much thinner soldier returned to duty with a newborn infant in "his" arms. It seems that "he" was a Scottish soldier's wife who had masqueraded as a common soldier alongside her husband. She had disappeared to give birth in a Tatar hut, helped by Tatar women. In an unusual act of kindness, the colonel of the regiment gave husband and wife leave in Constantinople to spend time together with their new baby.[34]

Some 300 British wives had been left behind at Gallipoli when the troops sailed for Varna, or they had returned there after spending some time in Bulgaria or the Crimea. They were said to be the dregs of the army wives. Whatever the truth of this assessment, they appeared to have neither bathed nor changed clothing since they left the troopships months earlier. After living in tents, vermin-ridden hovels, and open ditches, they had somehow taken possession of several cellars beneath the huge Turkish barracks at Scutari that now served as the British Barrack Hospital. These cold, dank cellars had little ventilation or light, and pools of urine, blood, and feces seeped into them from hospital drainage pipes.

These women, along with some convalescent soldiers and a few deserters, slept on decayed matting covered by filthy rags. In this hellish place, without beds, mattresses, blankets, or privacy of any sort, tormented by hordes of rats and fleas, they existed on scraps of food stolen or begged from the hospital, and on near-poisonous arrack, a rough brandy sold to them by Greeks. Those women who could sold their bodies for money to buy the liquor, although it is difficult to conceive of any man who would be attracted to such filthy, scrawny women. Later, numerous babies were actually born in these cellars. A few women received some money from their husbands who lay wounded in the hospital, but most had nothing.

One cellar was reserved for the sick, where vermin-ridden women and children lay in pools of the liquid feces and vomit expelled by their cholera-infected bodies. No one tended to these people in any way. When they died, they were placed in shallow graves just outside the building, marked by a piece of wood inscribed with "a woman" or "a child." Word of the terrible degradation and suffering of these people slowly spread to England, and some inquiries were made by sympathetic visitors, including a writer for *The Times* of London who traveled to Gallipoli with a relief fund. He wrote that nothing he could say would possibly convey the horror of these women's and children's existence. Florence Nightingale did what little she could to help the women but explained that all her time was taken by the wounded soldiers, whom she nursed some sixteen hours a day. Not until the arrival of her friend Lady Alicia Blackwood, just before Christmas of 1854, did Nightingale have anyone willing and able to do anything for these soldiers' wives.[35]

With money and gifts sent from England and the occasional help of hospital orderlies, the indomitable Lady Alicia actually managed to help many of the wretched women. She arranged for supplies of food and bedding, and even, with no little difficulty, for medical attention. Reasoning that without privacy, the women could never have any feeling of self-worth, she arranged for partitions to be constructed that offered reasonable barriers to sight and sound, and she began the hard task of sanitation. A civilian doctor soon arrived to staff the separate hospital that Lady Alicia arranged for the women. She also established a nursery, complete with playpens, for the women's children and set up a laundry where they could clean their own clothes and earn wages by washing for others. She arranged for Sunday school services as well, and for a store that stocked the gifts and supplies that now flooded in from England. There would never be a solution to the fleas and rats, which seemed immortal, and some of the women were not redeemable, but the worst of their suffering had ended.[36]

When the surviving women returned home, many received great compassion from charitable organizations. They were given food, clothing, and a little money and were provided with transportation to their hometown or home village if they had one. Patriotism had its limits, however. None of the women were given an actual home, and few had relatives who would even acknowledge them. Those whose husbands had died, and they were the majority, usually found themselves entirely on their own. Charity did not extend to housing, jobs, or help with child care, and widow's pensions did not exist at that time. What became of these women is not known. Just as their identities were never recorded, what happened to them and their children is not a matter of record.

The wives of British officers were usually not keen to join their husbands in the war zone. Numerous wives sailed with their husbands as far as Malta, where they stayed living in comfort and waiting for the war to end, and a few went to Varna, where some died of disease, but initially, only three officers' wives followed the British army all the way to the Crimea. One soon left because her husband was killed. A second, Lady Errol, arrived with a pair of pistols stuck in her belt, and followed by her French maid and a cook mounted on mules.[37] She also left when Lord Errol was wounded. Until that time, they shared a tent, where he slept on the only bed and she slept on a mattress on the ground. Only one indomitable officer's wife endured the entire war in the Crimea. The wife of an undistinguished cavalry officer from a socially prominent family, Fanny Duberly was the twenty-four-year-old daughter of a wealthy banker. She loved riding, adventure, and gossip. A voluptuous blue-eyed blond woman of considerable beauty, she attracted men's attention wherever she went, but with the possible exception of Lord Cardigan, with whom she was rumored to have had a brief affair aboard his yacht, she used her charm and wit to enchant men without betraying her marriage vows. A British film made in the 1960s portrayed Duberly and Cardigan as lovers, but there is no confirming evidence.[38]

Fanny Duberly lived in relative comfort aboard various ships in Balaclava harbor until an admirer built a small house for her. She also had a cook and a maid. A French soldier "seamstress" made a beautiful riding costume for her that she flaunted as she rode among officers and men doling out brandy from a small keg that she always carried. Even the Turks saluted and cheered as she passed by. Mrs. Duberly was not insensitive to the horrors of war or the human suffering she saw, but she earned the nickname "Vulture" because of her practice of riding over battlefields, inspecting the dead.[39] She sometimes suffered from cold, heat, and illness herself, but she loved the role of the unattainable but charming beauty, and she played it magnificently until partially eclipsed by the arrival, in April 1855, of Lady Agnes Paget, a twenty-two-year-old blond woman of such remarkable beauty that seemingly, no man could take his eyes off her. Certainly, Lord Raglan could not: He invited her to dinner on numerous occasions. And there was also Soledad, the beautiful young Spanish wife of French Foreign Legion colonel Bazaine. Soledad arrived in the Crimea complete with a piano, which she played for the enchanted French commander, General Pélissier. She also wore his general's cap, sometimes letting him pinch her chin. Colonel Bazaine's feelings about all this are not known.[40] By the summer of 1855, more aristocratic ladies had arrived to enjoy the warm weather and the pageantry of war at a distance. They enjoyed elegant picnics and the romantic attention of so many officers in uniform. As a twice-wounded soldier remarked, "The ladies looked on while the lads were shot down."[41]

While these "ladies of quality," as they were referred to, rode about, to the delight of most of the men of the allied armies, it went largely unnoticed that women nurses were suffering terribly as they used their very limited skills to help wounded and diseased British soldiers. At the time of the Crimean War, the British army, unlike the continental armies, did not utilize women as nurses. Thanks to the dispatches of Russell of *The Times*, E. L. Godkin of the London *Daily News*, and especially, Thomas Chenery, the Constantinople correspondent to *The Times*, the British public became so outraged by conditions in the British military hospitals that the government asked Florence Nightingale to recruit some nurses to accompany her to Gallipoli.

A longtime friend of Florence Nightingale, Lord Sidney Herbert, the secretary of war, had been committed to improving conditions for troops on campaign since he read his father's diary about the terrible and unnecessary suffering of soldiers in the Flanders campaign of 1798. He was goaded into action by scathing exposés in *The Times*, including insinuations that he had done nothing for Britain's troops because he was pro-Russian. This accusation stemmed from his mother's being the daughter of a former Russian ambassador to Britain and a member of the princely Vorontsov family, whose palace was located at Yalta, only a few miles from Balaclava. Despite government opposition, on October 15, 1854, Herbert asked Nightingale to go to Scutari in command of a party of nurses whom she would recruit, all at government expense.[42]

Nightingale needed no urging. She actually had a letter in the mail to Herbert asking his permission to take nurses to Scutari and had already begun to recruit them. Improving conditions in hospitals was the passion of her life. Rejecting an offer of marriage from a charming, socially prominent suitor, the tall, slim, plain, but iron-willed Nightingale had toured hospitals throughout Europe, reading everything there was on the subject of nursing, and over the loud protests of her upper-class parents, she had volunteered as a nurse during the 1854 cholera epidemic in London.

The women she recruited had none of the skills associated with nursing today, not even those possessed by French or Russian women nurses of that time. In reality, they were little more than chambermaids.[43] Nightingale persuaded a few entirely untrained upper-class women to serve as nurses, and other respectable women came from various religious orders, but almost all of the secular nurses she found, like army wives, came from the very bottom of society because no "respectable" woman of that time would become a nurse. Dressed in crude, mannish uniforms, many proved so coarse, drunken, and sexually promiscuous that they had to be sent home in disgrace.[44] At least one was brutal.[45] Dickens's portrait of the coarse, immoral, drunken, foulmouthed Sarah Gamp in *Martin Chuzzlewit*, published a decade earlier, became their stereotype.[46]

So many of these newly arrived nurses married sergeants, or tried to, that the nurses became known as the "New Matrimony at Any Price Association."[47] But many proved kind, hardworking, and devoted to the suffering soldiers. At least one worked such long hours that she collapsed and died. In addition to these Protestant women, there were several dozen Irish Catholic nurses, who drank as much as the Protestants and were equally promiscuous. There were also nuns, who tried to convert their patients to Catholicism, but most of these women, too, worked hard, long hours, doing what they could to ease men's pain and to cope with the horrors of cholera, dysentery, typhus, scurvy, and gangrene.

Almost all of these women became ill, and several died, mostly of cholera. Florence Nightingale rightly received international acclaim for instituting hospital reforms, but the women who spent days and nights comforting men in pain, cleaning their filthy, vermin-infested bodies, and smelling the stench of their diarrhea before falling ill themselves have received too little praise. At the time, the sick and wounded men they helped could not praise them enough. Many men were so grateful that they wept. One patient pleaded with a nurse not to touch him because he was so filthy that he would not let his own mother touch him.[48] She did so anyway. There was also a small, hardworking, thoughtful British doctor named James Brady who somehow managed to hide from the British authorities the fact that "he" was a woman. Brady had remarkable success in treating cholera victims and went on to serve in the army for forty-six years as a man.[49]

Neither the French nor the Italian soldiers ordinarily took wives with them to the war, but French regiments were accompanied by vivandières, often attractive, sometimes even stunning young women, dressed in trousers, military tunics, and pretty glazed, black leather hats with white feathers. Some were married to men in the ranks. When the army was not on the move, they acted as sutlers, selling liquor and delicacies. They were not prostitutes, and although some must have had romances with soldiers, they were discreet and usually much loved by all the men. They often went into battle with the men of their regiment, and at least one was killed in action at Inkerman.[50] One married vivandière was wounded several times and was recommended for a medal.[51] Nevertheless, the British were suspicious of the virtue of the vivandières, sarcastically referring to them as "hors de combat."[52]

There were many more French than British nurses in the Crimea, and they were greatly admired by all who saw them at work. These observations were made by a British admiral not ordinarily given to praising the French:

> The invalids derived inappreciable solace from the presence of Sisters of Charity amongst them. These self-denying women tended them as mothers and sisters are expected to attend sons and brothers. They fed those unable to feed themselves; they nursed the wounded with gentle hands; they cheered the desponding by their gaiety; they smoothed the pillows of the sleepless. We saw many a poor fellow's eyes light up as one of those good spirits, noiseless and smiling, approached his bed-

side, if only to say a kind word and pass on to another. In our unworthiness we have been unable to elevate our thoughts to that frame of mind which leads women, many of them fair and young, to devote themselves, uncheered by fame, their names and garb conventional, to the service of humanity in its most repulsive form. They seemed to be ubiquitous. Wherever suffering lay, there they were sure to be found. . . . In one of the wards that day we witnessed an interesting scene. A French soldier, a handsome brown-bearded fellow, was lying on his back in bed; his left arm had been amputated, and his right arm, bound in splints, lay useless on the coverlet. By his side stood a Sister of Charity, feeding him. She had broken bread in suitable morsels, and lain them on his broad chest, and she held a basin of soup, in the composition of which eggs seemed to have a large share. All the while chatting, that he might not eat too fast, she alternately put a spoonful of soup and a morsel of bread into his mouth. When they were disposed of, she raised his head higher with her left hand, and with her right hand held a cup of liquid to his lips. Good sister, we thought, the recording angel is noting thee down![53]

Many of these Sisters of Charity died during the war.

One of the most remarkable women to participate in the Crimean War was Mary Jane Grant Seacole, the very stout daughter of a Scottish officer in the British army and a free black Jamaican. Like her mother, Mary had learned a great deal about traditional Jamaican medicine and a little about more modern healing, as well as both kinds of nursing. She also had many entrepreneurial skills as a well-traveled hotelier and shopkeeper. Despite encountering racial prejudice, especially that of Americans, she had amassed a sizable fortune when war broke out in the Crimea. At her own expense, she immediately traveled from Jamaica to London, where she offered her nursing skills to various authorities but was refused, partly, it seems, because nurses were not wanted by the army, but no doubt also because of her mixed race. With the help of a shipper named Day, who helped to finance her, Seacole then sailed on her own to Balaclava, where she spent a large sum of money to build the "British Hotel," a large complex of buildings she had constructed out of ships' wreckage. The hotel included a large store that sold everything from "anchors to needles," as one customer marveled; a canteen for enlisted men that dispensed food and drink; a kitchen that employed several Caribbean cooks to provide delicious meals for officers; an actual small hotel; and a medical dispensary and sick bay. There were also stables for horses and fenced areas for cattle, sheep, goats, pigs, chickens, geese, and turkeys.[54]

She was known to the officers and men of all four allied armies as "Mother" Seacole, and her clean rooms, good food, and cheerful disposition guaranteed that the so-called British Hotel would always be packed. Despite many losses (forty goats and seven sheep in one night), mostly to Zouaves who stuffed everything they could into their baggy red trousers, she initially made a tidy profit. The plump, vivacious, and ingratiating Mother Seacole was always surrounded by allied officers who were cheered by her companionship, food, and drink. One of those most charmed by her was a Turkish pasha, who became notorious for drinking all the liquor she could provide.

Mother Seacole became best known and respected for her skills and compassion as a nurse and doctor. She had brought a remarkable array of modern medicines with her from London, and she now prescribed antidiarrheal and antiscorbutic medicines, among many others, to her favorites, the officers and men of the British 97th Regiment, whom she had known in Jamaica. But she treated French, Turks, and Sardinians as well. She nursed badly wounded men in her little hospital, too, and the men often wept with appreciation at the touch of her soft, motherly hands: "Many a man was later to confess that his most abiding memory of the war was that of Mother Seacole, seated by the death-bed of a young soldier who was comforted by the illusion that the black breast pillowing his head was really that of his mother."[55]

She was also known to the men in the trenches, where she frequently visited despite extremes of weather to see if she could aid the wounded or sick—British, French, Turk, and Sardinian. She also sold them food and drink. Delirious men sometimes took her for their wives, speaking to her about their children, their lives together, and how terrible the war had been. Once, as she helped wounded men to board a ship at Balaclava, an admiral watched sternly for some time before approaching her with tears in his eyes to tell her how touched he was to see what she was doing for the wounded. She did what she could for "half-starved" French soldiers, too, concluding that despite French censorship, which forbade publication of the number of dead and dying, the French had suffered even more than the British.[56]

After the battle of the Chernaya in August 1855, she rushed to the battlefield to do what she could for the wounded, Russian as well as

French and Sardinian. One Russian officer whom she treated kissed her hand and gave her his ring while smiling his thanks. Another Russian, badly shot through the jaw, accidentally clamped his teeth shut on her finger as she probed for the bullet. Others nearby had to pry the man's jaws open, and she bore a permanent scar from his bite.[57] She also took care of soldiers' wives and even nursed a wounded horse back to health. She nursed men with fatal cholera, doing what she could to ease their cramps, vomiting, and diarrhea, and was often seen treating men with frostbitten fingers and toes, a terrible task, which she detested because the flesh often fell away, exposing bones and tendons.[58] A young British doctor admired her greatly:

> In rain and snow, in storm and tempest, day after day, she was at her self-chosen post, with her stove and kettle, in any shelter she could find, brewing tea for all who wanted it, and they were many. Some times more than 200 sick would be embarked [on ships to Scutari] on one day, but Mrs. Seacole was always equal to the occasion.[59]

Mother Seacole made a good profit from her hotel and her food and drink early in the war, but she gave away much, too, and because the end of the war left her with a huge inventory of goods and livestock that could be sold, if at all, only for next to nothing, peace left her nearly bankrupt. Before leaving the war zone, she met some Russian officers, chuckling to herself as she wondered what they thought about the color of her skin, especially because British officers had playfully assured the Russians that she was Queen Victoria. She soon returned to England, where she became a masseuse to the Princess of Wales and was visited in her West End flat by many of the officers and soldiers she had nursed. Decorated by the French, Turkish, and British governments, she lived until 1881, still much loved by those who knew her.[60]

Menshikov's defeat and disorganized flight from the battle of the Alma created panic among the civilians in Sevastopol, but when it became clear that flight was not an option and that the allies were not planning an immediate assault, a new spirit of defiance arose, driven in large part by the determination of the women and children. To build fortifications, women carried dirt in their aprons, and children pushed wheelbarrows filled with dirt and rocks; day and night, they all carried gabions (bottomless baskets to hold dirt) and fascines (long bundles of rods and brush) and filled thousands of sandbags. Thanks to a corrupt contractor, only twenty serviceable shovels existed in the entire city, and there were no pickaxes at all. The Russians were forced to make crude wooden shovels. While Todleben waited for better tools to be shipped to him, fortifications were built by hand around the clock. In one thirty-six-hour period, over 100 guns were placed in newly emplaced batteries. A British officer was greatly impressed: "Daily fresh batteries sprang up as if by enchantment."[61]

When the fighting began, young Russian boys actually manned guns: "The seamen's children got themselves three-pound mortars—and were shooting at the enemy. These kids amazed everyone with their fearlessness and how carefully they treated their mortars! When it rained, they would put on their wool covers."[62] One boy decorated for his bravery was only eleven years old. He was Nicholai Pishchenko, the son of a sailor killed at his artillery battery. The boy refused to leave his father's gun and soon learned the craft of artillery so well that he became famous for his exceptional skill. He shared all the dangers of the siege, which he survived.[63]

Both the Russians and the allies used boys as buglers and drummers, but little is known about their experiences. It is reported that on one occasion, a British boy drummer met a Russian boy bugler in battle, battering him with his fists before returning with his captive and his bugle to a hero's welcome.[64] Another time, a Russian boy led Russian troops in a suicidal attack on British lines. He stood atop a British trench, blowing "attack" until shot down. After the battle, he was found to have seven lethal wounds.[65] Both sides in the American Civil War used boys as drummers, fifers, and buglers, but they were typically kept out of actual combat.[66]

Many Russian women also displayed great courage:

> During the battle, the heat was immense giving the young women a chance to show the strength, selflessness and courage of Russian women . . . Under a hail of bullets, they distributed first *kvass* (an alcoholic drink made from fermented rye), and then, when they ran out of *kvass*, water, in all the hottest areas of the battle.[67]

Many women and children were killed and wounded. The sight of their mangled bodies affected the men greatly. Tolstoy was particularly distressed by the plight of a young wife who lay in the hospital with an amputated leg. She had been hit while taking food to her sailor husband.[68]

*Two Russian boys who were captured outside Sevastopol sit with British Lieutenant Colonel Brownrigg, Grenadier Guards. They were eventually sent to England, apparently by their own preference. (Photo courtesy of the National Army Museum)*

Most women and children slept in Fort Nicholas, whose thick stone walls offered some protection against allied fire, but as the following description makes clear, an allied bombardment was a fearsome thing:

The firing was so frequent that, it seemed, there were no breaks at all; and all of this with screeching and a general din, was bursting in the air and falling on the city like hail. A more horrible picture of destruction is hard to imagine, ... With the horrible cries of the women and children, everyone in whatever they were wearing, in the middle of the night jumped out of their houses and ran for the harbor. ... Death ... in the full sense of the word feasted every minute. ... Thus continued this hell, unprecedented in the history of warfare, intermixed with fire from both sides, until late at night, ... not even slowing down for a single minute. The city was literally covered with bombs and rockets, but since all of the houses were stone and half-destroyed, there was nothing to burn. One bomb fell into a shop where rifle shells were pre-pared and where almost a thousand grenades were stored. Instantly, the shells flew up into the air, and the grenades tore apart one by one ... and to the external horror was added an internal one—there was no one to put out the fire. Then came the terrible night of the 6th; the enemy's fire grew noticeably more frequent and more powerful; bombs and rockets, tracing fiery radii, furrowed the sky; all of the batteries, ours and our foes', disgorged fire and death all around themselves.[69]

Through all of the bombardments, Russian nurses served in the forward batteries with the men:

With us at Malakoff Hill, lives one of the Sisters of Mercy. They call her Praskovia Ivanovna; I don't know what her last name is. She is a fighting woman; there are few like that! ... Soldiers gladly let her dress their wounds. ... And yet it's weird to see a woman under flying shells who's not afraid of them.[70]

She was not the only fearless woman:

One would bring her husband ... dinner, here, right next to the can-non. They'll sit and talk a bit as he eats and grieves over the losses, and the house getting destroyed, and the little girl killed, then back the sailor's wife will walk, with her dishes, not hurrying, hiding oncoming tears. And she won't jump aside at the sound of a shell whistling by, she walks quietly. She's gotten used to all the horrors of the siege.[71]

After the wounded were taken to the hospital, they encountered horrendous conditions, which were made only a little more bearable by the tireless efforts of nurses. This description is by Dr. Pirogov, the famed surgeon:

On the beds lay the foul-smelling wounded. . . . Mattresses soaked with blood and pus remain under the injured four or five days, for lack of bed-clothes and straw. . . . Each day, at the rebandaging, you can see three or four women, one of them the famous Daria, another a daughter of some official, about seventeen years old, and a soldier's wife. Besides this, I sometimes see another lady, middle-aged, in a veil, with a cigarette in her mouth. She's some seaman's wife, I think, and comes to give out tea, either hers or donated by someone, I don't know. Daria now shows up with a medal on her chest, which she got from Tsar Nicholas, who told the Grand Dukes to give her a kiss and 500 rubles. He ordered that she be given 1,000 more when she gets married. She is a young woman, good looking, and it seems, of light morals. She also assists during operations. . . . The women around us give the patients tea to drink and give each a glass of wine.[72]

Following the first heavy allied bombardments of Sevastopol, the wounded received excellent care, thanks to the supreme efforts of a few surgeons like Pirogov and dozens of brave women. Several nurses worked so hard that they collapsed, and one actually died of what appeared to be exhaustion: "Kartzeva (one of the Sisters of Mercy) is untiring, spends night and day in the hospital, looks after the sick, helps to dress wounds, does everything by herself, and every evening leaves me with new instructions (to improve patient care)."[73] Kartzeva was not the only zealous nurse. According to Pirogov, the Sisters of Mercy "have turned the hospital upside down, they worry about food and drink—it's just amazing—they give out tea and wine . . . ; if everything continues like this, if their zeal doesn't subside, our hospitals will somewhat resemble normal ones."[74]

Perhaps the most remarkable devotion was shown by Dasha Alexandrovna, the orphaned daughter of a sailor. Appalled by the suffering she witnessed after the siege began, she sold everything she owned to buy a cart and pony, bandages, and medical supplies. Every day, she exposed herself to allied fire as she bandaged and comforted wounded men in the front lines before taking them to the hospital, then turning her pony around and going back to the front lines. The Russian soldiers and sailors in the battered city so admired her courage and compassion that word of her actions reached St. Petersburg, where the tsar granted her a pension and a gold cross. Despite her recklessness in exposing herself to danger, she not only survived the siege but lived to an old age.[75]

The zeal and concern of Russian women nurses was not matched by the army's "dressers," soldiers assigned to work as hospital orderlies. A wounded officer lying in the hospital was asked by a friend if his wounded arm had been dressed:

> "Yes," said he, "but I was obliged to pay those swine to get them to wash and dress my arm; the dressers won't do anything without money—the brutes! But I must give all praise to a poor woman from Sevastopol; she is called Maria; she attends to us as well as she can—brings us tea, washes and dresses such wounds as she is able—in fact, takes care of us all." "Is not that the same woman," I asked, "whom I saw dressing the wounds of the soldiers in the courtyard?" "Most probably, as no one else is likely to care for them, poor fellows!"[76]

There was little disease and no cholera in Sevastopol when the siege began, but when cholera arrived a few months later and other diseases such as typhus and scurvy spread, the plight of women and children grew worse.

The day-to-day management of the hospitals eventually fell to nursing sisters, who distributed food, drugs, and alcohol to the patients based on doctors' orders rather than ability to pay, which had been the rule used by the army dressers and pharmacists:

> The sisters also helped to combat graft and thieving in the hospitals. The authorities gave sums of fifty to one hundred rubles to amputees, but as they had no place in which to keep the money safely, it was all too likely to be stolen by orderlies or medical assistants. Pirogov assigned some of the more reliable sisters to take care of this money and to keep records of it—no mean assignment.[77]

"The General Staff Doctor is a cipher. . . . In the hospital there is not one extra mattress, no good wine nor quinine bark, nor acid, even in case typhus spreads. Almost half of the doctors lie sick, and the only thing that is really fine is the sisters of mercy."[78] With little nursing training, these sisters provided devoted bedside care for the patients and looked after their feeding and their medication. Dr. Pirogov strongly supported the sisters in their quarrels with the pharmacists, even when their complaints led to the suicide of one of the offenders. Calling them "'true sisters of mercy— . . . ' Pirogov feared that when his tour of duty ended, 'the sisters would catch it,' for the chief doctors and commissars were spreading rumors that before the sisters had come 'it *had* gone better.'"[79] For these men, it had indeed gone better earlier because the nurses now prevented theft by hospital officials.

In June 1855, the large number of new casualties forced the Russians to ship 500 amputees to a safer area on the northern side of the harbor. However, with no building to house them, they had to be put in tents, their mattresses on the bare ground. Three days of heavy rain left the men lying in pools of muddy water. The already exhausted nursing sisters, now drenched and shivering, cared for them by kneeling in the mud. Some nurses fell ill from the exposure, and a few died. Fourteen of the surviving nurses were assigned to a first-aid station on McKenzie's Hill, where the wounded arrived in such numbers that everyone worked for days without rest. Only after sixteen consecutive days without changing their clothing were the sisters allowed to bathe in the sea.[80] For some, it was the last bath.

As dreadful as the conditions were facing the Russian nurses during the siege of Sevastopol, what the first British nurses encountered when they arrived in Turkey was even worse. Because there were no women nurses in the British army when the war began, physicians ran the hospitals, usually assisted by medical students. Feeding and bathing patients, giving them medications, and dealing with their daily needs was a job done by soldier-orderlies. These men, usually drunken outcasts from their regiments, when sober enough to provide any care at all, gave it only to those who could pay. This seldom happened, because whenever possible, the orderlies stole everything of value as soon as a patient arrived.[81] The orderlies also heaped verbal and physical abuse on the wounded men, who had no way to defend themselves and no one to complain to. These conditions, as well as an abiding concern about nursing, led Florence Nightingale to initiate the reforms that made her famous and that revolutionized British army hospitals. It should be noted that these dreadful conditions seldom affected wounded officers. As noted earlier, most of them received treatment in a separate, luxurious hospital reserved for officers only.

Despite her upper-class background, powerful social connections, wealth, determination, and intimidating temper, Nightingale had great difficulty obtaining permission for her nurses actually to do anything when they first arrived at the Scutari hospitals. Dr. John Hall, the same Hall who persisted in mismanaging medical care for the British, scoffed at her request for toothbrushes for soldiers and food for a balanced diet, calling them "preposterous luxuries." Opposing Nightingale at every step, Hall insisted that nurses had no useful role and would only cause trouble. Most of the surgeons were afraid to oppose Hall, and it was not until after the flood of wounded from the battle of Inkerman that the nurses were allowed to treat patients. When the medical staff finally met her decidedly matronly nurses, they no longer feared irresistible sexual temptation on the part of the patients. In fact, they should not have relaxed so quickly. Many of the nurses drank heavily whenever they could, swore mightily, and sought out sexual relations with soldiers, especially with sergeants, whom they hoped to marry.[82] Nightingale had to lock up supplies of liquor, and she actually sent several nurses home for various offenses, including theft, drunkenness, sexual promiscuity, and incompetence.[83] All nurses had traveled to Turkey first class; those who were sent home in disgrace traveled third class and received meals of salt pork.[84]

Admittedly coarse and drunken, most of these women were nevertheless kind to the men, and they were hardworking. They played a vital role in bathing the men, changing their clothing, cheering them with small favors, seeing that they had food and drink, and offering them hope. Nurses would kneel on the stone floors for hours, rubbing dying men's feet to give them some relief from their pain and would sit up with them all night to give them what comfort was possible. Nightingale herself often spent eight hours straight kneeling on stone floors while bandaging patients, and she rarely left a man alone when he was dying.[85] To the amazement of the surgeons, another nurse saved a man's leg that was scheduled for amputation by bathing it frequently.[86]

Nurses endured truly appalling conditions. They lived in cold, damp, crowded quarters with no semblance of privacy. Ten women shared one room, fourteen shared another, a room that had previously housed a decaying corpse. The water they drank was filthy, and tea was rarely available; their meals consisted of sour bread and tainted meat, and even this miserable ration was often unavailable. No bathing facilities existed. The nurses' quarters, like the two hospitals where they worked, were plagued by rats, lice, fleas, flies, and the stupefying stench of feces. Wounded men came to the hospital so covered with fleas and lice that their bodies shimmered, and nothing the nurses could do succeeded in removing them all. Nurses spent endless hours cleaning filthy and maggot-infested wounds. Others knelt in pools of vomit and feces as they tried to tend to soldiers dying of cholera.[87]

Exposed to deadly diseases every moment that they were in Turkey, many nurses sickened. How many died is not known, but the French, whose hospitals were initially more sanitary and better managed than those of the British, admitted that thirty-nine French nurses died early in the war.[88] The later typhus epidemic must have killed many more. All nurses in all armies had to endure the continual torment of young men dying in agony, calling out for their mothers or wives while reaching for a nurse's hand. They recalled with great pain patients like a young Scottish soldier who said he wanted to live so that he could take care of his mother. He died that same night.[89] One British nurse remembered finding a tall, seriously wounded young soldier, badly stooped by exhaustion and pain, sobbing like a baby as he staggered along outside the hospital. Lost and in despair, he collapsed in gratitude when a nurse rushed to help him.[90] The nurses' greatest reward was the gratitude of the men they served so faithfully.

These nurses in general and Nightingale in particular deserve much of the credit for a dramatic reduction in the death rate of men hospitalized at Scutari, although the recommendations of various government commissions that inspected the hospitals in early March 1855 were also important. Nightingale craved authority, acted pettily, and could be as tough and irascible as any drill sergeant, but no matter how self-serving her reforms may have been, they saved lives. She was said to have a "divided self which impelled her to fight, to cheat, to bully, to boast and to save lives."[91] And that she did. When Nightingale arrived in Turkey, close to 50 percent of all men admitted to the hospital died. During January 1855, the death rate fell to 36 percent. By May 1855, it had fallen to 5.2 percent, and from October 1855 through May 1856, it was only 3.6 percent—much lower than the death rate for soldiers hospitalized in the United Kingdom.[92]

Some of this improvement was no doubt due to the greater experience of the surgeons but this can account for only a small percentage of cases. Thanks to ten years spent studying European hospitals while her aristocratic family and friends looked on with undisguised distaste, Nightingale was responsible for many of the changes that increased patient survival: greatly improved sanitation, better food and medication, and compassionate patient care. She managed to replace most of the cruel, useless, and thieving orderlies and vastly improved the men's nutrition. Until her complaints finally brought about change, patients received only toast and tea for breakfast at 8 A.M., and no other food until 4 or 5 P.M. Even then, meals were often carelessly set down beyond the patients' reach or could not be eaten by men who had lost an arm.

Most important, Nightingale made the hospitals almost sanitary. Even though she vehemently denied the existence of germs—repeatedly pointing out that she had treated many cholera victims without "catching" the disease—she insisted compulsively on cleanliness, ordering that everything from the hospital walls to the patients themselves be kept scrupulously clean. She also spent much of her considerable fortune, plus money donated by *The Times*, to help the sick and wounded. She arrived in Gallipoli with a fund of £30,000. Because Dr. Hall and others blocked every reform, including the novel idea that patients should have clean clothing, Nightingale used this money to purchase shirts, trousers, and hospital gowns. Then, she rented a Turkish house, installed a boiler, and created an efficient laundry. Later, when word came from Balaclava that hundreds of British wounded would soon arrive at the overcrowded hospitals in Scutari, and the army authorities did nothing, she used more of her own money to hire 200 workmen to build a 500-bed hospital. She also purchased all the towels, dishes, and eating utensils the patients would need.[93]

She earned the sobriquet "Lady of the Lamp" by walking the wards at night to comfort suffering men as best she could. Like most nurses, she eventually fell desperately ill, nearly dying of typhus while visiting a Balaclava hospital. After the war, the thirty-six-year-old Nightingale received honors throughout Britain, while using all her fame, political connections, and iron will to overcome the resistance of the army medical establishment to her proposals for sanitary reform in their hospitals and barracks. Even after she showed that the mortality rate of "healthy" young soldiers in barracks in the London borough of Kensington was 17.5 percent, whereas the mortality rate of civilians in that borough, including children, the elderly, and the ill, was only 3.3 percent, it took all her strength and persuasion finally to achieve reforms. In doing so, she frequently ruined her health, at one point being unable to walk for six years, and was largely bedridden for the last fifty-four years of her life. Nightingale's legacy was strongly felt during the American Civil War. Twelve separate religious orders in the North put her teachings in place in their hospitals, and Dorothy Dix, every bit as difficult as Nightingale herself, was well aware of her reforms in hospital sanitation. And Clara Barton, one of a few women who nursed the wounded on the battlefields, was influenced by Nightingale as well.[94] She later established the American Red Cross.

Nightingale became perhaps the most beloved woman in Britain, and despite her ill health, she lived to be ninety. Many equally devoted nurses among the allies and with the Russians died during the war, and few received the acclaim they deserved. Most of these women died young, as did the beautiful Lady Agnes Paget, who died in childbirth at twenty-six, leaving two young sons, but the stalwart Lady Alicia Blackwood lived to be ninety-five.

With a few exceptions, such as Florence Nightingale and Fanny Duberly, we know very little about the women who took part in this war, and we know even less about the children. But we can say that the women and children were not simply victims of the war's violence, of disease, and of terrible weather, as they have been in most wars. Many took an active part in the fighting and in nursing the war's victims. A few received praise and medals. Many more deserved them.

So did many women and children during the American Civil War. As mentioned earlier, boys as young as thirteen enlisted in both armies, and many women served in the ranks disguised as men, often fighting gallantly. And women who served as nurses suffered many of the same horrors that confronted nurses during the Crimean War.[95] American women also lost sons and husbands, some searching battlefields for their remains. All too often, men who were killed in combat were buried anonymously, leaving their wives and mothers to hope in vain that they would one day return. Women and children also experienced hunger, and some saw their homes destroyed and their crops ruined. More than a few women were raped, and many were forced into prostitution in exchange for food. Terrible as the suffering of a good many women and children was during the four years of war, their counterparts in the Crimea suffered even more, although for a shorter time. For civilians, the siege of Sevastopol was far worse than any siege that Americans endured. The siege of Vicksburg brought great suffering to many civilians, as did Sherman's drive through Georgia into South Carolina, but many more women and children fought and died in Sevastopol, as they did in Kerch and Kars. American women and children suffered from the ravages of disease, but disease was even more widespread and deadly during the Crimean War. There are so many tests of courage that comparisons inevitably fall short, but it seems fair to say that even though many women and children displayed great valor during the Civil War, as a crucible for courage the Crimean War was even more demanding.

# 6

# PRIDE AND
# PREJUDICE

*The Turks at War*

I T IS NOT UNCOMMON FOR allied armies to lack respect for
one another. The Irish Brigade in the American Civil War was often scorned by fellow Federal troops and Confederate enemies alike.
And even though over half of the British troops killed at the Alma
River battle were Irish, they earned little praise. Instead, the long-
standing British-Irish hostility remained. Much of the enmity had to
do with religion. Only two Roman Catholic priests were made available for the 10,000 Irish soldiers in Raglan's army, and Florence
Nightingale rarely passed up an opportunity to criticize Roman
Catholic nurses.[1] But there were other reasons as well: a history of
conflict, difference in language, and accusations of cowardice, to
mention a few. German immigrant troops in the Federal army also
received little respect. And to no one's surprise, when former
slaves—over 200,000 of them—enlisted in the Federal army and
navy, it was not only the Confederates who loathed and murdered
them, a great many Northern soldiers detested them as well.

British and French officers and men alike detested their Turkish allies almost as much as white Americans hated African-American soldiers. Much of what has been written in the West about the Turks in
this war reviles them for cowardice, corruption, and incompetence. In
response, the Turks wrote next to nothing to defend themselves. For

one thing, although an Ottoman printing press had been developed in 1835 and several Ottoman newspapers existed, many of the Turks involved in the Crimean War, including many officers and government officials, were not literate, and except for a few French and British officers and surgeons who served with Turkish forces, the European allies did little to report the actual Turkish role in the war.[2]

Neither the British, the French, nor the Sardinians entered this war to "save" the Ottoman Empire or to protect the Turkish peoples. Their interests lay in blocking Russian expansion and promoting their own economic and political advantages. As they pursued these aims, the European allies openly deplored what they perceived as Turkish corruption, indolence, polygamy, sexual debauchery, and general backwardness, as well as the Turkish practice of slavery. They had no respect for Turkish soldiers, and even less for their leaders. They delighted in speaking derisively about the ignorance of "fat" pashas who knew nothing about Western ways. A British officer provided this account:

> The correct form is this,—you walk into the room; the Pasha gets up, salaams and shakes hands; you then sit down upon the divan, and he again bows to you, and you return it. The Pasha then claps his hands, and attendants appear with long pipes, with beautiful amber mouthpieces, already lighted, which they give to each person. The Pasha again claps his hands, re-enter attendants with small cups of coffee and sherbet for each of the company,—you smoke and drink coffee in silence for a short time till a sudden thought seems to strike the Pasha, and he asks you if you are well, to which knotty question you return a favourable answer, and the conversation becomes general. The Pasha of course exhibits an incredible amount of ignorance on every common subject, and takes everything you say for granted. After you have smoked yourself into a white heat, and then endeavoured to allay it with coffee, you rise, shake hands, bow, and retire; and the same scene, pipes, coffee, conversation, and ignorance, takes place at the next house you visit. They (the Turks) are far behind the natives of India, both in civilization and intelligence, and are a very debauched, good-for-nothing set.[3]

The European allies also laughed mightily about a ball given by French and British officers and diplomats in Varna, attended by a few British wives. Noticing that these unveiled, bare-shouldered women danced with one man after another, a high-ranking Ottoman government official assumed that they must be prostitutes. He proceeded to whisper outrageous obscenities into the ear of a British diplomat's wife. Her response left no doubt that the Turk had made a mistake.[4] Of course, the Westerners also had no love for Islam, and many declared that they wished they could fight Turkey instead of Russia.

The European allies derided the Turkish army as a polyglot, unpaid, poorly trained, badly equipped, ill-disciplined rabble, led by hopelessly incompetent and cowardly officers who thought only of their personal profit and new sexual delights with women, boys, or animals. When the war began with Turkish armies facing Russian troops along the Danube and in Russian Georgia in the east, Turkish atrocities only increased Western revulsion. Early in the war, a superior Turkish force, which was led by Mehmet Pasha and which included a large number of murderous Bashi-Bazouk cavalry, overran the Russian frontier outpost of Fort Nicholas on the eastern shore of the Black Sea. A Russian eyewitness survivor reported:

> They crucified the customs inspector and then used him for target practice. The priest had his head sawn off. The doctor was tortured to death while being questioned as to the location of the garrison's money. Women and children were slaughtered and, finally, a pregnant woman had her living child cut out of her and, before her very eyes, it was hacked to pieces.[5]

The more disciplined Turkish infantry did nothing to stop these atrocities and, in fact, mounted a good many heads of Russian soldiers on pikes and bayonets to receive the bounty that Mehmet Pasha had promised to pay for each head taken from a despised *Giaour* (infidel). Particularly handsome boys and girls were taken into slavery. The fact that the Turkish forces in the east next lost several battles to the Russians, in which many Turkish officers ran away, did nothing to increase the Westerners' enthusiasm for their Ottoman allies. In the western war zone along the Danube, Turks mutilated Russian dead, bayoneted Russian wounded, and took more heads.[6] Early in the war, a Russian officer said to a British counterpart, "What a pity two such nations as England and Russia should fight over such brutes as these Turks."[7]

When the French and British armies arrived at Varna, they were greatly surprised to discover that although most of the Bashi-Bazouks were outrageously undisciplined "savages" of little military value, the Turkish infantry and artillery had actually fought so well that the Russians had been driven back across the Danube in retreat. A British cavalry officer wrote that the Turks he had seen "are really good looking soldiers, much better than I expected to see; they must be brave fellows."[8] When news that the Turks had defeated the Russians arrived at French and British headquarters, it hit "like a bomb," leaving many British and French officers both amazed and bitterly disappointed that the "wretched" Turks had won without their help. As a senior allied officer lamented, "Nobody had expected the Turks to be able to repulse the Russian Force."[9]

The small Turkish force that sailed with its allies to the Crimea and took part in the battle of the Alma River did nothing to disgrace itself either, even though it was made up of older, married reservists with little military training and played no central role in the fighting. After this battle, the European allies treated the Turks with grudging acceptance until the battle of Balaclava, when all that changed. At five points on the British right flank near the harbor of Balaclava, the British had placed artillery behind earthworks. For reasons that have never been adequately explained, Lord Raglan accepted staff advice to assign these critical positions to Turkish troops without bothering to ascertain anything about their readiness for battle. He sent no British artillery officers to help them fire British guns and no British troops to back them up. The 500 ethnic Turks in the first gun position were attacked by a Russian force of 6,000 men, and despite these overwhelming odds, they held for an hour, even though they lost 170 men and all their artillery had been taken.

With still no sign of reinforcements from the British, who were very slow to move up in support, the Turks eventually broke, giving up the position and its guns. It was these guns that Raglan ordered the Light Brigade to save. The other four Turkish-held positions had not yet come under severe attack, but when the Turks began to retreat from the first position, the ill-trained Tunisians who were manning the other four positions fled in terror. Those not cut down by pursuing Cossacks ran for Balaclava harbor, where they attempted to find safety aboard British ships. The Russians did not exploit the rout, and potential disaster was averted, but from that time on, the British and French thought of the Turks as despicable cowards.[10]

That the first Turkish position had been held so gallantly did not matter, nor did the fact that the troops who ran were Tunisians, so poorly trained that the Turks themselves had previously used them almost exclusively as porters.

After this episode, the European allies treated all Turks in the Crimea as miserable curs—cursed at, spat upon, kicked, and slapped, their only duties to carry supplies, maintain roads, and stay out of sight. After winter struck, starving Turkish soldiers tried to stay alive by stealing food. When caught, they were flogged. One British officer wrote:

> The Turks are to be set to work to build us huts; this sort of work . . . is all they are good for. Everyone out here . . . hates the name of a Turk, while a Russian is certainly the more noble and braver man. (The Turks) are the most rascally-looking rabble in the shape of an army that any nation could produce. French and English look at them with contempt.[11]

Another officer confirmed this opinion: "The Johnnys [Turks] are made to do all the dirty work, that is as much as the idle rascals can be forced to do. Everyone pushes and cuffs them."[12]

Many Turkish soldiers in the Crimea simply accepted misery as their fate and slowly starved to death.[13] According to British war correspondent N. A. Woods, the horrors suffered by the British army during the winter of 1854–1855 were "trifles" compared to the suffering of the Turks. The European allies had agreed to take responsibility for feeding the Turkish troops in the Crimea, but the British, whom the Turks camped closest to, could provide only dry biscuits, salt pork, and rum. Because of their religion, the Turks could accept only the biscuits, and their commanders were too proud to ask the French for help. After eating all the dead horses that could be found, Turkish soldiers began to starve:

> Soon, every morning the Turkish soldiers could be seen coming in from the plain of Balaclava, carrying with affectionate care their dying comrades on their backs. These they deposited in little huts about the village, and the places became filled with them. Bye-and-bye, each morning the road was dotted with the corpses of those who in the night had perished, unaided, in trying to reach the houses, for the comparative warmth and shelter of some obscure nook.[14]

Turkish bodies lay in grisly rows until famished comrades could gather the strength to bury them under a few inches of dirt. Each night, wild dogs dug up the bodies and ate their fill. Each day, the process repeated itself as dead bodies were carried to the burial ground from a nearby Turkish hospital. The Turkish surgeon in charge, who had been trained in London and spoke very good English, showed Woods the hospital: "The deadly fetid air which issued from this charnel-house made me involuntarily shrink back from the door with loathing."[15] The building had previously been used for Russian prisoners, many of whom had died of cholera. After all the Russians had died, the "hospital" was given to the Turks, but despite "ankle-deep" blood and feces, it had never been cleaned. Hundreds of starving Turks now lay in this filth without beds, blankets, or even clothing. The dying men lay covered with maggots, rice water the only food available. The Turkish surgeon commented sadly, "None of those poor fellows will come out alive. I have not saved a single man who has entered that fatal building."[16] When Woods asked if he had no medicines, the surgeon pointed to two large tents amply supplied with medical supplies, saying, "But they are useless. The men are dying of hunger and medicine is of no avail."[17]

Neither the British nor the French general staff paid any heed to the dying Turks, but a British admiral who spoke some Turkish and had previously served with the Turkish navy managed to borrow a British steamer to take 158 of the worst cases to Constantinople. Half of the men died during the voyage, but had they stayed in Balaclava, all would have done so. In response to the growing horror experienced by the sick and starving Turks, the Turkish government showed surprising concern by converting a sixty-gun frigate into a fully equipped, 300-bed hospital ship. Staffed by four surgeons, two apothecaries, and several male nurses, the ship arrived in the Crimea only to stand at anchor for ten days waiting for a berth in any one of the three allied harbors. Even though several of the large ships then berthed in those harbors housed only a handful of senior officers, the French and British shamelessly refused to create space for the hospital ship, which was forced to return empty to Constantinople.[18]

Allied contempt for the Turks had no limits. When malnourished Turkish prisoners joined British prisoners in Russia, they were badly beaten by their "allies," then ostracized. After that, the Russians wisely kept the two sets of prisoners apart as much as possible. As one British prisoner put it, "We soldiers despised the whole of the

Turkish race for their cowardice in running away. . . . The sailors detested them for their filthy habits [presumably homosexuality] and for making their ships lousy."[19]

It is difficult to generalize about the Turks in this war because their diverse army included troops equal to any in the world and others that proved utterly hopeless. However, although the Turkish artillery consistently performed very well, with a very few exceptions senior Turkish officers who had not been trained in European armies proved worse than useless, not only stealing everything they could but refusing to take responsibility for anything. Officers often boxed their soldiers' ears or yanked on them in anger, and a French officer saw a Turkish battalion commander brutally attack an elderly, decorated sergeant for a minor infraction.[20] A British naval officer reported that the captain of a Turkish frigate ordered his cook beaten to death for preparing a bad meal.[21] However, a few junior officers displayed military skill and bravery, and some officers felt close to their soldiers, playing backgammon with them and walking with them hand in hand.[22]

So-called Turkish troops—more correctly, troops of the Ottoman Empire—took part in several major actions in addition to the debacle of Balaclava. As mentioned earlier, their advance into Russian Georgia achieved few victories, but it did not collapse. Several Turkish forces remained in action in eastern Anatolia near the Russian border throughout the war, and one of these, which defended the city of Kars, proved to be no less than heroic. At the war's onset, Omer Pasha, the Turks' Austrian-trained commander, had led his 90,000-man army against the Russians along the Danube with such skill that the French and British armies had nothing to do. The British preferred to attribute the Turks' success to two brave and enterprising British junior officers who volunteered to join their effort. But in fact, the Turkish army as a whole did very well despite the incompetence and lack of resolve of many of its officers, and even though many of its battalions consisted of overage reservists never before called to service and not at all keen to leave their wives and children. Many feared that they would die and their families would never even be informed. In fact, of the 14,000 aging Egyptian reservists sent to the Danube, half did die; that any survived their harrowing twenty-eight-day voyage, seated the entire way, with only dry biscuit and a single gulp of water each day, was remarkable.[23] Of 10,000 Tunisians sent to the Crimea, 7,000 died.[24]

The British and French refused to believe that the Turks could have fought so well, or that Omer Pasha's Turks would fight capably in defense of Yevpatoria, defeating a large Russian attack. Later, the Turks proved successful, if brutal, in helping to sack the eastern Crimean city of Kerch, and still later in the war, a large Turkish force under Omer Pasha made a spirited reconnaissance in force near Sevastopol that earned the admiration of allied officers. He also led an attempt to relieve Kars. The mission was too late, but his Turkish forces achieved a smashing victory over the Russians at the Ingour River in Georgia.

The 20,000-man Turkish force that held the small port of Yevpatoria, north of the Alma River, threatened the Russians as a dagger pointed at their lifeline of supplies from the Russian mainland. Protected by the guns of British and French warships offshore, Omer Pasha had done a capable job of fortifying the port as well as emplacing some thirty-four heavy guns and many smaller ones. But he lacked cavalry and had not the least intention of taking offensive action against the Russians, rich in cavalry and outnumbering him greatly as well. In fact, when Russian cavalry rounded up 10,000 beef cattle grazing nearby, Omer Pasha could do nothing to interfere. Prince Menshikov took his inactivity as a sign of weakness and ordered an attack on the port. The Turks easily defeated the Russians, throwing them back with substantial losses. They also cut off a good many Russian heads and mounted them on bayonets before the few British and French officers at Yevpatoria protested, and Omer Pasha had the offenders arrested.[25] News of the defeat crushed the tsar, who relieved Menshikov of command after indicating that he had foreseen defeat and had ordered that the attack not take place. The tsar had issued no such orders, but he would not live to feel guilty about his mendacity. Three days after relieving Menshikov, on March 2, 1855, he died. According to his physicians, Russia's defeat by the Turks at Yevpatoria was the "final blow."[26]

The allies believed that the Turks could fight, if they would fight at all, only behind impregnable fortifications. Omer Pasha put the lie to this belief through his capable handling of large forces in bloody offensive actions on the Danube. In April 1855, Omer Pasha moved almost 30,000 of his best troops (primarily Africans from Egypt and Syrians) to Sevastopol, where they languished, being allowed no meaningful military role. The Turkish commander was well aware that his few surviving troops in the Crimea were being used only as laborers by the European allies, so when a large Russian army under

General N. N. Muraviev began its siege of the eastern Turkish city of Kars in the summer of 1855, Omer Pasha asked his allies for permission to sail his forces from the Crimea to relieve Kars and fight a war of movement against the Russians. Inexplicably, the British and French insisted that his troops remain in the Crimea, where they were said to be needed even though the 17,500-man Sardinian contingent had begun to arrive, the French had been greatly reinforced, and even the battered British had regained much of their strength. In all, the European allies deployed over 160,000 men and 500 heavy cannons at Sevastopol. This reluctance to let the Turks leave the Crimea is all the more puzzling because the new French commander, Pélissier, had no respect for either Omer Pasha or his troops.

Turkish troops in the Crimea did no duty in the trenches and took no direct part in the siege of Sevastopol. It was rare enough that a British or French officer expressed any concern about the Turks, but Sir Evelyn Wood, then a young midshipman, wondered why they were not used because, as he noted, they had done well on the Danube, and "their courage and resignation were remarkable, even under sufferings beyond description."[27]

On April 19, 1855, for reasons that still remain unclear, Lord Raglan approved (and may even have requested) a major reconnaissance by the Turkish forces toward the Russian lines to the northeast of Sevastopol. Led by Omer Pasha, his face haggard and his beard now snow-white, twelve battalions of newly arrived Turks, Syrians, and black Egyptians from the Sudan (which was then a part of Egypt), accompanied by small numbers of French and British cavalry and some horse-drawn artillery, began to march north over the same ground that the Light Brigade had covered during its ill-fated charge of the previous fall. A large number of onlookers rode along behind the Turks, and one of these, The Times correspondent, "Billy" Russell, recorded what he saw in detail. The much-derided Turks looked the part in their drab dark blue uniforms with no flashes of color, their gray woolen socks pulled well up their calves, and their crude sheepskin sandals looking decidedly unmilitary. The rank stench of sweat-soaked men that came from their ranks did nothing to enhance the impression they made. Yet observers noted that they marched well and that the steel of their weapons was highly polished.[28] When they tramped over the thousands of wildflowers, mint, thyme, parsley, and sage that literally covered the valley floor, a pleasant scent gradually overcame all else.[29]

As the Turkish columns moved north, they passed by the body of a dragoon from the Light Brigade. All the buttons had been cut off his jacket, presumably as souvenirs, but he had not been buried. Nor had the body of a red-haired Russian that lay nearby. Half-decayed bodies of artillery and cavalry horses lay all about, and human arms and legs often protruded from shallow graves. Led by fifes and drums and a band incongruously playing a quick-step waltz, the Turkish soldiers marched on, their thoughts about the graveyard beneath their feet unknown.[30] As the troops moved farther north, they were led by a skirmish line of infantry, incongruously urged on by a man armed with only a bow and arrows and an ancient pistol. Russian officers and Cossacks now appeared on a ridge still farther north, where they stood watching the Turkish advance. While French artillery blasted the ridge with rocket fire, Turkish infantry charged up the incline, driving the Russians away. Omer Pasha, Lord Raglan, and several French generals then spent some time lunching and surveying the Russian lines before the entire force turned around and marched back to where they had camped near the British.

The allies were pleased by the Turkish performance, but a few days later, news arrived that the Russians were once again threatening Yevpatoria, so Omer Pasha and his men boarded ships and sailed back to the north. The Turkish maneuver accomplished little of military value, but it did provide a welcome, and largely bloodless, respite from the horrors of siege warfare, and it also improved the image of the now somewhat less despised Turks. A little later, 5,000 Turkish troops rushed to the support of the French and Sardinians at the battle of the Chernaya River but, through no fault of theirs, arrived too late to play a significant role.

While Omer Pasha sailed his troops to and fro, a 40,000-man Russian army under General Muraviev was marching west from the Russian border through eastern Anatolia, toward the Turkish city of Kars some forty miles away, where an 18,000-man Turkish force had assembled. Kars consisted of thousands of two-storied mud brick houses, clustered around a craggy cliff topped by a medieval castle. Originally an Armenian city in the center of a high, treeless plain close to the border of Russian Georgia, Kars now included as its residents many colorfully dressed Greeks, Arabs, Kurds, Turks, and Circassians, as well as mountain tribespeople such as the Daghestanlis and Lazis, the latter a warlike people who specialized in kidnapping children and selling them into slavery in Turkish harems. In addition to the rifle, long knife, and two pistols that all Lazi men carried, each wildly long-haired Lazi had a coil of rope hanging from his belt for use in tying any captive he succeeded in taking.[31]

But the most picturesque people were the Kurds, seen everywhere on the streets of Kars. Kurdish chiefs wore enormous silk turbans made of yellow, black, green, and white handkerchiefs:

[The chief's] nearest follower carries a bamboo lance, tufted with ostrich feathers: each cavalier has a small shield suspended from his neck, fringed with green and red trappings, and covered with steel bosses (ornaments); he is armed besides with pistol, scimitar, and dagger: hung around him are powder horns, flint and steel apparatus, drinking cups, and a variety of appendages useful or ornamental.[32]

Erzerum, a difficult five-day ride to the west of Kars, was a major city of over 50,000 people, with thirteen public baths and seventy mosques, as well as Roman Catholic, Greek Orthodox, and Armenian churches. It was even home to two American Christian missionaries. As a major arms depot, it should have been able to supply Kars with everything needed to survive a long siege. It should also have been able to supply a large number of troops. Not so. The government officials in Erzerum got off to a good start by sending (or, more correctly, allowing to go) a number of foreign military men to take over the direction of the defense of Kars. Although the Turkish forces fell nominally under the command of a Turkish "field marshal" named Zarif Mustafa Pasha, he had no military experience at all and gladly yielded command to a British officer, Colonel (later General) Sir W. Fenwick Williams, an extremely competent and energetic officer. Williams was assisted by Colonel Atwell Lake, a skillful artillery officer; a brave young captain named C. B. Teesdale; another enterprising captain named Henry Thompson; and Humphrey Sandwith, a vigorous surgeon with fifteen years' experience in Turkey, who would head some fifty Turkish and European physicians, surgeons, and apothecaries in Kars.

When the British officers reached Kars, they joined a veritable foreign legion of officers from Poland, France, Italy, Prussia, and Hungary. Many of the Hungarians had fled their homeland after the failed rebellion of 1849, retaining vivid memories of the day when scores of aristocratic Hungarian women were herded into a city square in Budapest, stripped to the waist in public, then flogged—something never to be forgotten. Williams's second in command was a stalwart sixty-five-year-old Hungarian general named Ismail Pasha Kmety. He also received good service from other foreigners already in Kars: a brave Circassian, a skillful Italian engineer, and two Americans, Nevis and Bonfante, both of whom had previously fought in the war between the United States and Mexico.[33] Nevis, a wealthy adventurer, happily served without pay.[34]

Williams and his countrymen rode east to Kars over high mountain roads, through dense pine forests, and across deep valleys and plateaus dotted with lovely wild flowers. They marveled at the profusion of birds and would soon learn that the 6,000-foot-high area was amazingly healthy as well. Williams expected to find a useless garrison, but matters seemed initially to be even worse than he had feared. Much of the army that had occupied Kars since the onset of the war had died, its troops victims of earlier fighting, disease, or starvation. That garrison had been largely replaced by untrained peasants conscripted by force. The muster role of troops given to the now General Williams when he arrived listed 30,000 men, but only 17,000 of these actually existed. Turkish commanders had maintained the fictional army of 30,000 so that they might sell or steal the rations and supplies meant for the missing 13,000 men. Even most of the 17,000 soldiers who did exist were seriously ill with scurvy.

Williams promptly replaced the drunken and corrupt Turkish commanders, laid down the new law to the others, and convinced Constantinople to send him more men, guns, ammunition, food, and other supplies. To be certain that the newly arrived food actually reached the soldiers, Williams and the other British officers regularly inspected the regimental kitchens, watching to be sure that the troops received the rations promised. Williams made another discovery: "In closely inspecting the troops as I rode through their ranks, I was struck by their healthy and soldier-like mien. I doubt if any army could produce better materials for working with in this country."[35] This assessment may have been wishful thinking at the time, but it proved to be accurate. Some of the Turkish troops were irregulars, but three battalions had modern rifles and several others had reasonably modern percussion muskets. By the summer of 1855, Williams had restored the Kars garrison and built formidable forts and earthworks.

Surgeon Sandwith also concluded:

The virtues of the Turkish private soldiers shone forth wonderfully during all this campaign: they had been ill-treated and abandoned by their officers, plundered of their dues, wretchedly clothed and armed, and there were many of them twenty-four months in arrears of pay; and yet the desertions were by no means so numerous as might have been anticipated. Their patience and long suffering, their sobriety and subordination, were beyond all praise; in short, there were traits observable in them which would mark them out as amongst the best troops in Europe, had they fought under better auspices.[36]

Captain Thompson was similarly impressed, although Erzerum still paid no attention whatsoever to General Williams's requests for supplies, wages, and reinforcements:

The poor soldiers never get their full rations, and many of them are twenty-eight months in arrears of pay. While such things are going on, it is a wonder to me that the soldiers don't lay down their arms, or desert by thousands; but strange to say, desertions are very rare, and the men are in the best of spirits. I think they are the finest soldiery (or stuff to make soldiers of) that the world can produce. Nothing comes amiss to them; they are literally in *rags*, and yet they never complain, although they are nearly always wet through. It would astonish you to see a regiment of them on parade. You could hardly pick out a worse (looking) lot from all the beggars in England.[37]

The British officers were pleased by the Turkish troops but appalled to discover that the Turkish officers had done nothing to fortify the medieval city. Despite their reputation for fighting only from behind strong walls and trenches, these Turkish officers proved notoriously inept at fortification. Colonel Lake called them "drunken, good-for-nothing rascals."[38] At the insistence of the British officers, the Turks now set to work. With the enormous help of the Christian population, who saw this as an opportunity to raise their standing with the Muslim authorities, the people of Kars joined with the army in constructing a formidable line of trenches and forts to encircle the city. When finished, it bristled with cannon and posed a tough obstacle to any attacking army. While the fortifications were being built, all manner of irregular soldiers marched or rode into

Kars, some of them said to be elegantly dressed, brave, and gentlemanly.[39] Bashi-Bazouks came in their hundreds, and 3,000 heavily armed Lazi tribesmen joined Williams's forces. The Lazis paid no attention to his orders and remained devoted to their leader, who wanted to kill Russians on his own terms.

At the same time, Dr. Sandwith outfitted a 2,000-bed hospital in anticipation of the carnage soon to come. Several of the so-called doctors on his staff were European charlatans without actual medical training, but some proved competent, and most of the Turkish doctors became energetic, dedicated, and reasonably capable. Their treatment of cholera victims, which combined hand massage to ease the pain of cramps and a chalky opiate drink to slow the diarrhea, proved to be every bit as effective as the Western therapies. However, Sandwith was horrified to find medical storehouses packed with every imaginable luxury, such as cosmetics and perfumes, but very few of the medical staples needed except for enough chloroform for 100,000 operations. There were no ambulances and few stretchers. Urgent appeals for basic bandages and surgical equipment went off to Erzerum. While Sandwith waited to hear from the never-prompt pashas in Erzerum, he set his men on such a diligent program of sanitation that throughout the siege, his hospital astonishingly did not suffer a single case of typhus or hospital gangrene. Amazingly, the quality of care he provided was superior to anything made available to the British, even after Florence Nightingale's successful reforms.[40]

The fortification of Kars had not yet been completed when General Muraviev's army reached the city, but the Russian general chose cautious reconnaissance over an all-out attack. In the first clash of cavalry, Russian dragoons routed a smaller force of Bashi-Bazouks and some regular Turkish cavalry, cutting the Turkish wounded to pieces. Colonel Lake, who rode with them, wrote, "I never saw such brutal butchery in my life."[41] A few days later, on June 16, the Russians launched a probing attack against the Kars fieldworks, only to be driven off easily with dreadful losses. This time, the Bashi-Bazouks surprisingly held their own against the Cossacks, who tried to lead the Russian attack, and Turkish artillery routed the Russian infantry, which withdrew across an open field of yellow flowers now blotched with blood. General Muraviev had timed his attack for the morning of the first day of the Bairem, a religious festival that called for idleness and the neglect of all secular duty. The Turks chose to fight instead, a holy fight, and boys as young as thirteen grabbed their dead fathers' ancient muskets or curved swords, rushing to join the soldiers at the trenches while their veiled mothers and sisters climbed onto rooftops to urge them on with cries such as "Kill the infidels" and "God sharpen your swords."[42]

July and August passed without a renewed attack, as fierce hailstorms alternated with stifling heat and plagues of flies. Many exchanges of artillery fire also took place, and the Turks proved to be better artillerymen than the Russians. Nevertheless, the Russian encirclement grew stronger day by day, and rations within the city had to be greatly reduced. Food shortages led to an increase in desertions by the irregulars, but the trained troops still had wonderful morale. Late in August, Williams ordered a strong force of cavalry and infantry, with many wagons, out of the fortress to harvest fields of corn and barley that had ripened nearby. They managed to return with their wagons full just before the Russians caught up with them. Once again, Turkish artillery caught Muraviev's men in the open and did great slaughter. In early September, cholera struck the Russians hard, and later, it appeared in Kars as well, but with far less loss of life. While Dr. Sandwith and his colleagues worked to contain the cholera epidemic, General Muraviev decided to try the Turkish defenses once again, this time in a full-scale attack in which Russia probably suffered its heaviest losses of any battle during the war.

At 4 A.M. on September 29, Turkish outposts heard the sound of wagon wheels and marching infantry. Because all the horses in Kars had starved or been eaten, cavalry could not be sent out to scout, but an hour later, the need to wonder about Russian plans ended. Dense columns of Russian infantry appeared on the murky valley floor, and the Turkish cannon and rifles opened fire. The Russian attacks came at many points along the circle of entrenchments. At one point, the Russians pushed aside a weak force of Lazi irregulars holding a position on the north side of Kars. Supported by artillery, and "seized with a raging desire for the fight," the Turks counterattacked with the bayonet, and the Russians gave way.[43] The Russians made several other breaches in the Turkish defenses, but they were always met by the bayonets and clubbed rifles of Turkish troops, Arabs, Lazi mountaineers, and even white-turbaned civilians swinging their curved swords. After no less than seven and a half hours of continuous fighting, the Russians withdrew, their surviving infantry running away down the same gradual slope they had marched up that morning. If the Turks had possessed cavalry, few Russians would have survived, but there could be no pursuit. General Williams later wrote that the Turks' bayonet attacks were "dashing" and that their defensive fighting had been tenacious.[44] Captain Thompson, who fought alongside them throughout the battle, was more graphic: "The Turks fought like heroes, almost like fiends; I never saw such desperate recklessness of life."[45]

Although Turks bayoneted some of them, Sandwith organized rescue efforts to save most of the Russian wounded, who lay everywhere in great pain; without horses, the work went slowly.[46] "Suddenly a band of music strikes up; . . . and the tune is a wild Zebek melody. At once a dozen of these mountaineers spring up from their repose, join hand-in-hand, and dance amidst the dead, dying, and the wounded."[47] Most of the Russian wounded lay all day in the terrible sun, then endured a frosty night before they could be helped. Providentially, no cases of cholera were reported during the battle or the next day. The great Turkish victory was attributed by many to the actions of "a sacred band of 10,000 men, all clothed in green, the Prophet's colour, fighting with our troops. These heavenly warriors disappeared when the Russians retreated."[48] The Turks buried over 6,000 Russians that first day. The full Russian loss in killed and wounded must have reached well over 12,000, probably more than died at Inkerman. The next day, the Turks recaptured two artillery batteries still held by the Russians, killing another 800 men with a loss of only 20 or 30 Turks.[49]

The total Turkish losses in these two days of carnage were comparatively low, amounting to 1,092 combatants killed and wounded, plus an unknown number of civilians. Most Turkish wounded bore their suffering without complaint, greatly impressing British doctors. Unlike European wounded, who often raged against death to the very end, Turks turned their faces to the wall and died without a sound. One British doctor referred to their "unequalled fortitude" and observed that their gratitude for what was done for them was also unequaled.[50] Russian wounded were also grateful for the care they received. One officer, whose jaw had been shot away by grapeshot, kept telling an interpreter that if only his lost ring engraved with the name *Eloise* could be found, he would recover. Incredibly, it was found, and the man leaped out of bed, "wild with joy," but died soon after.[51]

Despite his massive losses, General Muraviev tightened his choke hold on Kars until it became almost impossible to smuggle even a single donkey load of food into the fortress. Increasingly desperate, General Williams sent volunteers out at night, hoping that at least one would reach Erzerum with his plea for relief. Although many messengers were captured and executed, others got through. Still the Turkish commander in Erzerum sent neither food, ammunition, nor troops, forcing Williams to cut rations even more sharply. The usual diet of a Turkish soldier was thick rice soup and two pounds of bread in the morning, bread and olives at noon, and a large meal of lamb, vegetables, and pilaf at sunset. The troops were now on a daily ration of four ounces of bread and a bowl of soup containing less than two ounces of nutritious vegetable matter. No meat was to be had.[52] With starvation the inescapable outcome of the siege, everyone asked where Omer Pasha was. Some rumors had him only a few miles away. Others said that he was poised to attack the Russian rear. A few insisted that his cavalry had been seen only yesterday.

In July 1855, Omer Pasha again pleaded with the allied commanders to release his troops from the Crimea so that they could attempt to relieve Kars. Pélissier again refused, to the Turkish commander's great distress. After a nightmare of inactivity under the critical eyes of British and French commanders, in early September, just before the final assault on Sevastopol, Omer Pasha finally received permission to sail his now well-equipped army to the coast of Georgia, where he planned to drive south and attack Muraviev from the rear. Permission was granted perhaps because he had refused to join the attack on Sevastopol, and his army began to embark. Inexplicably, however, Omer Pasha then wasted six vital weeks while he received various medals and honors in Constantinople, was saluted by dignitaries, and awarded a grand estate by the sultan. Despite the delay, when the army finally sailed toward the coast of Georgia on British steamers, the soldiers were singularly patient and good-tempered. For two and a half days, they received nothing but water, some very hard and tasteless British army biscuits, and a small morsel of mutton fat. They also suffered terribly from snow and rain as they lay uncovered on the decks of their transports. A few even froze to death, yet the morale of the survivors remained excellent: "In the evenings, one would see a little knot of them gathered round a musician who alternately piped a melancholy tune on a little metal flageolet, or chanted a low, monotonous song."[53] They also carefully knelt to pray to Mecca, and after a Turkish major discovered he had

been praying to the northeast rather than the southeast, they used a
ship's compass to orient themselves.

Instead of landing in northern Turkey, close to Kars, the troops
landed in Georgia, directly under the magnificently snowcapped
twin peaks of 18,500-foot Mount Elbruz. Although the peak lay
some eighty miles inland, it was so clearly defined that it seemed
near enough to touch. While Omer Pasha gathered troops and supplies but could not find the transport horses he needed, his army sat
within this magnificent sight for another six weeks. Each evening in
camp, roll would be taken, and three cheers for the sultan would be
shouted out before dinner was served, followed by coffee and the inevitable pipes.[54] When Omer Pasha finally felt ready to march south,
he discovered that the heavily forested coastline, cut by numerous
streams, rivers, and deep ravines, was anything but ideal terrain for
his advancing wagon trains and artillery, most of which soon broke
down. Even the cavalry had difficulty, and in the first major skirmish, Skender Bey, Omer Pasha's dashing sixty-five-year-old cavalry
general, was wounded. His loss was felt, but heavy rains in this
mountainous country proved still more difficult to overcome.

Nevertheless, on November 5, Omer Pasha's men, led by the
British Colonel Simmons and a few other British officers, decisively
defeated a Russian force sent north by Muraviev at the River Ingour.
Attacking across the river into heavy Russian artillery and rifle fire,
the Turks drove the Russians back in disorder. A young British officer was killed, but the other British officers were elated by their success. A British observer wrote:

> It is impossible to speak too highly of the gallantry which the Turkish
> soldiers displayed throughout the action. Not only did the rifles [elite
> Turkish battalions armed with rifles] exhibit the greatest steadiness
> while exposed for upwards of six hours to the fire of the battery, but
> those infantry which took the battery by assault dashed forward with
> all the bravery and *élan* of the Zouaves. It is in this latter quality that
> the Turks have been supposed deficient; but they showed both under
> Omer Pasha and Colonel Simmons, that they possess it in a far higher
> degree than the Russians, and indeed as fully as any troops in the
> world.[55]

These troops made every effort to continue their drive south toward Kars, but tremendous rain flooded every valley, rivers became

impassable, and typhus, cholera, and scurvy decimated their ranks. Omer Pasha had lost so much time that his men would not relieve Kars. They would not even advance far enough to force Muraviev to send any appreciable force to oppose them.[56] Omer Pasha's lack of transport and the floods compelled him to withdraw. Why he delayed so long and why he did not march through Turkey, where he could easily have commandeered horses and wagons, is still not known.[57]

By October 17, when Omer Pasha was just beginning his drive south down the rugged Transcaucasian coast, the diet of bread and water had taken a visible toll on the troops in Kars. They were emaciated, the hospital packed with scurvy victims. Some impoverished soldiers, tempted to sell half their ration by the high price that civilians were willing to pay for bread, actually fell dead at their posts.[58] Wild dogs that dug up the shallow graves to eat their fill of corpses were followed by hordes of vultures that picked at the skeletons. All grass and roots had long since been eaten. On October 22, word came that Selim Pasha had landed an army of 20,000 on the north coast of Turkey and was marching rapidly on Erzerum. A week later, Selim Pasha reached Erzerum as starvation in Kars increased. Skeletal men with feeble voices and cold, clammy skin were carried into the hospital. A few who were treated with scarce horse meat soup survived, but so little horseflesh was available that most died. Every day, some 100 men starved to death, and women left more and more of their starving children on General Williams's doorstep.[59] Williams increased the bread ration, but the troops were still so feeble that they could do little more than sit at their batteries or lean against the parapet. Still, they called out, "Long live the sultan!" Surgeon Sandwith commented, "It would seem that the extremity of human suffering called for the latent sparks of loyalty and devotion not observed in seasons of prosperity."[60]

As the deaths by starvation increased, Selim Pasha was now said to be only three days march away. Desertions increased as Selim Pasha's army failed to appear before Kars, and brave men scouting on foot could see nothing of its advance guard. On November 22, a note in code arrived from a British diplomat, saying that Selim Pasha refused to advance and that there would be no help from Erzerum. At the time, Selim Pasha was reviled for his failure to advance, a charge repeated by many in subsequent historical accounts as well, but he commanded only 8,000 infantry plus 1,000 Bashi-Bazouks.

For him to have advanced against Muraviev's large army would have been suicide. Moreover, he had been ordered to Erzerum only to help defend it, not to relieve Kars.[61] Three days later, with all hope gone, General Williams requested peace terms from General Muraviev, who so chivalrously granted all his requests that Williams surrendered his garrison. Turkish irregulars were free to return to their houses, as were doctors and civilians. All regular troops became prisoners as did most officers, but they were allowed to retain their swords.

A short, pudgy nobleman of about seventy, who spoke Russian, French, English, German, and Turkish well, Muraviev was urbane, gracious, and thoughtful, feeding his prisoners well and demanding good treatment for them. When told of the surrender, most Turkish soldiers weakly stacked their muskets and feebly staggered off to the vast, well-appointed Russian camp, where well-fed, well-clothed troops lived in warm huts with glass windows, but many smashed their muskets against rocks, and some officers broke their swords, cursing, "Thus perish our Pashas, and the curse of God be with them! May their mothers be outraged [raped]!"[62] Those who had the strength to do so wept.

When Muraviev saw the condition of the Turkish troops who had surrendered to him, he was so appalled that he summoned the members of the Kars city council:

He reproached that gathering for its indifference toward the defenders of Kars, and reminded them that all of the riches they had acquired recently were stolen from the [Turkish] troops, the same troops whom they are now refusing to care for and feed. In conclusion, he told the head of the council, the most honored and wealthy of Kars' residents, to follow him. The Commander-in-Chief [Muraviev] led him to the nearest hospital and repeated his reproaches in front of the patients. He then immediately ordered that the elder be put on a free cot in the same ward, so as to force him, for an entire week, to suffer all of the deprivations that his indifference caused the patients to suffer. It was funny, and pitiful, to see the gold-sewn robes of the elder replaced with a dirty hospital gown, and his rich turban exchanged for a hospital cap. The loud laughter and joy of all of the sick served as the best kind of approval for this type of punishment. Immediately, measures were also taken by the Commander-in-Chief in order to supply Kars' hospitals with all necessary supplies.[63]

After their initial enthusiasm for the holy war against Russia, neither the Turkish people nor their leaders paid great attention to this battle nor, for that matter, to the war itself, in which so many brave men had fought, suffered, and died. Unlike the British public, now well informed about the suffering of British troops in the Crimea, few Turks knew anything about the suffering and death of their countrymen. Except for some people in eastern Anatolia, where heavy fighting took place, few Turks had any idea how the war was progressing, and even the surrender of the garrison at Kars went largely unnoticed. The best that Turkey could do for its dead was print this notice in the *Turkish Gazette:* "Drinking the sherbet of martyrdom, they gained eternal life."[64]

The drunkenness and violence of European troops in Constantinople was a more frequent topic of conversation among the Turkish public, as was the great influx of prostitutes to serve the foreigners. Turks were horrified when French troops lounged in mosques while prayers were being said, poisoned street dogs, ogled veiled women, mocked the muezzins as they called out prayers, and broke up tombs for paving stones. Nor were the Turks pleased when these soldiers amused themselves by shooting the seagulls flying over the Bosporus. The presence of unveiled foreign women in the city proved particularly troubling.[65]

But public expressions of patriotism by the Turks had long since ended, and no banners, speeches, or charitable works helped their soldiers. Throughout the war, Turkish dignitaries did everything in their power to grow rich at the expense of the Turkish soldiers, but when men of power visited the mosques on feast days, anything that might remind them of the war had to be removed from the routes their carriages would take.[66]

When the war ended, there were no monuments to fallen Turkish soldiers or sailors and no public thanks to the men who survived. Instead, the sultan provided a magnificent ball for foreign officers, diplomats, and their wives. Lady Hornby remembered it well:

I never shall forget the splendid scene when we entered the ball-room. Anything more beautiful it would be difficult even to imagine. Lady Stratford de Redcliffe, in a costume of the early part of the reign of George III., was standing about the middle room, surrounded by and receiving a most brilliant throng. Her crown of diamonds, her powder and pink roses, became her well. Miss Canning was dressed in the flowing white robes and oakleaf crown of a Druidess; Miss Catherine, as Mary, Queen of Scots. Mr. Odo Russell, first attaché, looked his ancestor, the Lord William Russell to perfection. His dress was black velvet; a white plumed hat, fastened with brilliants; a point-lace collar; and below that a splendid collar of diamonds. Mr. Doria was an Exquisite of Queen Anne's time, in a purple velvet coat, lined with figured satin; diamond shoe-bucks, snuffbox, and everything perfect, from patch to bow; Captain and Mrs. Mansfield in most tasteful dresses of the same date; one longed to pop them under glass cases, one at each end of the mantelpiece. It would take me a day to enumerate half the costumes. . . . Besides the gathering of French, Sardinian, and English officers, the people of the country appeared in their own superb and varied costumes; and the groups were beyond all description beautiful. The Greek Patriarch, the American Archbishop, the Jewish High Priest [Rabbi], were there in their robes of state. *Real* Persians, Albanians, Kourds, Servians, Armenians, Greeks, Turks, Austrians, Sardinians, Italians, and Spaniards were there in their different dresses, and many wore their jewelled arms. Some of the Greek yataghans and pistols were splendid. Two Jewish ladies were almost covered with diamonds. There were Fakirs, and Pilgrims, and Knights in real chain-armour, and Dervishes, and Maltese ladies, and Roman Empresses, English Shepherdesses, and Persian Princesses, and Turkish ladies without their veils. Of course, there were the usual oddities of a fancy ball. There was a Negro king, dressed in white and red feathers, and two gentlemanly Devils in black velvet, who waltzed with their long forked tails twined gracefully under their arms. . . . In fact, every costume in the known world was to be met with. . . . The flash of diamonds was something wonderful, especially among the Armenians and Greeks, who pride themselves, when wealthy, on the splendour of their wives.[67]

While Turkish pashas ate ravenously and drank vast amounts of champagne, the famous chef Alexis Soyer entertained the crowd with a "pet" bear—actually a friend dressed in a bear skin—while the crowd ate, drank, and danced until dawn. The war had ended, and Turkey carried on as before, its soldiers, both dead and alive, seemingly forgotten.

# 7

# SOLDIERS IN BATTLE

## *Courage and Cowardice*

A T THE TIME OF THE CRIMEAN WAR, and for years before, aristocrats were educated to exhibit courage, even fearlessness, as they were trained to practice dangerous sports, and to defend their honor and, if necessary, their countries. For them, honor was everything, and war was often seen as the supreme adventure, a time for charging horses, brilliantly uniformed men, plumes, trumpets, bugles—and after glorious battle would come praise, promotion, medals, and public acclaim. Viscount Wolseley wrote about how much he enjoyed combat, saying, "It is self-sacrifice of the most pronounced type, the acme of noble excitement, the apogee of patriotic enthusiasm."[1] Thousands of aristocrats went away to this war in search of glory, but most of those who fought were illiterate, impoverished commoners, even serfs. Not all of these sought glory, but most fought bravely; glory did not come without the conspicuous display of great courage.

Few wars have demanded more courage—and more different kinds of courage—than this one did. In repeated battles, the attacking army formed itself into close columns or ranks that made marvelous targets for its enemy's artillery, which tore men's bodies with solid cannonballs, shrapnel from exploding shells, huge shotgun shells called *canister* that sprayed tennis-ball-sized iron balls, and vicious discharges of smaller cannonballs known as *grapeshot*. Rifles and muskets blasted them with large-caliber lead bullets that expanded so much on contact that they produced huge, usually deadly wounds.

Military historian S.L.A. Marshall's influential book *Men Against Fire*, published in 1947, asserted that only about 15 percent of American combat infantrymen in World War II actually fired their weapons when they were in battle. He attributed this phenomenon in part to men's fear of exposing themselves to return fire, but even more to a deeply ingrained cultural and religious prohibition against taking human life. Marshall's book led to much concern in the U.S. Army and to changes in training procedures. Firing rates rose to 55 percent in Korea and 95 percent in Vietnam. Recent critics have argued that Marshall's research was badly flawed, but others have supported Marshall's contention that men have inordinate difficulty in killing others.[2] Whatever the truth about firing percentages in World War II, or about human nature, James M. McPherson has shown that even deeply religious American soldiers during the Civil War had little difficulty firing well-aimed shots at their enemies. Both sides firmly believed that they had a sacred duty to God and country to kill their enemies, and they did so in large numbers, often with great pleasure.[3] And so it was in the Crimean War. Men in all five armies, many of them Christians as devout as any Americans in World War II, killed their enemies in any way they could, often invoking God's will as their motive, and glee was often their reaction. Their letters and journals sometimes revealed later remorse, but the killing went on unabated.

When the attacking forces finally reached their enemy's position, often after marching through killing fire for over a mile while comrades fell dead or wounded all around them, their blood and flesh flying into the faces of the living, those who had survived this long and terrible ordeal met desperate men stabbing and slashing at them with bayonets, clubbing them with rifle butts, throwing hand grenades, thrusting and hacking with swords, even throwing stones and kicking. Men actually resorted to using their teeth as weapons, as a French officer did when he bit off the end of a Cossack's nose. The Cossack bit him back and took him prisoner.[4] During the battle of Inkerman, many men fought by throwing rocks, and in a failed attack on Sevastopol, British General Lacey Yea was killed by a Russian soldier who crushed his skull with a boulder.[5] In more recent wars, few generals have been killed by privates, especially not ones wielding large stones.

*Staged photograph of British soldiers skirmishing under
conditions not unlike those outside Sevastopol.
(Photo courtesy of the National Army Museum)*

Men in all these armies were trained to rely on their bayonets, and
it was not uncommon to find that a sizable proportion of the dead,
often over 20 percent, had been killed by bayonets. One British soldier was found lying dead surrounded by eight dead Russians. He
and one of the Russians had bayoneted each other. Before he died,
he had grasped the Russian's coat collar with one hand and clenched
his other fist as if to throw a punch. Nearby, three French soldiers
lay dead, their bayonets through three Russians.[6] And many men
who lay wounded by shells or bullets were later killed by bayonets.
In contrast, neither army in the American Civil War made much use
of either bayonets or swords. Of 7,302 Federal soldiers wounded at
Fredericksburg, only 6 were injured by swords or bayonets, and only
922 Federal troops were wounded by these weapons during the entire war.[7] Similar information about Confederate wounded is not
available. It is known that Civil War cavalrymen rarely came close
enough to their enemies to use their swords. In fact, many cavalry
units on both sides did not even carry swords. Both sides usually
went into battle with fixed bayonets, although Confederates some-

times chose not to, but when the fighting became hand to hand, most men preferred to swing their rifles like clubs, as did many soldiers in World War I.[8] So did some men in the Crimean War. A huge British sergeant killed twelve Russians with his rifle butt during the war's first battle, at the Alma River.[9]

Before the war, only a few of the officers and men in any of the armies had known what to expect from the war's first battle at Alma, but when that battle ended, everyone knew, and what they had learned horrified them. A British colonel left us with this memory: "Before our own men were buried, I wandered amongst them. What ghastly wounds! What varied positions!" He described one man who was in the act of loading his rifle when hit. He died so quickly that his muscles never relaxed; he held his rifle in an unbreakable death grip. Another soldier lay on his back with all his blood beside him in a pool. Others lay in every conceivable position, their bodies shattered gruesomely. "Such scenes of woe picture what the human heart is subjected to endure, and the human frame to suffer. Hear those piercing cries. Men don't often cry, but now they rend the air with life's last shriek of agony." He later met General Sir John Pennefather:

"Did you ever hear anything so terrible as the screams of those poor fellows?" he said. "I am going away to get out of hearing of such misery. They are all about my tent there, lying day and night on the wet ground, starving and dying, and screeching in agony!"[10]

A British war correspondent left this account:

One poor fellow of the 95th had been struck by two round shots in the head and body. A shell afterwards burst on him and tore him to pieces, and it was only by the fragments of cloth, with the regimental buttons attached, that you could tell the rough bloody mess had ever been a human being. Some had their heads taken off at the neck, as if with an axe; others their legs gone from their hips; others their arms, and others again hit in the chest or stomach, literally as smashed as if they had been crushed in a machine.[11]

Despite these scenes of horror and the knowledge survivors shared that their bodies could very well be torn to pieces as these had been, men in all these armies continued to risk their lives with memorable courage. A tall, elegant African officer serving with a Turkish regiment impressed many observers with his utter disregard for danger, as did a six-foot six-inch Italian captain in the same unit.[12] At Inkerman, a lone Russian officer valiantly hurled himself into a crowd of British soldiers and was bayoneted to death.[13] At Alma, another Russian officer risked his life again and again by riding back and forth in front of his wavering men to encourage them. So did a Turkish officer at Kars; he led his men under heavy fire while calmly smoking his pipe, despite having two horses killed under him.[14] A British officer continued to lead his men forward at Alma even after his arm had been torn off by a cannonball, and a Zouave bugler who had his mangled hand amputated returned to duty the same day.[15] Turkish soldiers often amazed onlookers by their courage, Zouaves impressed everyone by their reckless bravery, and some Russians at Sevastopol amazed those around them by pulling the fuses out of allied shells before they exploded rather than running for cover.

British navy Captain William Peel—son of Robert Peel, who created London's "bobbies"—was one of the kindest, most sensitive men to serve in any military force, and he was also so brave that his men revered him. He often rallied them by climbing up on a parapet to expose himself to Russian fire while waving a British flag. Once, when a forty-two-pound shell fell into the artillery battery he commanded, all his men dove for cover, but the tall, thin Peel calmly picked up the sizzling shell and dropped it over the parapet just before it exploded.[16] We can seldom know the state of mind of men who performed acts like these. We do know that Russians who disarmed allied shells received decorations as well as exemptions from any future physical punishment, but even so, not many men chose to perform such heroically reckless acts. We also know that some Russians repeatedly risked their lives to save wounded comrades, led raids against allied trenches, or exposed themselves to great danger by engaging in sniping duels with an enemy. But we do not know why they performed these acts, or how they felt as they did so. Perhaps they did not know themselves.

Only rarely did men of that time write about the emotions they felt as they were putting their lives at such risk, but a few did so revealingly. One British infantryman said that he felt simply "dazed," but some cavalrymen of the British Heavy Brigade spoke about quite different feelings as they charged pell-mell into a much larger troop of Russian cavalry at Balaclava.[17] Saying that he could not describe the feeling of being in the middle of such superior numbers of the enemy, one man wrote, "I certainly never felt less fear in my life than I did at that time; and I hope God will forgive me, for I felt more like a devil than a man."[18] Another British dragoon was even more specific about his feelings, which mirror those of men in so many wars that the concept of *combat frenzy* has been recognized.[19]

> Oh, such a charge. . . . From the moment we dashed at the enemy I knew nothing but that I was impelled by some irresistible force onward, and by some invisible and imperceptible influence to crush every obstacle which stumbled before my good sword and brave old charger. I never in my life experienced such a sublime sensation as in the moment of the charge. Some fellows speak of it as being demonic. I know this, that it was such as made me a match for any two ordinary men and gave me such an amount of glorious indifference as to life as I thought it impossible to be master of. Forward—dash—bang—clank—and there we were in the midst of such smoke, cheer and clatter as never before stunned a mortal ear. It was glorious, I could not pause. It was all push, wheel, frenzy, strike, and down down they went.[20]

The charge of the Light Brigade is one of history's most celebrated epics of courage. We know that these British cavalrymen were intensely disciplined troops who would obey any orders to charge. If ordered, they would probably have charged off a cliff, and that might, in reality, have been safer than the charge they made at Balaclava. Many must have muttered prayers before their horses moved first from a walk, then to a trot, and finally to a charge. Cardigan remembered saying out loud, "This is the end of the Brudenells" (the name of his ancient family), and a trooper said, "Oh, Lord, protect me and watch over my poor mother."[21] As the doomed charge came under heavy Russian artillery fire, men fell from their saddles, some shrieking with agony, others without a sound. One man whose head was blown off rode for fully thirty yards tightly clutching his lance before he fell.[22] Another fatally hit man turned to his friend and managed to say, "Domino chum," before he fell dead.[23] *Domino* meant "The game is over." A private who survived the charge described his emotions as fluctuating between fear and paralysis, followed by a frenzy of anger.

What kept these men going remains a matter for speculation, but we know that regimental pride and competition had much to do with it. Men in each regiment "knew" that they were the finest cavalry on earth, something that would not often be disputed after this charge—and never by the Russians who tried to withstand it. As the British lines of charging horsemen drew closer, they actually rode faster, each regiment apparently competing with the others to reach the Russians first. As an officer fell from his dead horse, he heard another officer shout, "Don't let those bastards of the 17th (Lancers) get in front, come on, come on."[24] The audacious French Chasseurs d'Afrique thrived on similar competition.

So did the infantry. Sick and slightly wounded men often insisted on joining their comrades when fighting began, and one former officer of the 1st Rifle Brigade came all the way from England to do so. George Evelyn, then serving in England with the Surrey Militia, paid his way to the Crimea to visit his former comrades, who welcomed him warmly. Even though he was a civilian, when the brutal battle of Inkerman broke out Evelyn insisted on being in the midst of the combat. Using a dead soldier's rifle and his own revolver, he fired at least fifty shots, hitting at least one Russian. Later, he saved the life of the brigade's colonel, who wrote him an effusive letter of thanks.[25] Not all civilians—or "amateurs," as the British called them—proved so brave. One Peter Morrison was courting a wealthy British lady who refused to consider any man who had not "fought and bled" for his country. Attaching himself to the ever-accommodating Alexis Soyer, he went to Balaclava in search of glory, only to find that exposing himself to Russian fire was not for him. After cowering every time a shell or bullet could be heard, he fled the battle scene, declaring, "I see no fun in glory."[26]

But it was not just competition that drove the men on; discipline was also a key. During the charge of Light Brigade, both commissioned and noncommissioned officers shouted, "Don't swear," to a man who was ventilating his feelings rather freely but, one would have thought, appropriately under the circumstance. Others shouted, "Steady," "Rally on me," and "Fall in." In a memorable moment, "Coom 'ere, coom 'ere" was shouted by a large Nottinghamshire corporal named Morley, who also roared obscenities as the men he gathered together crashed into Russian cavalry and cut them down with surprising ease. Overlooked for a medal, the embittered

Morley later emigrated to the United States, where his accent would not be held against him. He reached the rank of captain in the Union forces during the Civil War but was twice captured by Southerners and spent a terrible year in a prison camp.

A few men admitted to fear during this charge by the Light Brigade. A British private later recalled that his "heart grew still like a lump of stone within me," and he felt momentarily "paralyzed," but as the wild charge continued and he could actually see the Russians, he soon felt "neither fear nor pity."[27] Neither did handsome Lieutenant Alexander Dunn, a powerful young man of six feet three inches who used his longer-than-regulation sword to cleave one Russian from his shoulder to his waist and to slash several others to death. His valor proved so inspirational that he was later awarded the Victoria Cross. Incidentally, Dunn was not only brave but also enormously wealthy, and after the war, he retired to his huge estate in Canada with the former wife of Lieutenant Colonel John Douglas, his commanding officer in the 11th Hussars.[28] The handsome Douglas had also fought bravely at Balaclava and survived the charge. Just how this exchange of husbands took place is not recorded.

Another man who showed neither fear nor pity was John Veigh, the regimental butcher of the 17th Lancers, who was busily engaged in his occupation when he heard that a cavalry charge was about to take place. Still wearing his blood-soaked apron, he ran for his horse, shouting, "I'll be damned if I'll be left behind and lose all the fun."[29] Smoking a short black pipe, he caught up with his regiment in time to make the charge. After killing six Russians with his sword, he returned unhurt, still smoking his pipe. What shade of meaning should be put on behavior like this it is impossible to say. Was Veigh an unfeeling lout for whom killing men, like killing an animal, was simply part of a day's work? Was he oblivious of danger, or was he simply caught up in the thrill of the action, in "combat frenzy"?

For their part, the Russians did not know what to make of the recklessness displayed by the Light Brigade. Some declared that the British must have been mad—"valiant lunatics," one Russian said—and others wrote about the "amazing bravery" of British cavalrymen who, even when wounded, fought on until the end. But a Russian cavalry officer insisted that all this was only possible because they were drunk, adding that he saw "Lord Lucan" drunkenly swinging his saber from side to side.[30] This officer was not noted for his reliability. In truth, Lucan was nowhere near the charge of the Light Brigade and Lord Cardigan, who was there, was entirely sober, as were his men.

Commanding general P. P. Liprandi (a Russian of Greek ancestry) insisted on interviewing the British prisoners taken during this charge because he, too, could not believe they were sober. They were, as wounded prisoners indignantly told him. One trooper snapped, "By God, I tell you that if we had as much as smelt the barrel, we would have taken half Russia by this time."[31] A wounded sergeant major painfully got to his feet, saluted, and apologized for the trooper's lack of respect, but he confirmed the brigade's sobriety. Impressed, General Liprandi praised their courage and graciously ordered vodka for them, along with pencil and paper to write letters home.

The most common sentiment expressed by the survivors of this charge was happiness because they had had their chance for glory instead of letting the "Heavies" (the Heavy Brigade) have all the glory for themselves. The French, whose cavalry also made a valiant charge to help save the British, were as amazed by them as the Russians. Senior British officers immediately looked for someone to blame for the mad attack, and there were accusations aplenty, but most of the surviving troopers and many of the junior officers preferred to revel in the glory of it all. This was an era when the glory of war was praised as it has seldom been since, and British officers shouted "Death or glory," to their men as they rode into the muzzles of Russian cannon. It was not just officers who felt this way. After the charge, Lord Cardigan addressed several of its survivors: "Men, it is a mad-brained trick, but it is no fault of mine." One trooper replied, "Never mind, my Lord; we are ready to go again."[32]

In retrospect, the charge of the Light Brigade was a mere skirmish compared to the war's great battles, in which thousands of men were killed on each side. Only 157 British cavalrymen died. As a surgeon noted, the British would very soon bury three times that number every week from disease, and no one would blink an eye. But there was no glory in that kind of death. There was no glory in endless, exhausting trench duty either. A brave but sick and malnourished Zouave veteran who could barely drag himself to and from the trenches killed himself rather than live what he said was such an "inglorious" life.[33] As that awful winter wore on, many British troops became heedless of their lives in the trenches, too. A sergeant explained, "Oh! Sir, the men don't mind being shot: They are sick of this work, and don't care whether they die or not."[34]

There was glory in proving one's own regiment braver than any other, and perhaps most important, there was iron discipline. But not all armies were equal in this respect. Once the cavalry charge at Balaclava had been ordered, it was unthinkable that anyone in the British Light Brigade would not charge all the way. The French cavalry also charged bravely in several battles, including this one, but Russian cavalry wavered as the British charged, then broke, and after the British charge, they held back cautiously rather than attack the surviving remnants of the Light Brigade. Other Russian cavalry had been routed by the Heavy Brigade earlier in the day. No doubt there were brave men among them, but during this war, Russia's celebrated cavalry regiments never displayed the collective will to charge with no concern for danger.

Strangely enough, many less prestigious Russian infantry regiments did have the will to attack until killed almost to the last man. To be sure, many of the inexperienced and badly led Russians broke and ran away at the battle of the Alma, but in later battles, such as Inkerman, regiments fought hand to hand with British and French troops until so many had been killed that the survivors had to step on the bodies of dead men to continue the fight. They fought just as courageously many times during battles around Sevastopol. Sometimes, the French and Russians would each lose 3,000 men in a single night's struggle over the possession of forward trenches and rifle pits.[35] As we have seen, the much-derided Turks would attack with fanatic gallantry that dazzled foreign observers and earned the respect of the Russians. And everyone who wrote about the Russians' September attack against Kars, where some 8,000 Russians were killed and many others wounded, was impressed by Russian bravery. A British general who was there referred to their "undaunted courage" in a battle that lasted over seven hours. A Hungarian officer who served with the Turks referred to the Russians' "wonderful contempt of death" as they advanced through a murderous cross fire.[36] And the seemingly fearless French Zouaves almost always did the same, although some ordinary French "line" regiments made up of conscripted soldiers were sometimes anything but audacious.

Men in all these armies learned to have great pride in their unit, to fear the disgrace that would come to them if they displayed cowardice, and to be swept along by the collective fervor of their officers and fellow soldiers. A good example took place in the battle of the Alma when one of Britain's proud Guards regiments, the Scots Fusiliers (said to be Queen Victoria's favorites), wavered after another British regiment reeled back into them and someone mistakenly shouted an order to withdraw. When men of another Guards regiment that was holding firm shouted, "Shame, shame," and "Who are the Queen's favorites now?" the Scots Fusiliers turned around and fought with such bravery that a Russian general who tried to stop them called the Guards the finest infantry in the world.[37]

The French had regimental pride, too, but like troops from the other armies, they were also driven by national patriotism. The British journalist Edwin L. Godkin described what happened to a young French conscript, "beardless, slender, hardly able to trot under his musket, fitter to be by his mother's side than amidst the horrors of a heady fight," who was stopped in panic-stricken retreat by a general. The general rushed toward him, tore one of his cotton epaulettes off his shoulder, and shouted in his ear:

> "Comment? Vous n'êtes pas Français, donc!" The reproach stung the poor boy to the quick; all his fiery, chivalrous French blood rose up in him to repel it; his face flushed up, and constantly repeating, "Je ne suis pas Français," he ran back, mounted the top parapet, whirled his musket about his head in a fury of excitement, and at last fell into the ditch, riddled with balls.[38]

This sort of appeal to French pride was a powerful engine of bravery.

The exceptional courage of both commissioned and noncommissioned officers in all armies often inspired not only their men, but their enemies as well. French general Bosquet, himself a man of great courage, felt so overwhelmed by the bravery of a Russian officer who rode back and forth continually exposing himself to French fire that he blurted out, "What a brave officer! If I were next to him now, I would cover him with kisses!"[39] Many other officers were equally inspirational to their men. The following example is typical of the kind of thing that happened again and again. At Inkerman, as

Lord Raglan looked on with uncharacteristic anger, two French battalions marched rapidly away from an oncoming body of Russian troops. They passed by Colonel Thomas Egerton, who commanded 200 survivors of the highly trained 77th Regiment, which had engaged in brutal bayonet fighting earlier that day. Said to be the tallest man in the British army at six feet eight inches, Egerton roughly seized a French officer and in bad French demanded to know where he was taking his men. Seemingly amazed that Egerton should ask such a stupid question, he pointed to the oncoming troops: "Mais, monsieur, voilà les Russes!"[40]

Whatever Egerton said next inspired the French to turn around and march back toward the Russians. As they did so, accompanied by the men of the 77th, coolly returning fire while they advanced, another British colonel, named Daubeney, led the thirty men he had with him in a flank attack on the leading Russian column of 3,000 men. Confused by this attack of such an absurdly small band of men, the Russians stopped, and the British soldiers fired at them point-blank. The Russians recoiled and avoided further combat with the allied troops. Another colonel, this one named Henry Clifford, led another handful of men in a bayonet attack on the huge Russian force. Only Clifford and two of his men were not killed or wounded.[41] Next, the French, led by sword-swinging officers and urged on by drums and bugles, charged through the men of the 77th, now kneeling to reload. The excited French proved unstoppable, sending the Russians reeling back.

Only a few senior generals inspired their men in any of these armies, and General Menshikov may have been the least inspirational of the lot. A hopelessly inept general, as we have seen, Prince Menshikov was also detested by his men. He performed badly at the Alma River, and he provided no leadership at Sevastopol, where he rarely made himself seen, remaining instead at his comfortable headquarters twelve miles away. When Todleben pointed out the need to fortify the city, Menshikov first tried to ship the talented engineer away, then ordered him not to do anything. Todleben ignored him and accomplished wonders. His fortifications were brilliantly conceived, but much of his success was due to the round-the-clock labors of a gifted young engineering officer, Captain A. V. Melnikov (known to admiring troops as "chief mole"), who lived with his workmen in a battery. Todleben inspired the city's defenders by riding everywhere despite being under fire, making himself and his courage known to everyone. He was unwounded until late in the siege.

Three Russian admirals also proved to be remarkably brave leaders. Because early in the siege most of the defenders of Sevastopol were sailors, and Menshikov's army was miles away to the east, three admirals took control. V. I. Istomin was everywhere, risking his life, as was the immensely popular P. S. Nakimov, probably the only Russian officer known to his men by his first name. Only thirty-four years old, young Nakimov had commanded the Russian fleet that devastated the Turkish ships at Sinope at the start of the war, and while the allies accused him of ordering his ships to fire on helpless Turkish sailors in the water, he emerged as a hero to the Russians. Admiral V. K. Kornilov was the senior admiral and the heart of the defense. Kornilov, who had spent years in England and spoke good English, seemed never to rest as he made the rounds of the defenses he had informally taken responsibility for. When the allied fire became so heavy that his horse refused to move, he was heard to say to the animal, "I don't like it when I'm not listened to."[42]

Unlike his horse, his men listened to him attentively. He always greeted them by asking, "If you must die will you?" and they responded, "We will your excellency, we'll die." Count Leo Tolstoy, who served at Sevastopol as a young artillery officer, insisted that they meant it.[43] On October 16, knowing that a heavy allied bombardment would take place the following day, Kornilov wrote to his wife, "Many of us will not be alive tomorrow night." An aide pleaded with the admiral in advance to stay under cover when the shells fell, but Kornilov replied, "If I am not seen everywhere out there tomorrow, just what will they think of me?"[44] Joined by Nakimov, Kornilov kept his word. Nakimov was soon slightly wounded, and his aide was drenched with the blood of a sailor blown apart by a heavy shell, but now accompanied by Istomin, Kornilov continued his rounds until hit by a round shot that smashed his leg and tore into his abdomen. Rushed to the naval hospital, Kornilov told surgeons not to waste their time on him. He died only minutes later and was buried in a plot on a nearby hill. Not long after, both Nakimov and Istomin were buried next to him. Admiral Istomin and British admiral Sir Edmund Lyons had become close friends who regularly played cards together when both had been stationed in Athens some years earlier. Just before the October 16 barrage began, Lyons sent Istomin some Cheshire cheese and a friendly note. Istomin reciprocated with the gift of a young deer and a letter expressing the hope that they would meet again under more pleasant circumstances.[45]

Men who fight in proud groups and those who inspire them to fight even more bravely are the heart of any army, but the bravery of men who fight more or less alone is every bit as admirable and a good deal less easy to understand. Recalling his own experience, Winston Churchill once observed that he had found it easy to be brave when others were watching, but by no means as easy when no one could witness his actions: "I rode my grey pony all along the skirmish line where everyone else was lying down in cover. Foolish perhaps but I play for high stakes and given an audience there is no act too daring or too noble. Without the gallery things are different."[46] Whether brave men in this war were as honest as Churchill, we cannot say, but they could seldom have been unaware that many eyes were often watching them.

A British lieutenant, ordered to lead his men on an extremely dangerous and physically exhausting attack on a Russian battery at Sevastopol, could not convince them to follow him. "Then I'll go myself," he shouted and ran forward all alone. His shamefaced men took heart and followed him.[47] But such heroics did not always succeed. In another attack on a Russian fortification, a British officer tried desperately to rally his shaken men for another assault, but they all ran away leaving him behind. He was clubbed over the head and taken prisoner.[48] During the last battle at Sevastopol, when the French had succeeded in taking a key fort known as the Malakoff, a tall, gallant Russian officer led a handful of troops in a desperate attempt to retake the fortress. He fell, badly wounded, with all his men killed. The French raved about his heroism.

Other brave men risked their lives only to have their valor ignored. When the Heavy Brigade made its charge at Balaclava, two men—Captain Elliott and a large sergeant major named Shegog—rode fifty yards ahead of some 300 other horsemen and crashed into the Russian ranks like "madmen." Lord Lucan not only did not recommend medals for either man but did not even mention their names in his dispatch about the battle, an honor that men eagerly sought. He did, however, mention the gallantry of one of his own aides who took no part in the battle at all. Lucan also sat idly by watching the charge with the remainder of the Heavy Brigade, once again earning the epithet "Lord Look-on." He also ignored the valor of the general who commanded the Heavy Brigade. General, the Honorable, James Yorke Scarlett, a graduate of Eton and Cambridge, was a stout, red-faced fifty-five-year-old with a huge white mustache. Much beloved by his men, Scarlett led the charge although outdistanced by younger, thinner men. Still, he plunged into the mass of Russian horsemen, swinging his sword like a youngster, and emerged unhurt, though exhausted. In fact, as in all wars, most of the exceptional bravery of men in all these armies went unrewarded.

Despite the dangers and the absence of rewards, many ordinary soldiers repeatedly chose to expose themselves to death. Even though the Zouaves often said that Sevastopol had become so well defended that the allies would not take it until there were "three Thursdays in a week," they nevertheless repeatedly amused themselves by crawling up to the Russian trenches at night and draping a French flag over the parapet.[49] Time and again, Russians volunteered for night raids against allied trenches. Although they sometimes succeeded in surprising the exhausted, hungry, and freezing British or French soldiers, these raids more often resulted in ferocious bayonet duels. Because of the dark, however, unless someone was lucky enough to capture a prisoner, no one knew who had performed what acts of bravery. Nevertheless, one Russian sailor named Pyotr M. Koshka became "famous" by participating "in all of the raids, and not only at night, he also performed in raids in broad daylight, under streams of bullets."[50] He took part in some twenty raids, often bringing back three prisoners at a time. He also crawled out alone one night to unearth the remains of a comrade, crudely buried by the British. He brought the body back for a Christian burial. His miracles ended, at least temporarily, when he suffered his second wound, from a bayonet thrust in the stomach. Nevertheless, he lived until 1882.[51]

Many spies were enormously brave, too. The allies routinely shot the spies they captured, but this did not deter many Russians from risking their lives in search of information. Surprisingly, sometimes no risk was necessary. Todleben learned the exact locations of the French tunnels that were being dug to blow up Russian batteries at Sevastopol from a detailed lithograph published in Paris, and Russian officers found considerable information by reading *The Times* of London, the *Morning Herald*, and the *Illustrated London News*, all of which frequently made their way to Sevastopol. The Russians also obtained useful information from prisoners, many of whom were French outposts captured in night raids by being lassoed or gaffed with boat hooks. When General Canrobert complained about this "barbaric" behavior, the new Russian commander of Sevastopol, chivalrous Count von Osten-Sacken, ended the practice.[52]

But some Russian officers took daring chances to learn more about their enemies. Early in the war, their virtually nonexistent intelligence service engaged in some ludicrous failures, as, for example, sending a prostitute from Sevastopol to British headquarters to see what she could learn while plying her trade. Not surprisingly, the British guessed whom the woman represented and detained her. Whether she actually practiced her profession is not known.[53] As the fighting progressed, some Russian soldiers took apparent pleasure in crawling up to French and British trenches to learn what they could about allied defenses, and Russian officers sometimes brazenly put on disguises and strolled about allied positions before escaping to Sevastopol:

> One of these, disguised as a Zouave officer, rode round Balaklava for one whole day, and, towards evening, galloped back over the plain towards (the Russian lines). Another, as a Rifle officer, actually went out with the Rifles during a short *reconnaissance* from Balaklava, adroitly gave them the slip, and joined his countrymen before the eyes of our astounded troops, who were reluctant to fire, and only called on him to return, thinking it was one of their own officers who used to ramble out shooting. But the most daring spy of all was one who suddenly came down from the English camp into the trenches, in the undress uniform of an officer of one of our line regiments. He spoke perfect English, and represented himself to be an assistant-surgeon who had just arrived from England. He was permitted to go all over the batteries, and, after a careful survey, visited those of the French. He prolonged his stay till evening; and then, coolly getting over the most advanced parallel, ran straight into Sevastopol, which he succeeded in reaching in spite of the shower of shot, shell, and bullets which were sent after him, and where the Russian soldiers hailed him with tremendous cheers.[54]

The French took some similar risks, as well as employing Tatars as spies, but Raglan refused to allow spying, regarding such "ungentlemanly" activities with contempt. Nevertheless, some of his officers took it upon themselves to hire Tatar spies.[55]

One of the most dangerous activities that soldiers engaged in during this war was sniping, or "sharpshooting," as it was known. Snipers would crawl toward their enemy's lines at night, dig a foxhole, and wait for the dawn to reveal a target—which was often themselves. Many men became expert at this form of killing, and many others died in the practice of it. Camouflaged as much as possible, and armed with long-range rifles, these snipers posed a constant danger. After one abortive attack against Sevastopol, the redoubtable Colonel Egerton carried the dead body of a popular young officer back to the apparent safety of a British trench. Putting the body down, he reached for his pocket flask, only to discover that it had been dented by a bullet. As he showed the flask to a comrade, he was shot through the head. Egerton had apparently forgotten that because he was so tall, if he did not duck his head it extended above the trench. Admiral Nakimov was also killed by a sniper, as he peered through a telescope at the French trenches.

Some snipers combined comedy with a deadly display of bravado. For example, a Russian sniper named Ivan Grigorieff shot at a partially exposed Frenchman but missed. The Frenchman waved his cap to show Grigorieff he had missed, then fired back. Grigorieff stood on his head and waggled his legs back and forth to show that he was unhurt and undaunted.[56] The deadly game continued, as sniping did during the American Civil War: Men on both sides shot the unwary as easily as if they were "deer," and officers took part in the shooting with "pure gaiety."[57]

As we have seen, day-to-day survival required courage, too. At various times, first the Turks, then the British, and later the French and Russians—all suffered grievously from hunger and cold. Despite profound weariness, loosened teeth, night blindness, and maddening hunger pangs, the great majority of men in all these armies endured bravely. They did what they could to forage, and they stole a little, but they committed remarkably few crimes, and with rare exceptions, morale did not collapse.[58] Many men became too weak to perform ordinary duties, such as carrying supplies any distance or digging new latrines when the existing ones overflowed, but few desertions took place and no mutiny. Not even the terrible cold that killed sentries and horses broke the discipline of these remarkable men.

An example can be taken from early February 1855, following the coldest night of the winter. In one British regiment that night, only one man could be found fit for outlying picket duty, and he sat pathetically on a wet frozen saddle, "looking perfectly helpless." His starving horse had neither mane nor tail, its eyes were closed, and chunks of ice hung from its legs. Nevertheless, this wretched horseman was placed in the center of the Balaclava Plain as a sentry. A few days earlier, five British soldiers had frozen to death as they slept in their tent. There was no fuel for a fire, and they had neither warm clothes nor blankets.[59] A few days later, a British officer wrote that the wind had shifted to the north, and a terrible storm of rain, snow, and sleet had followed. The thermometer fell to four degrees below freezing, with snow drifting everywhere. Nevertheless, sentries, like pillars of ice, were on duty, jogging back and forth to stay alive:

> "Halloo! there, outside!" I called several times. "I say, sentry?" — "Yes, sire." "'Tis a bad night out there; are you cold?" "Freezing to my firelock, sire." "Come over to my tent door." "Af I can find the way, Colonel." "This way; do you hear me?" "I'm near you now, sir, I think, but the snow's in my eyes." "Come up close to the tent door. I have a totfull of rum for you in my hand. Take care now; order your arms, and put out your hand." "Be dad, I've got it, sir. God bless you, an' your health. O! it'll save my life, sir." And lucky it was that on many a night like this, I had a spare bottle of rum in my tent for such purposes.[60]

The same officer recalled a night when the temperature fell fourteen degrees below freezing! The wind was gusting, blowing snow into the men's eyes. He wondered how the freezing men were able to cling to life despite night after night of incessant rifle fire in the dark and shelling throughout the day. When there was a lull, men would fall into such a deep sleep in the trenches that they could not even be roused by the nearby explosion of a shell. Scores of sleeping men and a few officers were bayoneted to death by Russian raiders. When time came to return to the camps, the nearly frozen men would collect the wounded, bury the dead where they had fallen, and return to their frozen tents, where, without fire or warm clothing, they attempted to sleep.[61]

Death became so commonplace that few men even took notice of the blackened corpses washed out of their shallow graves or the newly dead bodies that so often lay unburied. During a truce to bury the dead in the summer of 1855, an allied officer referred to the terrible losses his men had suffered. Choked with emotion, a young Russian officer replied, "Losses? You don't know what the word means. You should see our batteries; the dead lie there in heaps and heaps. Troops can't live under such a fire of hell as you poured on us."[62] The young man was right. As terrible as it had been in the allied trenches outside Sevastopol, it had been much worse inside the city. During the first ten days of the bombardment, the allies fired 130,000 shells into Sevastopol, many of them powerful 200-pound explosive mortar shells.[63] It was the heaviest bombardment in history. Before the Russians evacuated the city, perhaps 150,000 had been killed or wounded in it, and at least double this number had probably died of disease.

A Russian civilian described the first heavy allied bombardment of the city:

> A terrible battle started: the ground began to moan, the nearby mountains began to shake, the sea began to boil. Imagine, simply, that out of a thousand cannons on the enemy's ships, steamers, and land-based batteries, and at the same time, from our side, a hellish fire burst out. The enemy ships and steamers shot at our batteries in salvos; bombs, red-hot cannonballs, and case-shot hailed upon us; crackles and explosions were everywhere; all of them combined into a single loud roar; you could not distinguish single shots, you could just hear one wild and terrifying rattling; the ground, it seemed, was shaking under the weight of the battle. . . . And this fierce battle never became silent for even a minute, lasting exactly twelve hours and ending only when complete darkness had fallen. The bravery of our artillerymen was indescribable. They, it seems, did not treasure their lives.[64]

Some of the cannonballs fired into the city were solid iron balls that smashed through walls, horses, men, and almost anything else in their path, and because many had been heated red hot, they started fires as well. However, most of the shells were explosive. A shell could be set to explode while still in the air or, more often, some seconds after it landed. The black powder that filled these projectiles was not as powerful as that used in World War I, but it still had a devastating impact. Some shells merely hurled in all directions their own metal fragments, which were capable of killing over a radius of 500 yards, but others contained several smaller shells or grenades that flew out for considerable distances before they, too, exploded. There were incendiary shells as well, and large rockets.

During the day, approaching shells trailed a spiral of smoke, and at night, the flaming fuses lit up the sky. Even the smaller shells, weighing thirty-two or sixty-eight pounds, could be devastating, whereas the 200-pound explosive shells that the allies also fired could lay heavy fortifications to waste. When one of these landed, most men ran or lay flat, depending on how close the shell was to them, but sometimes, three or four brave Russians would roll the sizzling monster over a parapet, where it would explode more-or-less harmlessly.[65] On one memorable occasion, a soldier named Pavlink rushed toward a shell to put its sizzling fuse out with a cupful of water. It exploded just as he was about to pour the water, but despite a tremendous blast, he was miraculously unhurt.[66]

And so it continued for month after month. Shells fell, and disease ravaged even the most healthy, killing hundreds of soldiers and sailors each day, their bodies roughly dragged away to shallow graves. The horror of the siege would be impossible to imagine had it not been for so many firsthand accounts. Count Tolstoy wrote one of the most moving records of the siege as it neared its end. After describing the terror of the bombardment and lamenting the closure of all the restaurants and hotels, not to mention the houses of prostitution, Tolstoy wrote:

> But enough on this subject. Let us watch that ten-year-old boy, with an old worn cap on his head which doubtless belonged to his father, with naked legs and large shoes on his feet, and wearing a pair of cotton trousers, held up by a single brace. He came out of the fortifications at the beginning of the truce. He has been walking about ever since on the low ground, examining with dull curiosity the French soldiers and the dead bodies lying on the ground. He is gathering the little blue field-flowers with which the valley is strewn. He retraces his steps with a great bouquet, holding his nose so as not to smell the fetid odour

*The effects of allied shelling on Russian fortifications around Sevastopol.
(Photo courtesy of the National Army Museum)*

that comes on the wind. Stopping near a heap of corpses, he looks a long time at a headless, hideous, dead man. After an examination, he goes near and touches with his foot the arm stretched stiffly in the air. As he presses harder on it the arm moves and falls into place. Then the boy gives a cry, hides his face in the flowers, and enters the fortifications, running at full speed.[67]

As time passed, women and children like this boy finally left the battered city, an option that Turkish civilians at Kars did not have. The Turks could only endure, hoping to be relieved by a Turkish army, or surrender to captors known to detest them and their religion. The Russians could leave Sevastopol by crossing the harbor to the north at any time, either taking ferry boats or crossing a newly built half-mile-long bridge made of huge timbers shipped in from over a thousand miles away.[68] But the Russian soldiers and sailors remained, facing their daily ordeal of death by disease, shells, and snipers' bullets.

When they finally evacuated Sevastopol after the French had captured a strong point that dominated what remained of the city, only 15 of its original 15,000 buildings stood undamaged and only some 60 others proved repairable.[69] After the French assault, some Russian regiments panicked and fled, but others actually refused orders to retreat, shouting to one another that they could never retreat from a place where so many of their friends had died: "Let's die here, boys! Let us lay down our bones, but we won't give up Sevastopol!"[70] The sailors had come to think of Sevastopol as their city, where their fleet had been harbored and where they had been the first to die in its defense. They were outraged by the order to retreat, as an army officer observed:

> It is hard to describe what was happening at that moment in the souls of the defenders of Sevastopol. . . . Their feelings poured out, uncontrollably, and many men had tears in their eyes. Others, especially the older seamen, were sobbing like children. . . . Shells and bombs would drop into the water, every once in a while, on either side of the [floating] bridge. . . . The weather was still; there were stars in the sky, their light dimmed by the bright blaze of the burning buildings and bastions and by the equally bright light coming from the shells which were piercing the sky in various directions. . . . Quietly, without any noise or crowding, this entire mass moved along across the bridge to the north.[71]

While most men in all armies experienced the war stoically and courageously, some men did their best not to experience it at all. A few soldiers from all armies took opportunities to desert. Officers did so as well, although more rarely, but when they did, they sometimes took valuable intelligence with them.[72] A surprising number of British officers who found the horrors of the Crimea not to their liking sold their commissions and returned home. Lord Wolseley, then a young officer, called them "curs," saying that they "sneaked aboard ship or to Scutari or to England on the plea of an extra pain in the stomach." He asked, "How could they sleep at Scutari in clean sheets, or live at home with every comfort around them, knowing that the men of their own troops and companies were literally dying of want and misery before Sevastopol?"[73] One officer later wrote that he knew of three officers—two of them noblemen—who had been openly accused of cowardice.[74] At the start of the war, as

Russian troops battled the Turks along the Danube, the Russian commander, Marshal Ivan Paskevich, the tsar's personal favorite and an illustrious, proclaimed hero, claimed to have been wounded, jumped into his carriage, and rode off leaving his army behind.[75] He never produced evidence of a wound. Others, like Lord Paget, tried to return home pleading illness or injury, only to be shamed into returning. Lord Paget had actually applied to resign his commission shortly before the war began, citing the death of his father and his marriage a few months earlier. When war came, he withdrew his request and fought gallantly at Balaclava, surviving the charge of the Light Brigade. With the destruction of the Light Cavalry, he asked for and received Raglan's permission to return to England, where he was treated with such contempt that he quickly returned to the Crimea, although in the company of his beautiful young wife.[76] Most Russian officers could not walk away from the war quite so easily, but thanks to several corrupt doctors, it proved possible for some officers to purchase a certificate declaring that they had suffered a wound incapacitating them for further active service. Each ticket back to Russia cost 400 silver rubles.[77] And there were so many desertions from the two battalions of the French Foreign Legion that the French considered sending these unreliable troops back to Algeria.[78]

Some officers and men in all armies did their best to avoid death by feigning injury, hiding in gullies, offering to carry wounded to the rear, or, sometimes, simply walking away from combat. After Inkerman, a Russian captain, described this episode:

The first company . . . of the battalion to which I belonged, came out of the quarry ravine under the arches. It was commanded by Sub-Lieutenant Ivanoff, whom I asked what had become of Captain _____ whose company it was. "He is gone to the field-hospital," was the reply. "Is he wounded?" "Oh, no." "Then how could he leave his company?" "Very simply. With our company was Colonel Gordeieff. Captain _____ came up to me and told me to do his duty for him while he went to the field-hospital. After this he made the best of his way out of danger."

I put it to all—is it not enough to disgust one that a man, because he is the son of a Major-General and the former Colonel of a regiment, can with impunity desert his post in the field of battle? Not only was nothing said about a court-martial, but this man was one of the first to be rewarded for his *distinguished* conduct; while others, who faced all the dangers and were in the thick of the fight, were overlooked altogether.[79]

Near the end of the same battle, Lieutenant General Kiryakov, who had run away at the Alma and had stayed out of danger in this battle as well, rode up to some retreating Russian soldiers shouting for them to halt. When they ignored him, he slashed at some of them with his whip. Not only did the troops ignore the despised general, but some of the men shouted back, "'Go up there yourself!' One added loudly, 'He was not to be seen during the fight but he makes himself felt now it's over.'"[80] Kiryakov was not unique; other senior Russian commanders became known to their men and subordinate officers as cowards. The Russian commander at Inkerman, Prince P. D. Gorchakov, was said to be vain, excitable, muddleheaded, and stupid as well as cowardly, but he was well thought of by the tsar, and that, after all, mattered most.[81]

Some Turkish officers also refused to expose themselves to danger, and at least one prominent French general found it necessary to remove himself from combat and reside in comfort in Constantinople. Because Emperor Napoléon III felt that it was imperative for a member of the imperial family to serve in the Crimea, he gave command of a division to Prince Napoléon Joseph Bonaparte, his cousin and a nephew of the great Bonaparte. He was a tall but plumpish man and, despite his Napoleonic eyes, no warrior. Known derisively as "Plon-Plon" because of his habit of ducking his head and muttering, "Du plomb, du plomb" (the lead), every time a bullet flew overhead, the prince soon acquired a reputation for cowardice.[82] In spite of repeated requests, he did nothing to help embattled British troops at Inkerman, and soon after the battle, he declared himself ill, leaving for the comforts of Constantinople, where a prince could live like one. A French count wrote, "This wretch may be a Prince, but he certainly isn't a Frenchman."[83]

Like most armies in history, all of the armies in this war had some problems with soldiers who held back from combat or ran away, and whose actions affected the courage of others. Even so, they were few in number, and none of the five armies felt the need to use "file closers"—soldiers or military police with loaded rifles and fixed bayonets who followed the advancing men of their own army, prepared to kill anyone who retreated. Both sides in the American Civil War made ample use of this tactic to ensure forward movement should bravery not be enough. Russian commanders at Inkerman were ordered to wheel artillery up behind their advancing columns to open fire if the infantry failed to press home the attack, but the threat, though no doubt real, proved unnecessary. The Russians advanced bravely.

Inexperienced troops often ran when they first met the enemy. Newly conscripted French troops did so on several occasions, as did young British replacements near the end of the war. Earlier, mistakenly thinking that the Russians were attacking, these same young soldiers had panicked and fled through their regimental camp, shouting, "Run boys, run, they're acomin', they're acomin'!"[84] And other troops dreaded some kinds of fighting more than others. The French line regiments were reluctant to attack against artillery fire, and the British soldier was, as one officer put it, "a bit of a coward at night," adding that British troops have a "perfect horror of night assault."[85] Even some of the Guards, who would fight as bravely as any men in the world when they could see their comrades near them—or "shoulder to shoulder," as they preferred—did not like night fighting. One Grenadier Guardsman in the throes of cholera insisted on joining his comrades at the battle of Inkerman, and another, who was seen by an officer to be hanging back, was so mortified that he promptly shot himself to death.[86] However, even the Guards were initially terrified by outpost duty in the dark.[87]

Just as it is difficult to know what men think and feel when they attack with apparent unconcern for their lives, it is often not easy to determine why men waver under fire, then run away. It can be the lack of leadership by both commissioned and noncommissioned officers, contagion of fear from a nearby unit, or simply such overwhelming fire that no group of men could advance against it. At Balaclava, as mentioned earlier, the Turks earned the contempt of the French, the British, and the Russians alike by abandoning their position on the British right flank. This first position had been the first to be attacked, and its men had fought so well that Lord Lucan praised them to his Turkish-speaking interpreter. But after losing many of their men and their cannon, they withdrew. Seeing this, the other Turkish positions followed suit. Later, the surviving men of the first position, many of whom had been wounded, demanded to know why no support had been sent to them, a reasonable query. One man pointed out that much of the artillery ammunition they had had would not fit their guns and, moreover, that they had been almost out of even that ammunition. Another man wanted to know why they had received nothing but biscuit to eat for two days and virtually no water to drink. A third man said, "What can we do sir? It is God's will."[88] It should also be noted that these men were not Turks at all, but largely untrained Tunisians who had previously served under the French as porters and had had no combat experience. For troops like these to run under such circumstances should have neither surprised nor disgraced anyone.

A similar rout of allied troops took place very near the end of the war, when young, inexperienced British troops attacking a Russian strong point at Sevastopol known as the Redan, ran away in total disorder. A British colonel who was there wrote in a letter home: "And what almost breaks my heart, and nearly drove me mad, I see our soldiers, our English soldiers that I was proud of, run away."[89] Other surviving officers were equally shocked and disgraced by this rout. Lord Raglan, there consoling wounded officers, died a few days later, many said of a broken heart after a wounded officer heatedly blamed him for all the bloodshed. The French were hardly pleased either, but the Russians were overjoyed. They stood on their parapets waving to the British to try again, shouting, "Come on, Ingliski!"

The attack took place because earlier that day, the French had attempted an assault, only to be driven back in good order with over 3,000 casualties. Raglan, like every other officer there, knew that it was hopeless to attack the Russian bastions across 400 yards of completely open ground, and into a host of cannon firing grapeshot and thousands of soldiers firing rifles. Although the attack order was "idiotic," in the words of Viscount Wolseley, who took part in it, the order came because Raglan believed he owed it to the French to support them. While bands played and aristocratic ladies looked on with gay anticipation, two divisions of British troops, many of them carrying heavy scaling ladders that could by lifted only by four men, struggled forward toward glory, to be shot down in huge numbers before they had gone fifty yards. With most of their officers and sergeants already dead, the troops wavered, and despite the desperate attempts of the surviving officers, they turned and ran back to their trenches, where they cowered, refusing all efforts to send them into the killing fire again.[90]

In reality, the Russian fire was so heavy that it is doubtful whether even British Guards or French Zouaves could, or would, have crossed the empty ground to the Redan. And most of the troops asked to do so were fresh young recruits from England, some of them so poorly trained they did not know how to fire their rifles.[91] That soldiers like these under the conditions at the Redan ran away in terror should be no more surprising or dismaying than the retreat of the Tunisians at Balaclava. It is true enough that the utter rout of these troops was shocking to their officers, but these untrained boys in scarlet should never have been given this impossible task.

A look at the American Civil War may help to put this kind of panic in perspective. Troops on both sides often attacked with the utmost gallantry, and they bravely endured the deadly trench warfare that came late in the war. The term *last-ditch stand* comes from this war, when a trench was called a ditch; soldiers often held onto their last "ditch" with stubborn courage. But both Northerners and Southerners sometimes fled in panic. Late in 1864, entire regiments of veteran Confederates ran away from battle. Southern women who watched them stream by tried without success to shame them into returning to combat.[92] This was only one of several such embarrassments for the usually brave Southern as well as Northern troops. Also, desertion was far more common during this war than it was during the Crimean War. Before the war ended, one in seven Northerners and one in nine Southerners deserted. Federal deserters were typically able to vanish in the heavily populated Northern states, but the Southern deserters usually formed bands of 20 to 100 lawless men, heavily armed and led by officers. By the end of the war, they posed a major threat to social order in several Southern states.[93] As the war turned against the Confederacy in late 1864 and 1865, desertion increased dramatically. An entire Confederate brigade deserted in March 1865, and at war's end, more Confederate soldiers were missing without leave than were actually on duty.[94] To see this decline in military ardor in perspective, it is important to realize that three-quarters of Southern men of military age served in the army and one-third of these men died.[95]

Some men in the Crimean War were unbelievably brave, others only sometimes showed great courage, and some were not brave at all. More than a few allied soldiers held their left hands above the parapets of the trenches hoping to receive a wound that would take them away from the combat.[96] But most men showed courage in battle and against the horrors of disease, and most endured suffering that would test any person's will. It was also a time when the pursuit of glory possessed men as it rarely did again, after World War I rapidly disillusioned the world. But even during the Crimean War, most men eventually learned to be cynical about glory. Major Sir Thomas Troubridge, a bearlike six-foot one-inch artillery officer said to be unnaturally calm and brave, had both feet shot off at Inkerman. His men pleaded with him to let them carry him back for treatment, but he refused to leave his post. Later, as Troubridge lay with the stumps of his legs stuck into barrels of gunpowder to slow the bleeding, he mournfully said to a fellow officer, "This is what's called glory."[97]

Cynical, despairing comments like this one were made by officers and men in all five armies. Expressions of hopelessness took place every day in every army. Yet somehow, these men not only endured but did so with courage that can seldom have been exceeded. How they managed to endure is the next question.

# 8

# THE MANY
# FACES OF
# MEN AT WAR

Throughout the Crimean War, men endured "life *in extremis*," as William James once described war. The suffering of men in all these armies can scarcely be exaggerated, and a good many women and children shared their ordeal. How they coped with these horrors can never be fully understood, but it is clear that although cultural differences were at work and individual differences existed as well, some common means of lessening the pain that might otherwise have been unendurable appeared among these national groups. Many men found comfort in the shared camaraderie of their unit, and others escaped their misery through gambling, organized games, sport, and theater. They also relied on humor, religion, and magical devices such as amulets, charms, lucky clothing, and protective rituals. As we have already seen, men and women also survived by numbing their senses with nicotine and alcohol, as well as by habituating themselves to horror through psychological numbing. For others, fatalism was the best survival mechanism. For still others, a sense of duty and of personal honor would allow nothing less than carrying on no matter what befell them.

From the earliest military historians to the present day, attempts have been made to understand the experiences of men at war. Psychological mechanisms of denial, displacement, and ritualization all helped to protect soldiers against the stresses of combat, as did alcohol, drugs, and humor. All of these factors can be seen at work during the Crimean War, but others sometimes took on greater significance. There are many reasons. For one thing, there are many different experiences of war, each stressful in its own way. Experiencing the charge of the Light Brigade was a very different thing from enduring artillery barrages within Sevastopol. A night trench raid was not the same experience as an exchange of sniper fire. And much of the experience of war consisted of dealing with disease, cold, biting insects, hunger, fatigue, and the deaths of friends—not bullets, shells, or bayonets. Of course, there is little reason to expect that the Turks, with their cultural heritage, would experience war in just the same ways as the Russians or the British. What is more, there was no single British, Turkish, or Russian experience of war. Most Irish troops were far more emotional than the typically stoical Scots, while stolid English farmers and more excitable English city boys were somewhat different kinds of men as well. And no army could be more diverse than that of the Turks—many of whom were Christian, others Arab, and still others African slaves—unless it was the Russian army, with its Cossacks, Poles, Jews, Muslims, Latvians, Georgians, and many others who were not ethnic Russians. Even so, there were common experiences shared by all, or almost all, of the combatants that helped to buffer them against pain and terror.

For one thing, even before the fighting began, all armies in this war, like those in almost all previous wars, looked forward to the chance to loot. When the opportunity came, they looted with abandon and also shared a great glee in destroying property.[1] It began with Cossack ravages of Tatar villages, followed by a senselessly savage destruction of the homes and possessions of Russians and others living outside Sevastopol. Retreating Russians, followed by pursuing British, French, and Turkish troops, left mansion after mansion in ruins. The house of a retired Russian general will serve as a case in point:

> Nearly all the rooms in this house were spacious and lofty, enriched with handsome gold moldings and with floors "parqueted" or inlaid with coloured woods. I never saw such a scene of wreck and destruction as these rooms presented in a few minutes. The superb rosewood and damask furniture was overturned and lying about in broken

heaps, mixed with books, vases, costly china, bronzes, pictures, and shattered mirrors. Over these the soldiers were trampling recklessly, and apparently with wanton delight, searching for articles of value or such as might be of use to them on their march. In another room was a handsome and well-selected library, containing about 2,500 volumes. The books, which comprised the standard works of the English, French, and Italian literature, were scattered about and trodden under foot, while the bookcases themselves were torn from the walls in the search for hidden doors and secret panels, which the soldiers expected to find concealing immense treasures. . . . In the corner of the room stood a handsome piano with a guitar and some volumes of music. The two . . . instruments soon fell victims to the desperate efforts of in-harmonious Zouaves, who pulled away the wires and broke the keys in mere wantonness. I was quite disgusted with the way in which both French and English destroyed everything. . . . The estate also contained a magnificently maintained orchard of fruit trees. The general had left a note in several languages asking the allies not to harm his precious trees. They responded by slashing the trees to pieces to spite the old general.[2]

Perhaps the worst and most senseless devastation took place in May 1855, when an allied expeditionary force of 7,500 French, 5,000 Turks, and almost 4,000 British troops sailed to the eastern Crimea, a resort area frequented by Russia's wealthiest families. Amid luxuriant semitropical shrubs and vines, fruit trees, and tall stately oaks, ash, and maples, Russia's nobles had built grand manor houses near several charming coastal cities such as Kerch and Yenikale. The raid was intended to open the way to the Sea of Azov, which the Russians used to ferry supplies to the Crimea. The raid succeeded, leading to the destruction of 240 small Russian ships and enough rations to feed 100,000 men for four months. But it also led to dreadful mayhem and destruction.

Despite extreme heat that caused the collapse of many allied soldiers, including almost all the British Royal Marines who had landed, weak Russian forces made little effort to resist. The allies happily consumed the vast amounts of caviar, dried sturgeon, and local wine they found on their way toward Kerch, which proved to be a handsome and wealthy town of 12,000 people, with public baths, libraries, schools, literary associations, and academies; a large, clean, well-equipped hospital; and many shops filled with expensive goods, including fine beef and champagne. The large, elegant mansions, complete with wine cellars and icehouses, were elegantly appointed with mirrors, carpets, expensive paintings, ornate furniture, lovely view windows, and well-appointed kitchens. Those residents of Kerch foolish enough not to have fled now experienced rape and pillage worthy of the worst band of Bashi-Bazouks.

Many women were raped, and everywhere *The Times* correspondent, Billy Russell, looked, he saw soldiers carrying away everything of value they could lift.[3] What they could not steal, they smashed. Finally, they set fire to everything, leaving the once lovely city and the mansions around it empty shells.[4] Many women barely escaped alive, carrying their small children away in their arms. Most of the outrages resulted from the indifference of French and Turkish officers to atrocities by their men, but despite the attempts by British officers to control their troops, British marines, sailors, and Highlanders committed their share of pillage and destruction. How many people died is not known. When happy Tatars in Kerch welcomed the Turks as liberators, pointing out Russian shopkeepers and merchants against whom they had grudges, the Turks took revenge for them. A few French patrols did what they could to prevent the worst of these Turkish outrages, shooting some Turks who were caught in an act of rape or who had just hacked a child to pieces with a sword, but the atrocities continued.[5]

The urge to destroy was so great that even a well-born, kind young British surgeon was barely able to restrain himself. Calling his feeling a "strange psychological fact," he wrote:

> I found myself obsessed by an inclination to imitate the wanton proceedings of those who had spared scarcely anything in their reckless efforts. I recognized a strong impulse in myself to smash to pieces mirrors and windows and, generally, to spread destruction around![6]

This same impulse was in evidence during the American Civil War. Sherman's destructive march to the sea left a seventy-five-mile blackened swath through Georgia and culminated in the devastation of Charleston, South Carolina. It is less well known that in 1863, Lee's Confederate troops pillaged and robbed Pennsylvania homes and enslaved free blacks. In 1864, Confederates burned the Pennsylvania town of Chambersburg to the ground.[7]

Killing wounded enemies could also be cathartic in many ways. Some men in all Crimean armies also took obvious pleasure in treating the enemy's wounded savagely. When the Turks and Russians fought in the east, the hatred was so intense that it was common for the enemy's wounded to be killed, something that had happened in earlier wars between these two enemies and would happen when they fought again some two decades later. But it also happened between Russians and their Christian enemies, the French, British, and Sardinians. At the war's first battle, at the Alma River, both Zouaves and other French troops killed Russian wounded.[8] A British sergeant saw wounded Russians ask for water, drink it, and then pull out hidden pistols to kill their benefactors.[9] The sergeant did not say what happened next, but others reported similar incidents, in which the Russians were bayoneted.[10] In later battles, the Russians had orders to kill allied wounded, and they did so with a vengeance. Russian officers shot allied wounded, and Russian soldiers often bayoneted them. Some bodies were found with a dozen or more bayonet wounds. Wounded British soldiers who survived bayonet wounds like these told of their attackers "grinning" as they stabbed them.[11] The cathartic value of destroying the property of one's enemies and killing their wounded has been noted in many wars both before and after this one, the American Civil War being no exception.

Sometimes, wounded men were callously neglected, as the Russian surgeon Pirogov noted:

> The French wouldn't let us carry away our dead in the trenches, and didn't remove their own, it seems, for two days; despite the fact that, from our side, the truce flag was raised three times, the French didn't raise theirs and so, for two whole days, the dead lay with some of our wounded, without water and their wounds undressed. This was probably done to quietly remove some of their dead and thus show that they had fewer casualties. The wounded who lay there for two days said that the enemy labored all night long, gathering his dead. One of our wounded said that he asked one of the French for a drink of water, pointing with his hand at the sky, but the Frenchman spit at him. Another wounded man, an Englishman who was lying next to him, took pity on him, and gave him water from his canteen and some biscuits.[12]

Officers in all armies often had to restrain their soldiers who were about to kill an enemy prisoner. For example, as wild Russian-

Albanian troops were battering a British colonel with their rifle butts, a young Russian officer shielded the wounded colonel and escorted him to Sevastopol, where he received great kindness, thanks to General Count Osten-Sacken, the city's courtly commandant.[13] And a young British officer at Kars risked his life to save wounded Russian officers from enraged Turkish soldiers.[14] When the Englishman was later forced to surrender himself, Russians recognized him and expressed their gratitude. Frontline soldiers in the American Civil War often treated prisoners with compassion but rear-echelon troops were frequently scornful, and both sides sometimes killed prisoners in cold blood.[15]

Chivalry did occur in the Crimean War, but it was often conspicuously absent. In a British-led raid against a fortress at Sevastopol, one company lost 100 men out of 113 and another lost 87 out of 96. A sergeant major who was unhurt but had nine bullet holes through his uniform later wrote, "I am sorry to have to record it, the enemy seemed to take delight in shooting down poor helpless wounded men, who were trying to limp . . . or drag their mangled bodies away from the devouring cross-fires."[16] The British, too, sometimes shot their enemies as sport. An officer reported that a soldier who saw a Cossack officer on a white horse some 1,300 yards away "thought he might as well try to knock him over." He fired and the Russian fell, his horse trotting away. The officer merely said that the soldier had "made a good shot."[17] Sometimes, the good shots were made by cannons. A French officer standing on a parapet a mile from a Russian battery was hit and killed by a single well-aimed shot.[18]

Snipers on all sides often referred to their shooting as "sport" and sometimes explicitly recognized it as such. Early in the war, a Russian officer came to the British lines waving a flag of truce. He proposed that their "champion" cannon exchange fire with "Jenny," said to be the most accurate British gun, a sixty-eight-pounder manned by sailors from the Naval Brigade. The British accepted the duel, and at noon the following day, all other firing stopped. The Russian gunners and the British sailors climbed onto their respective parapets and saluted each other as large numbers of officers on both sides looked on. By prior agreement, the British took the first turn in firing solid shot. The Russians fired back, and after turns had been taken seven times, the British gun knocked the Russian cannon on its side. The British sailors cheered wildly, and those Russians who had survived the direct hit took off their hats to acknowledge defeat.[19]

Later, a British colonel with his riflemen in rifle pits beyond the trench lines saw a wounded Russian get to his feet and limp away in obvious pain. He wrote with satisfaction that his men "very properly" did not fire at the man. But they did fire at other wounded Russians. On one occasion:

> The man who hit him [a wounded Russian] said with a laugh as he reloaded his rifle, "Bi-dad! and it's as good as rabbit shooting," and I heard another fellow say "Faith! and its paying five shillings that I'd rather be than lose this sport." Every man was taking the greatest interest in what they called the fine sport. I could not help laughing at their absurd remarks, and who would have thought to see or hear them, that they were playing a game of life and death.[20]

However, even in the heat of desperate hand-to-hand fighting, the idea of "fighting fair" sometimes held sway. This is from a British soldier named James Bancroft at the battle of Inkerman:

> I bayoneted the first Russian in the chest; he fell dead. I was then stabbed in the mouth with great force, which caused me to stagger back, where I shot this second Russian and ran a third through. A fourth and fifth came at me and ran me through the right side. I fell but managed to run one through and brought him down. I stunned him by kicking him, whilst I was engaging my bayonet with another. Sergeant-Major Alger called out to me not to kick the man that was down, but not being dead he was very troublesome to my legs; I was fighting the other over his body. I returned to the Battery and spat out my teeth; I found two only.[21]

When another British soldier saw a friend about to shoot at a Russian who was working on a fortification, he stopped him: "Let the poor beggar be; how would you like to be shot at when you was obliged to work?"[22] Russians were sometimes chivalrous, too. One day, a thoroughly drunken Zouave staggered out of a French trench toward the Russians, loudly singing *La Marseillaise*. Laughing uproariously, the Russians held their fire until he finally turned around and lurched back unhurt.[23] As a result of actions like this, many veteran soldiers developed a clear sense of reciprocity. And although there were not as many informal truces as Americans called during their Civil War, Crimean War enemies did fraternize. They also recognized some rules of combat. At the vicious battle of Inkerman, by which time all armies were thoroughly jaded, when a British lieutenant named Taylor and an unknown Russian officer squared off with their swords, Russian and British infantrymen stopped their own bayonet duels to form a circle around the swordsmen. After some minutes of deadly dueling, the two men lunged forward simultaneously, and each fell mortally wounded. The soldiers moved away to opposite sides, then began their killing again as if playing a game defined by clear rules.[24]

Despite the extreme demands of combat, men very often retained a strong sense of what was right. Before collapsing, a British private whose leg had been torn off turned to an officer to say, "I am hit, may I fall out?" He died soon after.[25] A colonel offered his brandy flask to a badly wounded soldier who rejected it: "Thank you, sir, it would be wasting it; I'm dying."[26] A wounded Russian soldier urged a doctor to treat another man first: "Your highness, don't examine me yet, but help that one first. He can't even ask for a drink of water."[27] And a Russian officer recalled this:

A soldier with a bloodied face and an open mouth looked into the house several times but never came in, just walking around. When all of the wounded were taken care of, the doctors, who hadn't noticed the man before, called him over and asked him what he needed. The soldier pointed to his mouth: a bullet had entered through his cheek and gotten stuck in his tongue—the doctors removed it. "Why didn't you come in earlier?"—"There were people here, sir, wounded a lot worse than me, who needed to be helped first; I was just worried about not swallowing the Turkish bullet."[28]

It appeared to help some men to believe that the civilities of peacetime might survive the mortal combat of war. At times, the need to believe this could go so far as to border on the absurd. While horrific combat was taking place at Inkerman, one young British officer whose men were about to be overwhelmed nevertheless felt obliged to defer to the social conventions of his class when he deferentially asked an aristocratic officer from another regiment for help: "My men can hardly stand their ground. Would you object to bringing yours into line with ours? I had the pleasure of being introduced to you at Lady Palmerston's [the prime minister's wife's] last summer."[29]

And after a battle, even badly wounded men could make light of the fighting. General Sir Evelyn Wood, then a midshipman with the Naval Brigade, later reminisced about the formal style of sword fighting taught to British cavalrymen. A man would first stab or slash, then return the sword to a guarding position to protect against his enemy's return blow. Each of the prescribed stabs or slashes was designated by a number. Wood remembered the following exchange between a large, wounded dragoon in the Heavy Brigade and his surgeon: "A doctor, dressing a wound in one of our men's head, asked, 'And how came you to get this ugly cut?' The trooper replied with much warmth, 'I had just cut five [a body cut] at a Russian, and the damned fool never guarded at all, but hit me on the head!'"[30]

The rage and fear that drove men to kill one another with swords and bayonets could sometimes be quickly replaced by the compassion born of a common human bond. A Russian officer recalled this incident:

On Saturday night, our men, at dawn ... attacked the English trenches. A few of their men were stabbed right there, a few wounded, and some taken prisoner. I saw two of them, when they were being led back. One, a dry, middle-aged man, the other, a beardless youth. The first walked silently and gloomily, the second, hand-in-hand with the sailor who was his captor. The captor and captive had exchanged hats and were conversing in a friendly manner. One spoke English and the other Russian; how they understood each other, I have no idea.[31]

A few days after he had cut off a Russian soldier's arm with his saber, a British officer was visiting wounded men in a field hospital; a one-armed Russian hailed him. He recognized the man as the one he had wounded. The two men embraced, and the Briton wept.[32]

Cossacks could be brutal to allied captives, dragging them behind their horses if they fell, and prodding them with their lances if they walked too slowly. But when the prisoners were handed over to regular Russian troops, their treatment typically changed. They were usually fed well, given vodka, and taken to hospitals to have their wounds tended to. After a rifle bullet had been surgically removed from his knee, a British lancer placed it on a windowsill beside his bed. A Russian sentry took a look at it, then asked if it had come from the lancer's leg. Told, "Yes," he swore, "Son of a bitch," and threw the bullet out of the window. A Russian cavalryman with two sword gashes in his head was watching a British hussar having his wounds dressed. After some time, he walked over to the wounded Briton and managed to demonstrate that it was he who had wounded him. The two men became such instant friends that the British soldier had all he could do to avoid being kissed.[33]

Of course, a sense of brotherhood did not always result when wounded enemies came together. As more wounded Russians—two out of four of them by bayonets—arrived at the same hospital after the battle of Inkerman, some of them spat on William Kirk, a British prisoner, who responded by going after them with his fists, something British soldiers often did during this war. Kirk was eventually overpowered and soon after was found dead. His comrades believed that he had been poisoned.[34] Turkish soldiers were sometimes quite cruel to Russian prisoners, and on one occasion, a British soldier shot a Russian prisoner simply because he was "troublesome."[35] And as a British colonel once watched two Irish soldiers carrying a Russian away to a burial pit, he saw the "dead" man move. He asked the men where they were going. "'To bury this Rooshin, your honour.' 'Why you rascals, he's alive.' 'Oh, yes, yer honour, but we had a consultation 'pon him; 'tis a mighty bad case, and ye see, he can't live long!'"[36] How many Russians were actually buried alive is not known. It is known that Russian officers and soldiers sometimes shot British prisoners in cold blood.[37] They also slapped them, something Russian soldiers were well accustomed to but British soldiers refused to tolerate. They fought back with their fists, much to the surprise of the Russian officers, who quickly learned not to strike them.[38]

Enduring captivity was yet another challenge to soldiers during the Crimean War. For the most part, once the heat of battle cooled, all of the armies were surprisingly kind to their prisoners. Even the Turks, who took the ears from some Russian prisoners at the Danube, were ordinarily not brutal, and both the British and the French typically liked the Russians who fell into their hands.[39] A British colonel recalled that his men treated Russian prisoners with good humor, calling them "Rooskies," and giving them pipes and to-bacco. For their part, Russian soldiers presented allied captives with cigarettes, then virtually unknown in the West, where men smoked cigars or pipes. The French often treated prisoners with kindness as well. Polish soldiers in the Russian army were especially kind to al-lied prisoners (one man gave away his shirt to a shivering prisoner). So were many Russians. It was by no means unheard of for allied prisoners and their Russian guards to become such friends that they marched along arm in arm, laughing and singing.[40] A Russian cadet, who had not yet been commissioned but would nevertheless be treated as an officer in the Russian army, had been in a British hospi-tal at Scutari, where he was treated as a common soldier with little to eat, bad tea, and indifferent care. Once it was determined that he deserved treatment as an officer, he was well provided for and be-came quite content.[41]

Many batches of allied prisoners were addressed by Russian digni-taries. On one occasion, a group of French prisoners complained to the grand dukes Michael and Nicholas (who had asked in very good French if they had any complaints) that the British prisoners had stolen their soup. The grand dukes laughed loudly, and one of them promised to tell his father, the tsar, that the French and British could not keep their alliance together when they were hungry. They or-dered that more soup be provided, along with excellent white bread.[42] Later, as a large crowd gathered to stare at them, the British prisoners were separated from the French and marched through a small town before being ordered to march through the open gates of a mansion and draw themselves up in front of the door. A flock of liveried servants came out to stare at the foreigners before a gray-haired "old man" in an ornate uniform with silver crosses and stars covering his chest came out. It was General Prince Menshikov, and despite everything said by his own officers and men about his churl-ish manner, he could not have been more courteous. Speaking in English, he asked the prisoners how they had been treated, and how each man had been captured. He then gave them the option of buy-ing their own food or being served rations. They chose rations if they could have white bread instead of black. He agreed and also told them that they could write letters. He told his little three-year-old grandson to shake hands with the captives, but the boy was afraid. Before the prince returned to the grand house, he said to the men, "Good by, my poor English. May God bless you and send you safe to your wives and mothers."[43]

Whenever possible, Russians began their day with a generous glass of vodka, and they often provided their prisoners with numerous bottles of the same liquor. Soon after allied prisoners arrived in Russia, they received regular payments in rubles and kopeks that allowed them to eat, and especially drink, quite happily. As soon as the weather turned cold, each of the captives received a warm sheepskin coat, knee-high leather boots, and leather gloves. Later, many officers and soldiers alike were entertained and fed in the homes of wealthy Russians. At one stop on their march deeper into Russia, the column of British prisoners (now joined by Turks and sailors) encountered a woman who had been educated in England and spoke fluent English. Filled with pity for the men, she took down the names of their loved ones, promising to write to them. With her husband's help, she also collected a large amount of clothing and gave each man a twenty-kopek coin, a considerable sum at a time when a good ham could be had for six kopeks and fifteen kopeks would buy half a sheep.[44]

At various stopovers along these prisoners' route to Voronezh on the Don River, Russian women came to them with bread, grapes, and tobacco. Tatars, who detested their Russian masters, proved even more kind. In one village, young women rushed to the men with freshly cooked dishes of food, and an old Tatar gave each prisoner a silver coin.[45] Later, some wealthy Russian ladies came to them with French rolls, huge German sausages, black puddings, cheese, tea, and sugar. Others gave them all manner of fresh fruit. One elderly nobleman invited the ragged, filthy, and louse-riddled men into his mansion, where he served them a true feast that included goose, mutton, roast turkey, black pudding, fruit, and decanters of fine vodka.

After dinner, there were cigarettes, more vodka, and much small talk in poor French. The old noble became so fond of a British hussar named Palfreyman that he asked him, in front of several pretty young ladies, if he would like to marry one of them. He was teasing but appeared to be so serious that the ladies blushed and appeared greatly confused. He was delighted with his joke. As the prisoners left, the ladies had them provided with as much tea, sugar, and fruit as they could carry. The men then discovered that someone had also loaded their wagon with two dressed sheep, bread, melons, cucumbers, and vodka. As the allied soldiers left, they gave the old nobleman three cheers. The ladies waved their handkerchiefs, and he doffed his hat.[46]

As the allied prisoners reached larger cities in the interior of Russia, they were so sought after as dinner guests that they often had several invitations each night, and not uncommonly, their hosts pressed several rubles into each man's hands as they left. Prisoners also went to balls, where they danced with pretty young ladies.[47] At one of these parties, where vodka and rum flowed copiously, a Russian officer told a British sergeant named Newman that he was on his way to the Crimea. He asked the sergeant if he would try to kill him if they were to meet in battle. The sergeant answered that he would if he could. The Russian laughed and translated the answer to the others. He then shook the sergeant's hand, saying to his Russian companions that Newman was a good soldier who could drink and dance today and fight and die tomorrow.[48] Good treatment of prisoners might ensure reciprocity, but it also bespoke a common humanity that could transcend war.

To be sure, not all Russians behaved in such a tolerant and friendly fashion. One Russian officer proved anything but well disposed. Speaking fluent English, he claimed that although he had formerly been one of the queen's subjects, he had become Russian because he detested British law and government. The prisoners reacted angrily. In response, the Russian cursed them all, damning them to Siberia, a place, he said, from which no one ever returned.[49] One night, Newman was billeted in the house of an old woman who bitterly accused him of killing her husband and a son, both at the Alma. Newman became so uncomfortable that he had to leave. At other times, Russians would approach the prisoners in public places to accuse them of bayoneting prisoners, an atrocity Russian newspapers claimed the allies regularly practiced. They also received many hostile glances from Russian militia that passed them on their way to the Crimea, and their guards often tried to make a profit by conspiring with the proprietors of vodka shops to cheat the thirsty allied prisoners.[50]

During one overnight stop on their long journey through Southern Russia, the British prisoners found themselves camped near many Russian troops, including some who had just been exchanged from

French and British captivity. Those who had been held by the French complained about their treatment, saying that they had been forced to work on the fortifications at Toulon and that if they had not completed their assignment, they had received no food. They also complained that they had been held in a prison when not at work. Those who had been prisoners in England had no such complaints. They had not been forced to work and had had good beds, good food, and ale. One Russian said this to a British survivor of the charge of the Light Brigade: "Very good stout, very good beer, very good beef. Brighton very good. Russia got no Brighton. Russia no good. Sorry to come back."[51]

To the amazement of the Russian officers and men who guarded them, the British prisoners regularly gathered together to sing raucously (they bribed their guards to bring them vodka), and while a trumpet major named Crawford struck up lively tunes on a flute, the men paired off to dance the polka, the schottische, the jig, and a spirited dance appropriately called the gallop. Sometimes they even slowed down to try a waltz or a quadrille. They also performed theatrical productions of all sorts and organized masked balls. In one of these, two beardless young soldiers made themselves up as women. One did so with such success "that one of our fellows, who did not know what was going on, enticed him into a corner to kiss him, and what else my modesty forbids me to say." Needless to say it was some time before the teasing stopped.[52]

The prospect of captivity is an inescapable part of men's experience of war. During the Crimean War, it was seldom a fearsome prospect. Not so during the American Civil War. Some prisoners were well treated before they were paroled or exchanged, but many others were sent to prison camps, where their treatment was barbarous. Andersonville Prison in Georgia was a killing field. The death rate was 793 per 1,000. No Federal prison was as terrible as Andersonville, but one had a death rate of 441 per 1,000.[53]

While most Crimean War prisoners fared reasonably well, those who remained in combat searched for means to cope with an increasingly horrendous war. Around Sevastopol, shelling and trench raids went on much of the time, and for the Russians, there was no escape. Most of the allied troops not in forward positions, however, searched for ways to forget the war. As soon as the weather warmed, French soldiers planted vegetable gardens, and British officers' fan-

cies turned to hunting. In the absence of foxes and other suitable ob-
jects of "blood sport," some officers rode around Balaclava shooting
stray dogs. A twenty-one-year-old British surgeon, Douglas Reid,
joined in one such hunt, which he referred to as "jolly fun but rather
expensive" because the dogs—or "curs," as Reid called them—belonged to the proprietors of a French canteen, into whose tent one of
the surviving dogs ran in terror. To "pacify the irritated female,"
owner of the dogs, the young officers had to buy a quantity of her
bad wine.[54] Many stray dogs roamed the plains near Balaclava, and
other officers continued to hunt them. Mother Seacole detested this
so-called sport and did everything in her power to put an end to it.
So did Fanny Duberly, who once confronted a group of officers on
horseback, shouting to them that the animal they hunted had more
intelligence in its head than "they had in the whole of theirs strung
together."[55]

But though she doubtless saved many dogs, overcoming this passion for the chase required more than Fanny's influence. When the
men could no longer hunt dogs, there was always someone who volunteered to act as a quarry. Sometimes, a solitary figure could be
seen, scrambling and sweating over the hills and down a valley, with
a crowd of horsemen behind spurring on their mounts, yelling and
firing pistols at the voluntary victim: "The French, not without reason, looked on the hunters as being only a trifle less insane than the
utterly demented quarry."[56]

At the same time that British officers saw nothing wrong in hunting stray dogs, they lovingly cared for their own pet dogs and
adopted many stray Russian kittens. One officer, who dearly loved
his kitten, observed that Russian cats were more intelligent and so-
ciable than their English counterparts. The Coldstream Guards
adopted a cat they named Pinkie; later an officer magnanimously
gave Pinkie to Mother Seacole as a present. Soon, however, the cat
found its way back to the Coldstream camp, and the soldiers were
delighted.[57] Other British soldiers had cats as pets as well, but the
Zouaves did their best to steal them for their cook pots. Nonetheless, the French were terribly fond of other kinds of animals. The
Zouaves had monkeys and parrots as pets, and one French officer
became so fond of his horse named Vulcan that "he caressed him, he
brought him things, he petted him with his hand: he told him about
the Russians, about Sevastopol, about battles." When the horse was

killed, "For everyone, this was just a dead horse; for him, it was a lost friend."[58] Another French officer remembered, "Among the animals that we bought, two became quickly popular in the battery under the names of Papavoine and Caroline. . . . Caroline, my mule, was the most charming, the most intelligent, and I would be tempted to say the most spiritual of mules."[59]

As the war wore on, men in all armies displayed a growing affection for pets, adopting turtles, wounded birds, and other small creatures. A British officer in the Turkish fortress of Kars adopted two cats, a deer, and a small bear.[60] Men's need to give affection and to receive it grew as the war continued. Two orphaned Russian boys of about eight were cared for solicitously by British officers, who took them to Britain after the war. And during a raid on a suburb of Sevastopol, troops of an Irish regiment astonished themselves by finding an abandoned three-month-old infant. Tenderly, they carried the child back to their trenches, where, according to an Italian liaison officer, "This child . . . was adopted by the entire regiment, officers and soldiers went crazy loving and caressing it."[61] This pent-up tenderness was expressed by the same men who drank themselves insensible whenever they could and fought with bare fists over the possession of worthless trinkets found in Sevastopol.[62]

Even before the bitter winter of 1854–1855 had ended, the French, Italian, and British passion for horse racing had led to the elaborate staging of numerous races. This is a description of the first one:

> The course was laid out with much care on the heights among the Fourth [French] Division; and though the wind blew with a cruel coldness, yet some three or four hundred horsemen mustered up sufficient courage to attend the "meet." French officers were there in all their glory, on long-maned, long-tailed horses, which would do nothing but canter and fret; and English officers were there, too, on rough-coated gaunt-looking quadrupeds—veterans which have survived not only the charge at Balaklava, but, worse still, a winter in our camp. . . . The races were like most other camp races in their general features—that is, there was a starting-post (which appeared to be the bane of the whole concern), and a starter, against whose start everyone but the winners formally protested; and last of all, a winning-post, with a very grand stand. . . . The jockeys, of course, were officer amateurs, some

few of whom appeared in the prescribed breeches and tops, and all of whom laid foundations for subsequent catarrhs, as, wanting distinguishing colours, they were compelled to ride in their flannel shirts. At each start, the soldiers who lined the course shouted amazingly, and their vocal efforts did more to stimulate the nags into racing speed than all the skill of their riders. Who were the winners it is almost impossible to say, as each decision was fiercely contested, and according to individual statements every one who started a horse won the race. Two, however, were won beyond all dispute by a little midshipman from the Naval Brigade, of the name of Molyneux; and the hurdle race, the very last of the day, and in which there was a couple of nasty jumps, by Captain Wilkins. These races, in which some heavy "croppers" might have been reasonably expected, passed off without accident; but in the mule race, to which all looked forward as a piece of fun, two of the riders got most severe falls, and had to be assisted from the ground.[63]

In the American Civil War, Confederate soldiers staged races of all kinds, including wheelbarrow races and heavily wagered races between lice.[64]

Some officers in the Crimea spent their off-duty time reading, sketching, and writing letters home, activities that were even more popular with the Americans during the Civil War. Ninety percent of the Federal soldiers were at least somewhat literate, and they read everything from dime novels to Shakespeare.[65] They also read newspapers aloud and helped one another to write letters, although most spelled in eccentric fashion: "Horsepittle" was standard for *hospital,* "axidently" for *accidentally,* and "fortigg" for *fatigue.*[66] In the Crimea, too, there was letter writing, but not as much reading. Instead, some officers explored nearby caves, towns, and monasteries in search of adventure and souvenirs. One British captain who frequented the lovely monastery of St. George, where the former Russian commandant at Balaclava had been allowed to live with his wife and six pretty daughters, married one of the girls.[67] Another who enjoyed exploring was a young Scottish lieutenant of the Royal Engineers, Charles "Charlie" Gordon. Like many cavalry officers, Gordon affected such a pronounced lisp that "nonsense" became "nonthenth," yet he was flamboyantly brave. Later known as "Chinese" Gordon for his military exploits in China in helping to put down the Tai-Ping Rebellion, and revered in England after he was killed in Khartoum shortly before a rescue column could reach him, Charlie Gordon spent his free time in the company of a Sardinian officer named Romolo Gessi who was fluent in English. The two men became lifelong companions, and it has been speculated that Gordon, who never married, was in love with the handsome and charming Italian.[68]

In search of entertainment, the French and the British both built theaters to stage plays, mostly light farces. One Zouave play, which drew large French audiences, lampooned the arrogance and stupidity of the British by having a ragged redcoat wearing a ridiculously huge leather stock announce grandly to the French that he would show them the way into Sevastopol. He thereupon marched straight toward the Russian lines until a cannonball took his head off. Only then did a rotund John Bull rush to him with a new uniform and delicacies from Fortnum and Mason.[69] During the American Civil War, stage plays were very popular, if sometimes surprisingly risqué. For example, Confederate troops staged all-male burlesque shows in which men stripped to the nude while some women in the audience watched.[70] In the Crimea, regimental bands played as well. The French played unceasingly, but all the allies agreed that the Sardinians were best. As French losses to typhus decimated the once healthy French army, the high command, powerless to defeat the disease, tried to encourage the troops by building a ballroom large enough to hold 3,000 people. Of course, there were no women, just beardless young soldiers who dressed as ladies.[71] There were plenty of women available to the troops in the American Civil War. Many thousands of prostitutes followed both armies, and it was calculated that during the war, Richmond, Virginia, held more prostitutes than Paris and New Orleans combined.[72] The soaring venereal disease rates indicate that they were popular with both armies. There was also a flourishing trade in pornographic photographs.[73] However, some young soldiers preferred pinup girls cut from ladies' fashion magazines.[74]

In the Crimea, the British built a hut large enough to seat 300 men that was known as the "Theatre Royal." Old tents were cut up to serve as a stage curtain. Officers, including Lord Raglan, often attended, sitting on benches in front of the men. Most of the plays required actresses, and once again, Mother Seacole played a crucial role. She enlarged and adjusted her own already sizable gowns and dresses to fit even larger Guardsmen. She also made wigs and caps for the "ladies." All this took place in her kitchen, where Guardsmen and dragoons could often be seen looking miserable as Seacole stuffed their dresses with the requisite padding in the front and the rear, while cinching up their waists. She also taught men how to make feminine hand gestures, how to walk gracefully, and even how to have fashionable fainting fits.

The French and the British both organized balls for their officers, who loved to dance even when there were no women available. Occasionally, the wife of a British officer or two would attend, becoming dancing partners for many of the officers, but the French had few wives with them, and their vivandières were not considered suitable partners for officers. It was a tremendous surprise, therefore, when a very attractive young lady made an appearance at a French dance. No one knew who she was or where she had come from, but everyone wanted to dance with her. She danced with many but answered none of their questions. Many held her tighter than decency allowed, and some pleaded for a kiss, which was never granted. As mysteriously as the young lady arrived, she disappeared. A few minutes later, the same young lady entered British officers' quarters, where she entertained a crowd of howling officers by describing the lovesick French officers. When she finally took off her wig, she was recognized as Lieutenant Lacey of the 63rd (West Suffolk) Regiment, a talented female impersonator who had brought his makeup and feminine attire with him from London.[75]

Men in all five armies gambled whenever they had the time and the money. Poker was common, as were dice games, and the Turks played dominoes. Men also bet on such things as where the next shell would fall and who would be the next to be wounded or killed. Singing was important, too. Troops sang as they marched and they sang around campfires. The Sardinians were especially fond of Verdi's new opera, *Il Trovatore*. But none of the Crimean armies sang as often as the Americans of the Civil War, who made singing together a vital part of camp life. Songs like "Cheer Boys Cheer," "Go Tell Aunt Rhoda," "Home Sweet Home," "Dixie," and "Who Will Care for Mother Now" were sentimental favorites. Once, when a wounded Federal prisoner sang "Home Sweet Home," his Confederate guards were so moved that they wept.[76] But there were ribald songs, too, and men might even sing during combat. When one Federal brigade was close to defeat, an infantryman began to sing the "Battle Cry of Freedom": "We'll rally round the flag boys, we'll rally once again, shouting the battle cry of freedom." Others took it up, and soon the entire brigade was singing; the brigade did rally.[77]

It is likely that song, gambling, sports, races, dances, and theater helped many war-weary men to forget the killing and to "normalize" their lives to some extent. But men also relied on their religious convictions to cope with the seemingly endless nightmare of the Crimean War. Most Russians, including the officers, were highly religious at this time, and the illiterate soldiers and sailors were true believers in all sorts of supernatural powers. In one description, before leaving Russia for the Crimea, "The soldiers pray zealously; they often bow down to the ground; many are kissing the soil of their homeland for the last time as they tie clumps of it into little pieces of cloth in order to wear it on their crosses."[78] The same officer recorded his own feelings on leaving Russia:

> One hears the sad sounds of the general march, like the farewell sobs of a leaving army; and my heart echoes them. Goodbye, Russia, goodbye to all that is beloved in her, for a long time; for a long time because I do not want to say forever. The more carefully you look into this faraway expanse, the bluer, darker, it looks. Is it because, beyond it, gapes for me an open grave? May Your holy wish be fulfilled, o Lord! You see my soul: with joy I go to the fight for the glory of my fatherland, but how can I at this moment force my heart to be quiet? How can I not see there, in the distance also, but in the opposite direction, my mother, prostrate before a miracle-working icon? How can I not see, at the door of my house, her, in whose embraces I not long ago, found out the cost of life, the sweetness of happiness? How can I forget her prayerful look, fogged with a sufferer's tears, and the kids, with fearful hands embracing my neck, my knees?![79]

Many Russians also believed that some among them had supernatural powers to prevent shells from exploding or to alter the flight of bullets, and holy icons were thought to have immense powers.[80] When Admiral Kornilov tried to sink some of his warships in the Sevastopol harbor's entrance at the start of the war, one of these ships took shell after shell along its waterline but would not sink. A sailor rushed up to explain that the ship contained a consecrated icon so holy that it could never sink. He pleaded to be allowed to bring the icon to the safety of land, saying, "How could you expect so holy a thing to sink?" He removed the icon, and the next two shots sank the ship, admirably sustaining the faith of this man and others like him. A cynical officer, who happened to be a Pole, described the episode as an example of the "fanaticism that exists among the lower orders in Russia, which is exploited by the government."[81]

It is certainly true that many priests marched with the men, thirty minutes of prayer took place each morning, and the men were required to pray far more for the tsar and "Mother Russia" than for their own souls. With the partial exception of the Sardinians, many of whom were openly anticlerical, the allies also took comfort from their religious beliefs. Despite the anticlerical French revolution, most French soldiers were still practicing Catholics; most British soldiers were devout, whether Protestants or Catholics; and the Turks outdid them all in their devotions. Each Muslim Turk carried a prayer rug, even into battle, and the rugs were put to daily use. Islam was central to all that the Turks thought and did, yet unlike the Russian priests, who were so conspicuous among the troops, imams were seldom to be seen.

For the Turks, this was often a holy war, a jihad, and Turkish soldiers often believed that Allah took an active role in the fighting. Surprisingly, a good many British officers and soldiers had a similar conviction. One of the most popular officers in the 7th Scots Fusiliers, the regiment that bore the brunt of the fighting at the Alma River, was Captain Hedley Vicars. Beloved for his good fellowship, Vicars was exceptionally devout, leading prayer groups and continually urging his men to accept Christ. When he was killed in battle, those who shared his Christian faith went berserk, killing Russians in a frenzied bayonet charge. At Vicars's funeral, men wept but also vowed revenge, invoking Christ as their master and inspiration.[82]

It is clear that religious convictions sustained many officers and men in all armies throughout the war, but most men also turned to various forms of tobacco, alcohol, and revelry to ease away some of the horror of their lives. Men in all five armies smoked tobacco incessantly, no doubt alleviating their tension somewhat as a result, and alcohol was even more sought after. Vodka and brandy played a crucial role in lifting Russians' spirits and deadening their fears. Most men in Sevastopol, including the surgeons, drank a good-sized tumbler of vodka with breakfast and another with dinner. Most soldiers also drank in between if their officers permitted it, and a good many men were seldom completely sober throughout the entire siege. Many officers spent their off-duty hours drinking heavily, singing, and playing the piano loudly before visiting prostitutes, as long as any remained in the city. Men with the Russian field armies outside the city also drank whenever they could and often did so heavily before an attack. The Russians who fought so fiercely at Inkerman were well fortified by alcohol, and most of the dead and wounded still had some vodka in their canteens.

During that fog-shrouded battle, the Tomsk Regiment mistook another Russian regiment, the Butirsk, for Frenchmen because they wore newly issued caps that resembled the French kepi. They opened fire, then charged with bayonets, stopping only when the Butirsk officers shouted their identity in Russian. One well-besotted Russian soldier nevertheless took a Butirsk sergeant prisoner: "In vain the sergeant assured him that he was Russian like himself, advancing as proof that he spoke his own language. 'No, no,' said the hero, 'that will not do. When you get into trouble you can all talk Russian! After this, nothing can persuade us that all Frenchmen don't know our language.'"[83]

Drunken excess apparently served many men well. For example, on special occasions, senior officers staged parties in the grand Russian tradition of unbridled revelry. This is Dr. Pirogov's description of New Year's Day 1855:

> The table seated about twenty; the guests were a brigadier-general, the regimental priest, various officers and several medical staff, including me. A dinner began, and what a dinner! We had jellied beef, meat-pie, wild game with truffles, paté, jelly, and champagne! How about that! And yet we complain about supplies, saying our biscuits are stale. If the French and the English had seen such a dinner, they would have surely gone home, having lost any hope of conquering Sevastopol. At the dinner, the divisional quartermaster, a drinker and a joker, made everyone roll on the floor with laughter. The host, a good man, too, a hero with his arm shot through, fed us marvelously. We drank to the health of His Majesty, music started playing, everyone started singing,

'God save the Tsar'! Near the end of the dinner, we heard noise in the courtyard—it was the officers, having drunk a bit in the next tent and pronouncing loud toasts. We all went outside. . . . The musicians, singers, and officers formed a circle, and inside it, in mud up to their ankles, people started to dance. The regimental doctor, . . . was doing the cancan with an ensign; the others couldn't stand aside and started doing the mazurka; the host, a colonel with his arm in a sling, and the battalion commander also joined the row of dancers. A huge feast started. I was dying of laughter—you couldn't help being joyous, seeing how happily and carelessly a Russian lives. There, behind the mountain, you could hear cannons firing; in the trenches, they were digging in and firing and here, they were doing squat-dances, while one soldier, with his sheepskin coat turned inside out, walked on his hands while clicking his heels in such a way that it was a joy to watch. It ended with the guests getting picked up and rocked in the air, all of it [the merriment] drunk down with a healthy amount of champagne. I myself got raised up like that three times, and was worried that I might fall into the mud. We got home late that night.[84]

Pirogov criticized Menshikov for spending a "gloomy and boring" New Year's Day and condemned such conduct as un-Russian.

As we saw earlier, all the allied troops drank as much alcohol as they could get their hands on, even the Turks who had learned to love sour Crimean wine. To be certain that their soldiers would take their quinine, Russian officers added it to their men's vodka ration. The British so institutionalized drinking that when troops traveled onboard transport ships, they were lined up before being handed a cup of a quarter-pint rum and a half-pint water, then ordered to take "two steps to front and swallow."[85]

Soldiers of all five armies, including many of the Turks, made drinking their primary recreation. A French officer wrote, "Thankfully the morale was good: sitting at night under the Turkish tent that served as a shelter for us, we warmed our feet with hot coals and our bodies with scalding brandy, we were almost cheerful."[86] A young British officer observed:

Almost every Regiment has a canteen, and at the door of each of these stood, no they did not stand, for very few could, but lay and rolled about, groups of French and English soldiers, in every state of intoxication. Merry, laughing, crying, dancing, fighting, sentimental, affectionate, singing, talking, quarrelsome, stupid, beastly, brutal, and dead-drunk. French just as bad as English and English just as bad as French. . . . Let him be English, French, Turk, Sardinian, give him enough money and he will get drunk.[87]

No one in all of these hard-drinking armies could outdrink the French Foreign Legionnaires. At a time when most soldiers drank almost anything containing alcohol, the Legionnaires were famous for their potent, almost lethal home brews, and when well-stocked wine cellars in Sevastopol fell into their hands after the Russian withdrawal, the Legionnaires drank so much more than any other troops that their consumption became legendary.[88] Early in the war, General Canrobert did not hesitate to use the Legionnaires to lead the most dangerous raids against Russian trenches, overlooking their thieving ways and even their growing rates of desertion. But the sight of a Legionnaire standing at attention during an inspection, his bare feet painted black to simulate shoes, proved too much. When Canrobert discovered that the soldier had sold his shoes to buy brandy, he delivered a tirade about the ranks of the Foreign Legion being filled with "thieves, murderers, lunatics, ruined noblemen, and—he concluded breathlessly—a former Prefect of Police in Rome."[89]

Religion, drunkenness, and revelry all helped men to face day after day of horror, but perhaps the most common and effective means of coping was for men to deaden their sensibilities so completely that nothing had the power to upset them any longer. A British civilian wrote that war "renders men selfish, cruel, and hard-hearted; they become indifferent to things present, reckless to things to come."[90] They also learned to take death lightly. A French officer wrote, "One makes light of dangers, like love affairs; and the raining of iron that too frequently dropped on the field of battle, seems to be something as natural as the bad weather of autumn at her decline."[91] Another Frenchman observed, that "One begins to play with death as easily and comfortably as one plays with cards."[92] At first, men of all the armies had great difficulty adjusting to the horrors of war. Inexperienced soldiers sometimes wept and vomited at what they saw, but as a British colonel observed, they would soon get used to anything. He quoted the Irish folk story about a gentleman who came upon an old lady skinning eels alive and asked her if it was not cruel to do so. She answered, "Law bless you Sir, it's nothing when they're accustomed to it."[93] And so it became for these soldiers. A British sergeant recalled that when a shell hit the man next to him, "his brains were splashed on to my biscuit. I thought so little of it that I wiped the biscuit and finished my meal."[94]

During truces to bury the dead, Russian, French, and British officers stood around chattering amiably, even laughing and joking as their men carried away for burial the gruesomely mangled bodies of their former comrades.[95] During another truce, a British soldier was startled to find a Russian soldier who spoke English with an Irish accent. He turned out to be a former Irish sailor who had jumped ship to marry a Russian woman. He said that there were two or three other Irishmen in his regiment. Warmly invited to come over to the British, he chose to remain with the Russians.[96] A French officer "amused" himself by laughing as he watched shellfire cut Russians in two, observing, "How the war makes one into a villain and cruel. . . . I am here in a strange school of sensibilities."[97] And many British soldiers became so hardened that they impassively watched British surgeons amputating the limbs of wounded Russians.[98]

A Russian officer inside Sevastopol affirmed his comrades' capacity to adapt to just about anything:

> Upon my return from Simferopol [a nearby city housing a large Russian hospital], I found everything here unchanged, except for the loss of one old comrade, . . . I found him delirious, he recognized me, then didn't recognize me. He had already been sick for several days. His illness lasted six more days, of interchanging delirium and silence; he was in the throes of death for three days, a veritable corpse, without a pulse, with cold arms, but breathing and moving convulsively. . . . Because of this, our apartment was something of a cross between a barracks and a hospital. Next to us lay the dying man, and we had to dine and hold conversations listening to the incessant moaning and seeing the agony of this dying man—you get used to everything.[99]

In their civil war, Americans experienced the same thing, referring to the process as "heart-hardening."

While men died all around them, soldiers in all these armies, except for the Turks, devoted as much time as they could to laughing, telling stories, and playing practical jokes. But the British were unique in their love of sport. They organized foot races with the French (the British won at all distances), leapfrog contests, football, and cricket.[100] In one game of cricket observed by Colonel Edward C. Hodge, the cavalry "easily" defeated the infantry.[101] Sailors were especially fond of rounders, the game said to have been the ancestor of baseball. There were shooting contests, too, and the British also loved bare-knuckle boxing. They discouraged organized fights because of the danger of serious injury, but men often fought anyway, and they were always eager to show foreigners how well they could fight with their fists. During one truce called to retrieve the wounded, instead of polite conversation with their Russian counterparts, some British soldiers thought it quite appropriate to suggest that they engage in fisticuffs. The horrified Russians declined the offer. American Civil War soldiers also had an interest in boxing as a sport, and they did not hesitate to punch one another in anger, but they also engaged in all manner of races; played baseball, quoits, and marbles; wrestled; played hopscotch and leapfrog; and enjoyed swimming and hunting. The favorite sport of the cavalry involved hanging a live gander upside down from a tree limb just out of a horseman's reach. Called "gander pulling," the game called for men to ride by and try to grab its neck and pull.[102]

In the Crimea, British soldiers also enjoyed demonstrating their boxing prowess to the Turks and the French. Sergeant Major Timothy Gowing, a six-footer with such enormous strength that he could lift weights no one else could budge and easily tear a pack of playing cards in two, put into words what most British soldiers and sailors believed: "Foreigners have no more idea than a child how to use their hands; they will scratch and kick, but if you give them a good go-along [a punch], they will not face up again."[103] As if to prove his point, Gowing related a confrontation between a few British soldiers and some fifteen French soldiers who began to shout, "Anglais non bon, non bon." A corporal who was said to be one of the strongest men in the British army said "Now, boys, if these fellows interfere with us, you sit down and leave this little lot to me." A cursing French artillery man walked up to the corporal and spat in his face. Gowing continued:

Our hero's arm at once came into play, and the frog-eater went head-over-heels down the cudd, a nasty slope of some thirty feet, studded with prickly pear bushes. The others rushed at him, and both his arms then went at it like mill sails. At each blow one of them followed their leader, till not a man was left. Our hero then put his hands into his pockets, and, looking over the cudd, shouted out that the English were *bon* enough for them on the field of Waterloo, and were so now, and turning round to us with "Come on, boys, let's go home," left the French to get out the best way they could. Next day there was a parade for all hands, in order to pick out the men who had so disgraced themselves and the regiment, as our friends had stated that they had been overpowered by numbers, and that those who had attacked them belonged to the Fusiliers. I must say they all looked in a most pitiable plight; some with their heads bandaged, some with black eyes, others with their arms in slings, and some limping with the assistance of a stick. They were accompanied by a French general officer (I think MacMahon). After a minute inspection up and down the ranks not a man could be picked out, but they still persisted that the party that had given them such an unmerciful beating belonged to us. The Colonel then formed square, with this nice little party in the centre. He then addressed us, expressing a hope that those who had disgraced themselves would step to the front. Four out of the five who had constituted our party at once complied. We were made prisoners, and the Colonel proceeded to question us; but when it was made known to him that *we* had been attacked and grossly insulted, and that one man, who was not then on parade, had settled the whole, without any assistance from us, the regiment was at once dismissed, and our gallant pioneer corporal sent for. As soon as our friends caught sight of him, there was no need to ask if they recognized him, for they at once commenced to jabber like a lot of magpies. When General MacMahon had satisfied himself that we had been the injured party, and that this solitary man had settled the lot, and further stated that he was ready for as many more, provided they came singly, the General laughed heartily, and applauded the man's conduct, requesting the Colonel not to punish any of us. We were at once released, and the case dismissed.[104]

Humor, especially in the form of pranks, also kept many men going. French soldiers were gifted pantomimists and pranksters who loved ribald jokes, and British soldiers usually preferred even less subtle humor. A favorite for them was an organized snowball fight in which entire regiments faced off and happily battered each other for hours.[105] The same practice was followed on both sides in the American Civil War. Led by their officers, American regiments faced one another throwing snowballs—some packed with rocks—so hard that many men were injured and some even killed.[106] Few senior officers in the Crimea had great reputations for hilarity, but now and then there were light moments. During one meeting of French and British commanders, General Canrobert began by issuing one of his by-now dreaded platitudes: "Gentlemen, we are here for the capture of Sevastopol." Incredulous, British admiral Lyons asked, "Oh, that's it, is it?" Admiral Stewart, notorious for his wild laughter, then burst into such an uncontrollable fit of laughter that he eventually had to walk out of the room, leaving Canrobert red-faced.[107]

With the exception of the American Civil War in which thousands of men suffered a psychosomatic stress reaction called *nostalgia*, as well as many other kinds of psychiatric disorders, stress reactions were seldom reported during wars of the nineteenth century.[108] The Crimean War was no exception. Personal accounts by men who survived this war rarely even hint at any stress reactions by them or by others comparable to the "shell shock" of World War I, the "combat fatigue" of World War II or the "posttraumatic stress syndrome" of the Vietnam War.[109] However, one evident exception was His Royal Highness, the Duke of Cambridge. Needless to say, accustomed to the utmost in luxury, he thought nothing of arriving in Turkey trailed by seventeen carts filled with personal baggage. In letters to his wife, he complained despairingly about the cold, the mud, the hunger, the endless fatigue, and the ghastly horrors of war, saying that the war had "completely worn out my nerves and spirit."[110] The Duke of Cambridge cared intensely about the welfare of the Brigade of Guards, which he commanded. At Inkerman, he led the Guards with reckless bravery during the day-long battle, having his horse killed under him as he rode through the Russian troops surrounding him. He escaped with only a minor flesh wound, but his exhaustion after the battle was profound.

He began to obsess about the Guards' losses, which amounted to some 40 percent of the brigade, bursting into tears in public when he visualized the dead bodies he had seen. When he became unable to sleep and physically ill with diarrhea, doctors ordered him aboard the ship *Retribution* to recuperate. The hurricane struck only a few days later, the battered ship very nearly sinking. As the storm ravaged the ship, the duke lost control, clutching the hand of a steward and wailing over and over, "Oh! We shall be lost!"[111] He then developed a fever and could not bear to think about the war, which he referred to as a "dreadful thing." He insisted that he could not bear to remain in the Crimea and asked the queen's permission to leave for England, citing ill health. She told him that she had already heard the rumors said to be flying about the clubs of London that the duke had lost his will, adding that his departure from the Crimea was unthinkable. Disregarding her wishes, he returned to England and, despite disdainful gossip, was eventually forgiven sufficiently to serve as commander in chief of the army for thirty-nine years.

In all probability, the Duke of Cambridge was not the only man to react as he did. Perhaps some of the officers who found ways to leave the Crimea were suffering distress comparable to his. But if so, they left no memoirs, and doctors in the various armies made no mention of symptoms of what would now be called posttraumatic stress among their patients. It is tempting to speculate that soldiers in the armies of the Crimean War had led such horrific lives that they simply could not express what they may well have felt. But we know that many soldiers were aghast at what they saw, at least early in the war, and that some officers did exhibit cowardice. It is also possible that because there was no concept like *shell shock* that would legitimize stress-induced symptoms, men could not show their symptoms without fear of scorn or punishment. It is apparent that as the twentieth century progressed, and stress-related incapacity for duty became increasingly legitimate in Western armies, more and more men were diagnosed with this disorder. Still, there is good reason to believe that the symptoms of posttraumatic stress syndrome were known in antiquity.[112]

# EPILOGUE

HUMANS HAVE ALWAYS LIVED during hard times and no doubt always will. The human condition has never been free of disappointment, hunger, disease, despair, pain, and the specter of death. That said, it must be allowed that for most people in Europe, the Ottoman Empire, and Russia, life during the 1850s was far harder than it is for most people in those places today. Hunger was widespread; actual starvation was hardly unknown. Technology could not yet temper extremes of heat and cold, nor could medicine control deadly epidemic diseases. This was also an age of great social inequality. Few social programs existed to alleviate the suffering of the poor, and there were few or no limits on the power of the wealthy. Many wealthy people lived luxurious, long lives, surviving into their eighties and even nineties, while most of the poor died much younger. When it came to war, poor men served at the beck and call of wealthy ones. With the partial exception of France, armies and navies were organized and commanded by pashas, counts, lords, barons, and other men of high social rank, wealth, and power, while those who served among the rank and file were usually the poorest and least powerful men in their countries.

When these soldiers and sailors left the many hardships of their civilian lives, they entered an even harsher world of military service, where they quickly became inured to brutal discipline, bad food, recurrent disease, and precious few pleasures. By the time these men encountered the rigors of actual warfare they were well used to fatigue, sleepless nights, extremes of heat and cold, vermin, little to eat, and the constant presence of death. Although no men could have been fully prepared for what they faced during the Crimean War, those who fought there were hardened in ways that their grandchildren and great-grandchildren were not likely to be. There was some cowardice, some desertion, and some grumbling, especially by officers, but most impressive was the steadfast determination of the great majority of men in all these armies to fight on.

To be sure, there were differences in how these five armies experienced the war. Superbly equipped and led, the Sardinians proved stalwart fighters, but they arrived after the ghastly winter of 1854–1855, suffered little from disease, and never went hungry. Of all the troops, they took the most romantic view of life, and if what they wrote is an accurate reflection of their emotions, they missed their loved ones more than any other troops. Except for the elite Zouaves, who had superb morale throughout the war, French troops frequently behaved unpredictably. Moody, excitable men, they often attacked with great dash, but at other times, they refused to advance, and when not in actual combat, they often gave themselves over to despondency. The Russians proved unpredictable, too, alternating between phenomenal courage in the attack and pell-mell retreat. Abused from the moment of their conscription, underfed, and often poorly led, Russian soldiers nevertheless never lost their patriotism. Often depressed, they fought nonetheless. The British troops had their differences—for example, most Scots being emotionally reserved and most Irish being ebullient—but despite their extreme suffering, they displayed the utmost doggedness. More phlegmatic and fatalistic than men in the other armies, the Turks showed as much bravery and devotion as any other troops, and sometimes even more.

Many cultural differences existed among these armies. To mention a few examples, the British favored manly sports, the Russians loved singing and storytelling, the French reveled in organized exhibitions of music and theater, the Sardinians adored opera, and the Turks spent many of their off-duty hours in silent comradeship. But preferences like these made little difference in how these men endured the war. Duty, honor, patriotism, unit pride, religious devotion, discipline, alcohol, gambling, humor, and deadened sensibilities—all appear to have sustained the men in these five armies to about the same degree. Readers will note that the pursuit of glory was not listed as a factor that universally led men to acts of gallantry or to the enduring of prolonged suffering. It only served this role for some men, some of the time. Dreams of glory were in the air, of course, but many men fought bravely without thoughts of glory, and many who endured terrible suffering and bravely exposed themselves to great danger were children, wives, nurses, soldiers, and sailors who cared little about glory.

Any student of military history would be quick to point out that these same beliefs and practices have sustained men during twentieth-century wars, and they would be right. Men at war still rely on patriotic fervor to keep them going; they still fight for their unit, whether it be a small one such as a platoon or a large one like the U.S. Marine Corps; and usually, nothing matters to them as much as doing well in the eyes of their closest comrades. Discipline still holds men together during combat, and religious beliefs are remarkably strong during battle, even among men who care little about religion when they are out of danger. The lull between battles is still made more bearable by alcohol and other drugs, by gambling, pranks, and other humor. And men still cope with the horrors of war by growing accustomed and insensitive to things that earlier in the conflict traumatized them profoundly.

In reflections on the Crimean War, then, the most lasting impression is not how much men from different cultural backgrounds differed in their reactions, but how much they were alike. If this similarity is true, it is not what we would expect, because the long history of war has emphasized differences among troops—these Bavarians so different from those Saxons, those Siberians so different from these Ukrainians, any Swede so very different from any Italian. Even within the same country, men from certain cities, or areas, have also been said to differ greatly in valor, discipline, and staying power. For all their differences, Federals and Confederates were very much alike in how they coped with the American Civil War.

Was there something about the Crimean War that reduced Turks, Russians, and western Europeans to the same primal reactions? If the troops in the allied trenches or the gun batteries of Sevastopol had been Japanese, communist Chinese, Zulu, or Aztec, would they have reacted in markedly different ways? There can be no certain answer, of course, but the evidence strongly suggests that this war was so horrendous, and so protracted, that it reduced those who fought in it to highly similar, perhaps nearly identical coping strategies. In less intense wars and in wars of shorter duration, the cultural backgrounds of the men and women involved have very likely stood out much more visibly. Is it correct to say that this horrific war reduced all who fought in it around Sevastopol to the same elemental beliefs and practices, blurring their national, class, and religious backgrounds? That is how it appears. It was a war—a total experience—so terrible that almost everyone involved in it responded in much the same ways. The search for survival reduced most of them to basic human responses, and in these, they were all equally human.

Perhaps the most fundamental lesson to be learned from a look back at the Crimean War is how easy it is for nations to blunder into wars that serve no purpose or cannot be won. Another lesson to be learned from the Crimean War applies to any war: Do not assume that the next war will necessarily be fought with the same tactics, strategies, or weapons. As military leaders were to learn so painfully, the development of airpower and the tank in World War II made most of the lessons of World War I meaningless. Just as nothing that had gone before prepared the armies that fought in the Crimea for the impact of steam-powered ships, long-range rifles, land and sea mines, and massive artillery barrages, so the development of night vision technology is likely to transform future wars into continuous and exhausting combat, as the brief Gulf War illustrated.

An important lesson has to do with the inability of so many senior military commanders to comprehend the military value of technological innovations. It should not have required more than a moment's thought for Russian commanders to realize that long-range rifles would mow down their massed columns of infantry. But this was hardly an isolated example. In 1849, the Prussians developed a breech-loading rifle called the *needlegun* that could fire seven rounds per minute. Despite its obvious potential to change warfare, German leaders rejected it, fearing that their soldiers would simply waste their ammunition. In the latter part of the nineteenth century, Maxim's new machine gun proved its worth in numerous small colonial wars, but senior generals still largely ignored the weapon during the Boer War, and not until late in the Russo-Japanese War of 1904–1905 was its potential finally realized. Ten years later, when World War I began, the destructive power of the machine gun was still neglected. So it was with the tank. It was actually during the Crimean War that a British inventor first proposed a steam-driven, heavily armored tank. He was ignored. The British finally did develop the first workable tank later in World War I, but Britain then neglected the weapon until World War II was well under way.

Poison gas had a similar history. The Spartans used a form of pitch and sulfur to create a poisonous smoke cloud used against the Athenians some 400 years B.C., but poison gas was rarely discussed after that until early in the Crimean War, when a venerable British admiral, Lord Dundonald, who was also a good chemist, offered the government a plan to use sulfur fumes to drive the Russians out of Fort Kronstadt in the Baltic and even to threaten nearby St. Petersburg. After some study, the British rejected the idea as inhumane, but Dundonald repeated the offer in August 1855, with Sevastopol now the target. This time, the offer was taken more seriously, but there were fears of wind shifts, something that would not have been a problem had the British earlier taken poison gas seriously as a weapon. Early in 1854, the British had developed a charcoal respirator that was effective against sulfur, to be used in London's chemical manufacturing plants. An army with these masks and sulfur gas would have been invincible in the Crimea. The idea of poison gas languished for years, although the Japanese used a crude form of cyanide gas against the Russians during their siege of Port Arthur in 1904–1905. But in 1908, the British inadvertently published Dundonald's formula for sulfur gas, a slip that is said to have inspired the Germans to be the first to use poison gas during World War I.[1]

In addition to these technological lessons, the Crimean War provides a sobering indictment of generalship. One Russian general after another proved to be an inept tactician and leader, and the British were no better. Only Pélissier among the French had any success, and he, like Grant in the American Civil War, did so by spending lives recklessly. Omer Pasha was alone in displaying any skill for the Turks, and at the war's end, he failed miserably. The Sardinians saw so little action that their leaders cannot be judged. In the perspective provided by subsequent wars, this failure of the leadership should not be surprising. For every Wellington, Napoléon, Zhukov, or Rommel, there have been dozens of mediocre or downright incompetent generals.[2] Even the late-twentieth-century Gulf War between Iraq and the Western allies appears to have been no exception.[3]

This is not to suggest that there have been no improvements in the management of war since the mid-1850s. With the possible exception of the Russian army in World War I, when the Russian government's loss of the ability to supply the army contributed to the Russian Revolution of 1917, armies since the Crimean War have almost always been better supplied than armies of that time were. To be sure, Japan was unable to supply all of its troops in the South Pacific in World War II—some starved as a result—and other troops have suffered shortages of food and ammunition from time to time, but never on the scale observed in the Crimean War. Medical care, too, has improved dramatically. As early as the Russo-Japanese War, now almost a century ago, the expectation that ten men would die of disease for every one killed in combat was overturned, and since then, battlefield medicine has improved enormously. Still, with the advent of biological warfare, there are new challenges for medicine, as the Gulf War has shown.

The Crimean War also provided many painfully clear lessons about creating and maintaining international, multicultural military alliances. It is also clear that those lessons have not proved easy to learn. As we have seen, failure to establish lines of command among the allies remained troublesome throughout the war. Raglan complained bitterly about the French but sacrificed many British lives in the attempt to appease them. French distaste for the British and their ways of waging war was made abundantly obvious during the war as well as in a history of the war approved by Emperor Napoléon III, and published before the war even ended.[4] The book was not only insulting but often inaccurate as well. The allies' mistreatment of the Turks and their failure to make good use of the Turks' abilities were particularly outrageous. And of course, the Russian army never resolved its internal rivalries and hatreds between Poles, Latvians, Ukrainians, Germans, Cossacks, Jews, and other minorities.

Following all this acrimony, it is perhaps no surprise that Turkey fought against the allies in World War I, or that the Soviet Union eventually splintered largely along ethnic lines. What is surprising is the ability of past enemies Britain and France to fight on the same side in 1860 in China, again in 1900 during the Boxer Rebellion, and then in two world wars. It should also come as no surprise that no multinational military alliance since the Crimean War has been free of confusion, rancor, and inefficiency. As two world wars and the Korean War have shown, even nations with cultural ties as close as those of Australia, Britain, and the United States have been unable to achieve trouble-free military alliances. Cultural and religious differences are likely to trouble any alliance, and a previous history of conflict or contempt will worsen matters still more. But a military alliance can survive all of these problems if it possesses a strong sense of purpose, and especially if it has a clear-cut chain of command. The Crimean allies had no clear chain of command, but they did have a purpose: to take Sevastopol.

Sevastopol became the symbol of this war for both sides. When it fell, the war seemingly had no further purpose. The allies blew up all of Sevastopol's naval and military facilities before leaving. It took six years under the expert direction of an American engineer to rebuild it. In 1941, almost a century later, Hitler's troops swept over the Crimea again, besieging Sevastopol for a second time. Its defenders held out almost as long as they had during the Crimean War. Despite their use of mammoth siege guns, the Germans never succeeded in driving the half-starved Russian defenders out of the rubble that had once been Sevastopol's residential district.[5] This time, Sevastopol was not the focus of the war. Its second heroic defense is little more than a footnote to the allies' victory in World War II.

# NOTES

## Chapter 1

1. Goldfrank (1994:289). Casualty estimates vary, but these figures represent a conservative reckoning, Turkish losses being the most difficult to ascertain.
2. Hibbert (1987:541–42).
3. Fremantle (1991:xxii); Wiley (1943:101).
4. Gagnon (1972).
5. Bettmann (1974:3).
6. Webb (1980:263); Hibbert (1987:596).
7. Goldfrank (1994:22).
8. Parish (1975:110).
9. Goldfrank (1994:9, 16). See also Wiley (1943, 1951).
10. Furnas (1969:589).
11. Hibbert (1987).
12. Williams (1957).
13. Royster (1991:383); Goldfrank (1994:5); Troubetskoy (1986:ix).
14. Shaw and Shaw (1977:136).
15. Goldfrank (1994:49). For readers wishing to read further about this period of history, Goldfrank provides a useful annotated bibliography, as does Rich (1985).
16. Fuller (1992:219).
17. James (1981).
18. Slade (1867).
19. Troubetskoy (1986:143).
20. Higginson (1916:79).
21. Gooch (1959:41).
22. Knightly (1975:4).
23. Barthorp (1991:11).
24. An Amateur (1855:68).
25. Hibbert (1961:19).
26. Bentley (1966:41).
27. Bell (1956:191).
28. Bonham-Carter (1968:38).

29. Slade (1867:217).
30. Slade (1867:283).
31. James (1981:48).
32. Barthorp (1991:95).
33. Selby (1970:182–83).
34. MacMunn (1935:134).
35. Kinglake (1887:Vol. 7, 49).
36. Seaton (1971:206).
37. Lambert (1990).
38. Greenhill  and Giffard (1988).
39. Lake (1856:118).
40. Lambert (1990); Baumgart (1981).
41. Zürcher (1993:56–57).
42. Shaw and Shaw (1977).
43. Clarkson (1962).
44. Dowty (1971:248).
45. Dvoichenko-Markov (1954:138).
46. Golden (1926:471).
47. Golden (1926:471).
48. Bemis (1959:188–89).
49. Warner (1977:199); Clifford (1956)

# Chapter 2

1. Barber (1973:28).
2. Barber (1973:48).
3. Collier's Encyclopedia (1995:Vol. 2, 763).
4. Massie (1980:551).
5. Barber (1973:44).
6. Barber (1973:44).
7. Barber (1973:58).
8. Massie (1980).
9. Zürcher (1993).
10. Zürcher (1993:16).
11. Troubetskoy (1986:7).
12. Barber (1973:138).
13. Barber (1973:139–40).
14. Zürcher (1993:42).
15. Buzzard (1915:123).
16. Ogden (1907:Vol. 1, 50).
17. Buzzard (1915:122).
18. Buzzard (1915:121).
19. Zürcher (1993:46).
20. Ogden (1907:Vol. 1, 76).
21. Slade (1867:28).
22. Slade (1867:116).

23. Shaw and Shaw (1977:138); Goldfrank (1994:22).
24. Hornby (1863:99).
25. G. L. Smith (1987:167).
26. Sandwith (1856:119).
27. Masquelez (1858:65).
28. Gooch (1959:102).
29. Buzzard (1915:62).
30. Seaton (1971:30).
31. G. L. Smith (1987:35); James (1981:62).
32. Bayley (1977:18).
33. Richardson (1977:149).
34. Barthorp (1991:16).
35. Bolster (1964:xxi).
36. Barthorp (1991:16).
37. Bayley (1977).
38. G. L. Smith (1987:36).
39. Vetch (1901:16).
40. Hibbert (1961:24).
41. James (1981).
42. Steevens (1878:16).
43. Judd (1975:67).
44. Strachan (1985:140).
45. Woodham-Smith (1953:140).
46. Strachan (1985:140).
47. Griffith (1989:76).
48. Griffith (1989:16).
49. Campbell (1894:399).
50. Griffith (1989:61, 129).
51. Gooch (1959:56).
52. McClellan (1861:61).
53. Calthorpe (1979:241).
54. Gooch (1959 :57). The minister in question was the formidable Adolphe Thiers.
55. Gooch (1959:49).
56. Chesney (1960:206).
57. Vulliamy (1939:267).
58. Kinglake (1887:Vol. 8, 42).
59. Gooch (1959:229).
60. Curtiss (1965:119).
61. Aksakova (1913).
62. Curtiss (1965:235); Stanislawski (1983).
63. Hodasevich (1856:50).
64. Curtiss (1965:125).
65. Thomas and Scollins (1991:16).
66. Alabin (1861:1–2).
67. Curtiss (1965:198). For a personal account, see Rodzianko (1939).

68. Curtiss (1965:192).
69. Curtiss (1965:214).
70. Alabin (1861:75–76).
71. Alabin (1861:28–29).
72. Fuller (1992:246).
73. Thomas and Scollins (1991).
74. Hodasevich (1856).
75. Curtiss (1965:141).
76. Fedorov (1909:63).
77. Hodasevich (1856:50–51).
78. Warner (1977:83). See also Kinglake (1887:Vol. 5, 216).
79. Barthorp (1991).
80. Pemberton (1962:96).
81. Selby (1970:202).
82. Baylen and Conway (1968:73).
83. Crawford (1992).
84. Wiley (1952:309); McPherson (1965).
85. Wiley (1952:307–10).
86. Wiley (1943:322).
87. Wiley (1943:331).
88. Linderman (1987:229–30).
89. Linderman (1987:234); Fremantle (1991); Rawley (1964).
90. Brooks (1966:12).
91. Linderman (1987:144).
92. Linderman (1987:39).
93. Wiley (1943:109–10).
94. Wiley (1943:24).
95. Wiley (1952:327); Mitchell (1993).
96. Royster (1991:88); Rawley (1964:41).
97. Lowry (1994:7).
98. Wiley (1943:18).
99. Rawley (1964:xxvii).

## Chapter 3

1. Wolseley (1903:Vol. 1, 92).
2. Lysons (1895:15).
3. Lincoln (1978:273).
4. Hibbert (1961:31).
5. Buzzard (1915:80).
6. Tisdall (1963:52).
7. Wachsmuth, Blake, and Olsvik (1994).
8. Woods (1855:Vol. 2, 200).
9. Woodham-Smith (1953:169–70).
10. Woodham-Smith (1953:167).
11. Woodham-Smith (1953:178).

12. Bazancourt (1855:Vol. 3, 243).
13. Rousset (1894:Vol. 1, 191).
14. Woodham-Smith (1950:131).
15. Peard (1855).
16. Woods (1855:Vol. 1, 376).
17. Steevens (1878:162).
18. Barker (1970:119).
19. Lincoln (1978). Wortman (1995) is skeptical about Nicholas's fidelity.
20. Hibbert (1961:54); Troubetskoy (1986).
21. Goldfrank (1994:117).
22. Seaton (1977:174).
23. Curtiss (1979:303).
24. Seaton (1977:67).
25. Woods (1855:Vol. 1, 364–65).
26. Hibbert (1961:90).
27. Seaton (1977:71).
28. Seaton (1977:76).
29. Hodasevich (1856:57).
30. Seaton (1977:74).
31. Vulliamy (1939:97).
32. Woods (1855:Vol. 1, 319).
33. Pemberton (1962:40).
34. Seaton (1977:82).
35. Seaton (1977:78).
36. Seaton (1977:78).
37. Seaton (1977:74).
38. Hibbert (1961:64).
39. Calthorpe (1979:45).
40. Calthorpe (1979:42).
41. Fenwick (1954:17).
42. Hibbert (1961:86).
43. Gooch (1959:21).
44. Pearse (1897:72).
45. Paget (1881:28).
46. Hibbert (1961:127); James (1981:47).
47. Hume (1894:93).
48. Lambert (1990:126).
49. Seaton (1977:108).
50. Tolstoy (1912:12).
51. Tolstoy (1912:63).
52. Hodasevich (1856).
53. Hibbert (1961:100).
54. Chesney (1960:92).
55. MacMunn (1935:47).
56. James (1981:23).
57. Hodasevich (1856:98).

58. Seaton (1977:182).
59. Kinglake (1887:Vol. 3, 238–39).
60. Barker (1970:134).
61. Hibbert (1961:105).
62. Tolstoy (1912:106).
63. Seaton (1977).
64. Thomas (1974:187).
65. Vulliamy (1939:126); Woodham-Smith (1953).
66. Carew (1954:178).
67. Thomas (1974).
68. Thomas (1974:193).
69. Thomas (1974:196).
70. *United Service Gazette,* September 2, 1854.
71. Gibbs (1960:92).
72. Woodham-Smith (1953:151).
73. Paget (1881:217).
74. Hibbert (1961:142-43).
75. Thomas (1974:240).
76. Thomas (1974:241).
77. Thomas (1974:241).
78. Pemberton (1962:113).
79. James (1981:58).
80. Groushko (1992:107).
81. Pemberton (1962:115).
82. Paget (1881:220).
83. Woodham-Smith (1953:280).
84. Clifford (1956:93).
85. Wolseley (1903:Vol. 1, 143).
86. Gooch (1959:145).
87. Wolseley (1903:Vol. 1, 170).
88. MacMunn (1935:180).

# Chapter 4

1. Buzzard (1915:13).
2. Warner (1977:124).
3. Hibbert (1961:200).
4. Wood (1906:54).
5. de Molènes (1886:130).
6. Woods (1855:Vol. 2, 190); Gooch (1959:151).
7. Tisdall (1963:108).
8. Gowing (1895:69).
9. Jocelyn (1911:291).
10. Stern (1961:304).
11. Clifford (1956:125).
12. Bentley (1966:160).

13. Woods (1855:Vol. 2, 222).
14. Porter (1856:174).
15. Gooch (1959:154).
16. Clifford (1956:164).
17. Warner (1977:121).
18. Seacole (1988:179); Vulliamy (1939:185–86).
19. Shepherd (1991:Vol. 1, 326); G. L. Smith (1987:178).
20. Clifford (1956:173).
21. Vulliamy (1939:115).
22. Shepherd (1991:Vol. 1, p. 331); Wood (1906:59).
23. Shepherd (1991:Vol. 1, 331).
24. Shepherd (1991:Vol. 1, 332).
25. Airlie (1933:150).
26. Clifford (1956:145).
27. Kinglake (1887:Vol. 7, 20).
28. Airlie (1933:183).
29. Bell (1956:275).
30. Calthorpe (1856:57); Wood (1906:61).
31. Bolster (1964:117).
32. Shepherd (1991:Vol.1, 312).
33. Windham (1897:87).
34. Hibbert (1961:218).
35. Clifford (1956:146); Knightly (1975:12).
36. Crawford (1992).
37. Hibbert (1961:4).
38. Shepherd (1991:Vol. 1, 302).
39. Shepherd (1991:Vol. 1, 161).
40. Carew (1954:179).
41. Gernsheim and Gernsheim (1954:55).
42. Hannavy (1974:14).
43. Gooch (1959:173).
44. Hibbert (1961:206).
45. *Report of the Sanitary Commission* (1857:Vol. 1, 159).
46. Vulliamy (1939:187).
47. *Report of the Sanitary Commission,* (1857:Vol. 2, 159).
48. Bell (1956:283).
49. Calthorpe (1856:23).
50. Parish (1975:148).
51. Woodham-Smith (1950:197).
52. Hibbert (1961:208).
53. Regan (1987:200).
54. Regan (1987:207).
55. Russell (1858:253).
56. Woodham-Smith (1950:157, 198).
57. Regan (1987:207).
58. Bonham-Carter (1968:27).

59. An Amateur (1855:134).
60. Shepherd (1991:Vol 1, 310).
61. Buchanan (1871:61).
62. Gooch (1959:160).
63. Airlie (1933:257).
64. Palmer (1987:197).
65. Barker (1970:222).
66. Morris (1938).
67. Hibbert (1961:195).
68. Pirogov (1899:148).
69. Tarle (1954:144).
70. Hodasevich (1856:164).
71. Clifford (1956:227).
72. Hamley (1968:319).
73. Woods (1855:Vol. 2, 143–44).
74. Kinglake (1887:Vol. 5, 324).
75. Hume (1894:112).
76. Bardeen (1910).
77. Tarle (1954:171).
78. Brooks (1966:66).
79. Guthrie (1958:301).
80. Guthrie (1958:301).
81. Baylen and Conway (1968:16–17).
82. Hodasevich (1856:214).
83. Bazancourt (1855:13).
84. Zverev (1956:79).
85. Richardson (1977:109).
86. Baylen and Conway (1968); Bonham-Carter (1968).
87. Hodasevich (1856:149, 179).
88. Selby (1970:193).
89. Bonham-Carter (1968:13).
90. Calani (1855:127).
91. Hume (1894:9).
92. Laffin (1970:142).
93. Alabin (1861:3–4).
94. Tarle (1954:90).
95. Tisdall (1963:123).
96. Bolster (1964:8).
97. Shepherd (1991:Vol. 2, 414).
98. *Report of the Sanitary Commission* (1857:Vol. 2, 489).
99. Bonham-Carter (1968:136).
100. Chesney (1960:169).
101. Osborne (1855:30).
102. Osborne (1855:43).
103. Bolster (1964:71).
104. Richardson (1977:47).

105. Bonham-Carter (1968:10).
106. Vulliamy (1939:196).
107. Vulliamy (1939:202).
108. Osborne (1855:21).
109. Judd (1975:123); Woodham-Smith (1950); Davis (1857).
110. Vulliamy (1939:87).
111. Osborne (1855:49); Porter (1856:181).
112. Shepherd (1991:Vol. 2, 438).
113. Porter (1856:181).
114. Vulliamy (1939:87).
115. Barker (1970:216).
116. Osborne (1855:2).
117. Woodham-Smith (1950:160).
118. Porter (1856:181).
119. St. Aubyn (1964:93).
120. Reid (1911:41).
121. Pirogov (1899:113–15).
122. Sandwith (1856). See also Slade (1867) and Buzzard (1915).
123. Chesney (1960:154).
124. Shepherd (1991:Vol. 1, 326).
125. Garrison (1922:172–73).
126. Guillemin (1981).
127. An Amateur (1855:98).
128. Gooch (1959:262).
129. Gooch (1959:262).
130. Calthorpe (1856:455–56).
131. Hodasevich (1856:129).
132. Russell (1858:161).
133. Clifford (1956:263–64).
134. Hamley (1968:322).
135. Tisdall (1963:162).
136. Hamley (1968:314).
137. Calani (1855:448).
138. Chesney (1960:184).
139. McPherson (1997:56).
140. McPherson (1997:56).

# Chapter 5

1. Jones (1997).
2. Lowry (1994:118).
3. Parish (1975:42).
4. Moore (1866:23).
5. Trustam (1984:152); Compton (1970:57).
6. Mayhew (1862:158).
7. de Molènes (1886:36).

8. Compton (1970:57).
9. Lowry (1994:70).
10. Trustam (1984:118).
11. Woodham-Smith (1950:373).
12. Trustam (1984:73).
13. Compton (1970:21).
14. Higginson (1916:87).
15. Compton (1970:23).
16. Compton (1970:32).
17. Compton (1970:27).
18. Hodasevich (1856:89).
19. Trustam (1984:175).
20. Mayhew (1862:163).
21. Compton (1970:77).
22. Compton (1970:99–100).
23. Bell (1956:256).
24. Compton (1970:122).
25. Compton (1970:123).
26. Compton (1970:31).
27. Compton (1970:108–9).
28. Hall (1993:16).
29. Hall (1993:27).
30. Petry (1955); Conrad (1990:169).
31. Conrad (1990:110).
32. Conrad (1990:111).
33. Conrad (1990:112).
34. Conrad (1990:104).
35. Calani (1855:454).
36. Blackwood (1881).
37. Selby (1970:48).
38. Selby (1970:3).
39. James (1981:110).
40. Mercer (1964:69).
41. Compton (1970:9).
42. Knightly (1975:13).
43. Woodham-Smith (1950:135).
44. Richardson (1977:19).
45. Bolster (1964:93).
46. Richardson (1977:19).
47. Tisdall (1963:110).
48. Woodham-Smith (1950:172).
49. Laffin (1970:97).
50. Compton (1970:104).
51. Cler (1860:153).
52. Tisdall (1963:125).
53. Slade (1867:371–74).
54. Seacole (1988).

55. Compton (1970:136).
56. Seacole (1988:179).
57. Seacole (1988:166).
58. Seacole (1988:144).
59. Bonham-Carter (1968:157).
60. Seacole (1988:xxxiii).
61. Calthorpe (1856:Vol. 2, 267).
62. Tarle (1954:Vol. 1, 172).
63. Zverev (1956:83).
64. Calthorpe (1856:Vol 2, 207). See also Cockerill (1984).
65. Wood (1906:Vol. 2, 66).
66. Bardeen (1910).
67. Tarle (1954:Vol. 1, 156).
68. Tolstoy (1912:15).
69. Tarle (1954:Vol. 1, 143–44).
70. Tarle (1954:Vol. 1, 144).
71. Zverev (1956:82).
72. Pirogov (1899:26–27).
73. Pirogov (1899:148).
74. Pirogov (1899:45).
75. Hodasevich (1856).
76. Hodasevich (1856:213).
77. Curtiss (1979:462).
78. Pirogov (1899:59).
79. Pirogov (1899:60–61).
80. Curtiss (1979:463).
81. Richardson (1977:95).
82. Bolster (1964:55).
83. Bolster (1964:93).
84. Woodham-Smith (1950:143).
85. Woodham-Smith (1950:206).
86. Richardson (1977:108).
87. Bolster (1964); Richardson (1977); Woodham-Smith (1950).
88. Slade (1867:373).
89. Richardson (1977:90).
90. Richardson (1977:90).
91. F. B. Smith (1982:202).
92. F. B. Smith (1982:48).
93. Goldie (1987); Richardson (1977).
94. Brooks (1966:52–53).
95. Royster (1991:249).

# Chapter 6

1. Bolster (1964:131, 180).
2. Shaw and Shaw (1977:128).
3. Lake (1856:35–36).

4. Grenville-Murray (1855:127).
5. Tarle (1954:Vol. 1, 293).
6. Alabin (1861:117).
7. Warner (1977:83).
8. Warner (1977:22).
9. Gooch (1959:88).
10. Barker (1970:154).
11. Warner (1977:90–91).
12. James (1981:134).
13. Wolseley (1903:Vol. 1, 139).
14. Woods (1855:Vol. 2, 227).
15. Woods (1855:229).
16. Woods (1855:229).
17. Woods (1855:229).
18. Slade (1867:333–34).
19. Inglesant (1977:98).
20. Bedarrides (1868:Vol. 2, 103).
21. Slade (1867:27).
22. Duncan (1855:Vol. 1, 100); Steevens (1878:137).
23. Slade (1867:116).
24. Slade (1867:273).
25. Slade (1867:376).
26. Seaton (1977:185).
27. Wood (1906:Vol. 1, 199).
28. Gernsheim and Gernsheim (1954).
29. Russell (1858:187).
30. Bentley (1966:185).
31. Sandwith (1856:142).
32. Sandwith (1856:143).
33. Sandwith (1856:104).
34. Duncan (1855:Vol. 1, 178).
35. Slade (1867:408–9).
36. Sandwith (1856:132).
37. Lake (1856:56).
38. Lake (1856:151).
39. Lake (1856:77).
40. Sandwith (1856:252).
41. Lake (1856:190).
42. Sandwith (1856:252).
43. Buzzard (1915:4).
44. Lake (1856:179).
45. Lake (1856:118).
46. Lake (1856:122).
47. Sandwith (1856:285).
48. Sandwith (1856:285).
49. Lake (1856:119).

50. Buzzard (1915:273).
51. Sandwith (1856:286–87).
52. Sandwith (1856:787).
53. Buzzard (1915:206).
54. Oliphant (1856:95).
55. Oliphant (1856:113–14).
56. Slade (1867:434).
57. Sandwith (1856:343).
58. Sandwith (1856:289).
59. Lake (1856:26).
60. Sandwith (1856:297).
61. Slade (1867:435).
62. Sandwith (1856:305).
63. Tarle (1950:Vol. 2, 538).
64. Slade (1867:138).
65. Slade (1867:355).
66. Barber (1973:148).
67. Hornby (1863:205–6).

# Chapter 7

1. Wolseley (1903:Vol. 1, 159).
2. Smoler (1989); Marshall (1993); Grossman (1995).
3. McPherson (1997:72).
4. Tarle (1954:40).
5. Airlie (1933:306).
6. Barthorp (1991:122).
7. Brooks (1966:7, 74).
8. Grossman (1995:123).
9. Compton (1972:70).
10. Bell (1956:248).
11. Woods (1855:Vol. 2, 142–43).
12. Duncan (1855:Vol. 1, 230; Vol. 2, 36).
13. Wood (1895:43).
14. Kmety (1856:30).
15. Pemberton (1962:47); Cler (1860:184).
16. Wood (1906:Vol. 1, 45).
17. Small (1898:29).
18. Pemberton (1962:85).
19. Dinter (1985).
20. Pemberton (1962:85–86).
21. Thomas (1974:244).
22. Thomas (1974:245).
23. Harris (1973:219).
24. Barthorp (1991:53).
25. Evelyn (1954:140).

26. Morris (1938:149–50).
27. Barthorp (1991:53).
28. Barthorp (1991:54).
29. Pemberton (1962:114).
30. Seaton (1977:152–53).
31. Woodham-Smith (1953:262).
32. Woodham-Smith (1953:258).
33. Cler (1860:232).
34. An Amateur (1855:114).
35. Curtiss (1965:79, 431).
36. Kmety (1856:26).
37. Curtiss (1965:79).
38. Ogden (1907:99).
39. Tarle (1954:24).
40. Gibbs (1960:239).
41. Pemberton (1962:134).
42. Tarle (1954:37).
43. Bestuzhev (1956:101).
44. Seaton (1977:125).
45. Calthorpe (1979).
46. Manchester (1983:254).
47. Pemberton (1962:159).
48. Tarle (1954:156).
49. Garrett (1974:31).
50. Pirogov (1899:69–70).
51. Thomas and Scollins (1991:34).
52. Kinglake (1887:Vol. 7, 17–18).
53. Russell (1858:199).
54. Woods (1855:Vol. 2, 267–68).
55. Calthorpe (1979:145).
56. Hodasevich (1856:131–32).
57. Linderman (1987:148–49).
58. Hamley (1968:122).
59. Bell (1956).
60. Bell (1956:280).
61. Bell (1956:280).
62. Calthorpe (1979:213).
63. Kinglake (1887:Vol. 7, 178).
64. Tarle (1954:43).
65. Vulliamy (1939:27).
66. Parsky (1903).
67. Tolstoy (1912:68–69).
68. Curtiss (1965:355).
69. Slade (1867:403).
70. Curtiss (1979:458). See also Tolstoy (1912).
71. Tarle (1954:199).

72. Hodasevich (1856). Hodasevich was a Russian captain of Polish ancestry who surrendered to the British.

73. Wolseley (1903:Vol. 1, 91).

74. Campbell (1894:259).

75. Palmer (1987:57).

76. Paget (1881:83).

77. Hodasevich (1856:217).

78. Calthorpe (1979).

79. Hodasevich (1856:217).

80. Hodasevich (1856:199).

81. Seaton (1977:177).

82. Frey (1895:276–77).

83. Gooch (1959:167).

84. Campbell (1894:228).

85. Campbell (1894:231).

86. Higginson (1916:158).

87. Higginson (1916:175).

88. Selby (1970:115–16).

89. Clifford (1956:259).

90. Windham (1897).

91. Chesney (1960:234).

92. Wiley (1943:86).

93. Lonn (1928:62).

94. Lonn (1928:23); Wiley (1943:145).

95. Mitchell (1988:181).

96. Small (1898:185).

97. Barthorp (1991:119).

# Chapter 8

1. For a discussion of such destructiveness in war, see Holmes (1985).

2. Woods (1855:Vol. 2, 392–93).

3. Bentley (1966).

4. Buzzard (1915:95).

5. Russell (1858:458).

6. Buzzard (1915:94–95).

7. Royster (1991:38); Mitchell (1988:155).

8. Carew (1954:173); Clifford (1956:59).

9. Gowing (1895:49).

10. Small (1898:89).

11. Fenwick (1954:55).

12. Pirogov (1899:122–23).

13. Kinglake (1887:Vol. 7, 96).

14. Lake (1856:244).

15. McPherson (1997:154).

16. Gowing (1895:120).

17. Calthorpe (1979:54).
18. Calthorpe (1979:54).
19. Thomas (1974:221); Lysons (1895:168–69).
20. Clifford (1956:185).
21. *Army Diary,* November 5, 1971.
22. An Amateur (1855:115).
23. Wood (1895:262–63).
24. *Illustrated London News,* December 16, 1854.
25. Brett-Smith (1969:110).
26. Lysons (1895:105–6).
27. Zverev (1956:48).
28. Alabin (1861:108).
29. Pemberton (1962:161).
30. Wood (1895:113).
31. Tarle (1954:86).
32. Clifford (1956).
33. Selby (1970).
34. Selby (1970:195).
35. Chesney (1960:152); Slade (1867:340).
36. Bell (1956:254).
37. Gowing (1895:181).
38. Gowing (1895:192).
39. Woods (1855:Vol. 1, 115).
40. Selby (1970:195).
41. Inglesant (1977:242–43).
42. Inglesant (1977:25).
43. Inglesant (1977:40).
44. Inglesant (1977:93).
45. Inglesant (1977:67).
46. Inglesant (1977:80–81).
47. Inglesant (1977:222).
48. Inglesant (1977:224).
49. Inglesant (1977:27).
50. Inglesant (1977:231).
51. Inglesant (1977:235).
52. Inglesant (1977:243–44).
53. Brooks (1966:111).
54. Baylen and Conway (1968:67).
55. Compton (1970:154).
56. Compton (1970:154).
57. Compton (1970:134).
58. Bazancourt (1855:xvii).
59. Thoumas (N.d.:45).
60. Lake (1856:82).
61. Calani (1855:449).
62. Pemberton (1962:204).

63. Woods (1855:Vol. 2, 296–97).
64. Wiley (1943:39).
65. McPherson (1997:viii).
66. Wiley (1952:186).
67. Hibbert (1961:262).
68. Garrett (1974); MacGregor-Hastie (1985).
69. Tisdall (1963:141).
70. Lowry (1994:30).
71. Lysons (1895:261); Calani (1855:434).
72. Lowry (1994:70).
73. Lowry (1994:60).
74. Galwey (1961:71).
75. Compton (1970:157).
76. Bauer (1977:73).
77. Wiley (1952:160).
78. Alabin (1861:11–12).
79. Alabin (1861:11–12).
80. Hodasevich (1856).
81. Hodasevich (1856:100).
82. Fenwick (1954:74–75).
83. Hodasevich (1856:198–99).
84. Pirogov (1899:53–55).
85. Russell (1858:55).
86. Thoumas (N.d.:146).
87. Clifford (1956:269).
88. Mercer (1964:68); Wellard (1974:48).
89. Mercer (1964:68).
90. An Amateur (1855:265).
91. Bedarrides (1868:76).
92. Bazancourt (1855:8).
93. Clifford (1956:124).
94. Small (1898:37).
95. Clifford (1956:190).
96. Small (1898:39).
97. Goedorp (N.d.:23).
98. Small (1898:36).
99. Tarle (1954:46–47).
100. Lysons (1895:261).
101. Anglesey (1971:122).
102. Wiley (1943:159–60).
103. Gowing (1895:232).
104. Gowing (1895:232–33).
105. Lysons (1895).
106. Wiley (1943:64–65).
107. Eardley-Wilmot (1898:391).
108. Holmes (1985:255).

109. Shepherd (1991:Vol. 1, 243).
110. St. Aubyn (1964:95).
111. St. Aubyn (1964:89).
112. Shay (1994).

# Epilogue

1. Fries and West (1921).
2. Regan (1987).
3. Gordon and Trainor (1995).
4. Bazancourt (1855).
5. Seaton (1971).

# REFERENCES

Airlie, M., Countess of. *With the Guards We Shall Go: Letters of Col. Strange Jocelyn, 1854–1855*. London: Hodder and Stoughton, 1933.

Aksakova, V. S. *Dnevnik Very Sergeevny Aksakovoi*. Sank-Petyerburg: Ogni, 1913.

Alabin, P. *Pokhodnye Zapiski v Voini 1853, 1854, 1855 i 1856 Godov*. Moskva: Viatka, 1861.

An Amateur. *A Trip to the Trenches*. London: Sanders and Otley, 1855.

Anglesey, Marquess of (ed.) *"Little Hodge": Being Extracts from the Diaries and Letters of Lt.-Colonel Edward Cooper Hodge Written During the Crimean War, 1854–1856*. London: Les Cooper, 1971.

Barber, N. *The Sultans*. New York: Simon and Schuster, 1973.

Bardeen, C. W. *A Little Fifer's War Diary*. Syracuse, NY: C. W. Bardeen, 1910.

Barker, A. J. *The War Against Russia, 1854–1856*. New York: Holt, Rinehart and Winston, 1970.

Barnett, C. *Britain and Her Army, 1509–1970*. London: Penguin, 1970.

Barthorp, M. *Heroes of the Crimea: The Battles of Balaclava and Inkerman*. London: Blandford, 1991.

Bauer, K. J. *Soldiering: The Civil War Diary of Rice C. Bull*. San Raphael, CA: Presidio Press, 1977.

Baumgart, W. *The Peace of Paris, 1856: Studies in War, Diplomacy and Peacemaking*. Santa Barbara, CA: A. P. Saab, 1981.

Baylen, J. O., and A. Conway. *Soldier-Surgeon: The Crimean War Letters of Dr. Douglas A. Reid, 1855–1856*. Knoxville: University of Tennessee Press, 1968.

Bayley, C. C. *Mercenaries for the Crimea*. Montreal: McGill-Queens, 1977.

Bazancourt, Le Baron de. *Cinq Mois au Camp Devant Sebastopol*. Paris: Amyot, 1855.

Bedarrides, J. P. *Journal Humoristique du Siège de Sebastopol*. Paris: Librairie Centrale, 1868.

Bell, Sir G. *Soldier's Glory*. London: G. Bell & Sons, 1956.

Bemis, S. F. *A Short History of American Foreign Policy and Diplomacy*. New York: Henry Holt and Co., 1959.

Bentley, N. (ed.). *Russell's Despatches from the Crimea, 1854–1856*. New York: Hill and Wang, 1966.

Bestuzhev, I. V. *Krymskaia Voina, 1853–1856 gg*. Moskva: Academii Nauk CCCP, 1956.

Bettmann, O. L. *The Good Old Days—They Were Terrible.* New York: Random House, 1974.

Blackwood, Lady A. *A Narrative of Personal Experiences and Impressions During Residence on the Bosphorus Throughout the Crimean War.* London: Hatchard, 1881.

Bolster, E. *The Sisters of Mercy in the Crimean War.* Cork, Ireland: The Mercier Press, 1964.

Bonham-Carter, V. (ed.). *Surgeon in the Crimea.* London: Constable, 1968.

Brett-Smith, R. *The 11th Hussars.* London: Leo Cooper, 1969.

Brooks, S. *Civil War Medicine.* Springfield, IL: Charles C Thomas, 1966.

Bryant, A. *Jackets of Green: A Study of the History, Philosophy, and Character of the Rifle Brigade.* London: Collins, 1972.

Buchanan, G. *Camp Life as Seen by a Civilian.* Glasgow: James Maclehose, 1871.

Buzzard, T. *With the Turkish Army in the Crimea and Asia Minor.* London: John Murray, 1915.

Calani, A. *Scene Della Vita Militare in Crimea.* Vol. 1. Napoli (no publisher), 1855.

Calthorpe, S.J.G. *Letters from Head-Quarters.* 2 vols. London: John Murray, 1856.

———. *Cadogan's Crimea.* London: Hamish Hamilton, 1979.

Campbell, C. F. *Letters from Camp.* London: Richard Bentley and Son, 1894.

Carew, P. *Combat and Carnival.* London: Constable, 1954.

Chesney, K. *Crimean War Reader.* London: Frederick Muller, 1960.

Christian, R. F. (ed.). *Tolstoy's Diaries.* Vol. 1, *1847–1894.* London: Athlone, 1985.

Clarkson, J. D. *A History of Russia.* New York: Random House, 1962.

Cler, J.J.G. *Reminiscences of an Officer of Zouaves.* New York: D. Appleton and Company, 1860.

Clifford, H. *Letters and Sketches from the Crimea.* London: Michael Joseph, 1956.

Cockerill, A. W. *Sons of the Brave: The Story of Boy Soldiers.* London: Leo Cooper, 1984.

*Collier's Encyclopedia.* Vol. 2. New York: Collier, 1995.

Compton, P. *Colonel's Lady and Camp Follower.* London: Robert Hale, 1970.

———. *Cardigan of Balaclava.* London: Robert Hale & Co., 1972.

Conrad, E. *General Harriet Tubman.* Washington, DC: The Associated Publishers, 1990.

Cook, E. *The Life of Florence Nightingale.* 2 vols. London: Macmillan, 1913.

Crawford, M. (ed.) *William Howard Russell's Civil War: Private Diary and Letters, 1861–1862.* Athens: University of Georgia Press, 1992.

Curtiss, J. S. *The Russian Army Under Nicholas I, 1825–1855.* Durham, NC: Duke University Press, 1965.

———. *Russia's Crimean War.* Durham, NC: Duke University Press, 1979.

Davis, E. *The Autobiography of Elizabeth Davis,* edited by J. Williams. 2 vols. London: Hurst and Blackette, 1857.

Dean, E. T., Jr. "We Will All Be Lost and Destroyed": Post Traumatic Stress Disorder and the Civil War. *Civil War History* 37:138–53, 1991.

de Molènes, P. *Les Commentaires d'un Soldat.* Paris: Librairie des Bibliophiles, 1886.

Dinter, E. *Hero or Coward: Pressures Facing the Soldier in Battle*. London: Frank Cass, 1985.

Dixon, N. *On the Psychology of Military Incompetence*. London: Jonathan Cape, 1976.

Dowty, A. *The Limits of American Isolation: The United States and the Crimean War*. New York: New York University Press, 1971.

Duncan, C. *A Campaign with the Turks in Asia*. 2 vols. London: Smith, Elder & Co., 1855.

Dvoichenko-Markov, E. America in the Crimean War. *Russian Review* 13:137–45, 1954.

Eardley-Wilmot, S. *Life of Vice-Admiral Edmund, Lord Lyons*. London: S. Low, Marston and Company, Limited, 1898.

Ellis, H. *The Sharp End of War*. London: David & Charles, 1980.

Evelyn, G. P. *A Diary of the Crimea*. London: Gerald Duckworth, 1954.

Fedorov, V. *Vooruzhenie Russkoi Armii v Krymskuiu Kampaniu*. Sank-Petyerburg: Ogni, 1909.

Fenwick, K. (ed.). *Voice from the Ranks*. London: William Heinemann, 1954.

Fortesque, Hon. J. W. *History of the British Army*. Vol. 8. London: Macmillan, 1930.

Francis, H. *Leaves from a Soldier's Notebook*. Colchester, Essex: C. W. Poole & Sons (N.d.)

Fremantle, A.J.L. *Three Months in the Southern States, April–June 1863*. Lincoln: University of Nebraska Press, 1991.

Frey, A. R. *Sobriquets and Nicknames*. Boston: Houghton, Mifflin and Co., 1895.

Fries, A. A., and C. J. West, *Chemical Warfare*. New York: McGraw-Hill, 1921.

Fuller, W. C. Jr. *Strategy and Power in Russia, 1600–1914*. New York: Free Press, 1992.

Furnas, J. C. *The Americans: A Social History of the United States, 1587–1914*. New York: G. P. Putnam's Sons, 1969.

Gagnon, P. A. *France Since 1789*. Rev. ed. New York: Harper and Row, 1972.

Galwey, T. F. *The Valiant Hours*. Harrisburg, PA: Stackpool, 1961.

Garrett, R. *General Gordon*. London: Arthur Barker, 1974.

Garrison, F. H. *Notes on the History of Military Medicine*. Washington, DC: Association of Military Medicine, 1922.

Gernsheim, H., and A. Gernsheim. *Roger Fenton, Photographer of the Crimean War*. London: Secker and Warburg, 1954.

Gibbs, P. *Crimean Blunder: The Story of the War with Russia a Hundred Years Ago*. New York: Holt, Rinehart and Winston, 1960.

Goedorp, V. *La Guerre de Tranchées*. Paris: Dorbon-Aine (N.d.).

Golden, P. Russian-American Relations During the Crimean War. *American Historical Review* 31:462–76, 1926.

Goldfrank, D. M. *The Origins of the Crimean War*. London: Longman, 1994.

Goldie, S. M. *"I Have Done My Duty": Florence Nightingale in the Crimean War, 1854–56*. Manchester: University of Manchester Press, 1987.

Gooch, B. D. *The New Bonapartist Generals in the Crimean War*. Den Hague: Martinus Nijhoff, 1959.

Gordon, M. R., and B. E. Trainor. *The Generals' War: The Inside Story of the Conflict in the Gulf.* Boston: Little, Brown and Co., 1995.

Gowing, T. *A Soldier's Experience: A Voice from the Ranks.* Nottingham: Thomas Forman, 1895.

Gray, J. G. *The Warriors: Reflections on Men in Battle.* New York: Harcourt, Brace & Co., 1959.

Greenhill, B., and A. Giffard. *The British Assault on Finland, 1854–1855.* London: Naval Institute Press, 1988.

Greiner, J. M., S. L. Coryell, and J. R. Smither (eds.). *A Surgeon's Civil War: The Letters and Diary of Daniel M. Holt, M.D.* Kent, OH: Kent State University Press, 1994.

Grenville-Murray, E. C. *Pictures from the Battlefields.* London: G. Routledge & Co., 1855.

Griffith, P. *Battle Tactics of the Civil War.* New Haven: Yale University Press, 1989.

_____. *Military Thought in the French Army, 1815–51.* Manchester: Manchester University Press, 1989.

Grossman, D. A. *On Killing: The Psychological Cost of Learning to Kill in War and Society.* Boston: Little, Brown and Company, 1995.

Groushko, M. *Cossack: Warrior Riders of the Steppes.* New York: Sterling, 1992.

Guillemin, R. *La Guerre de Crimée: Le Tsar de Toutes les Russies Face à l'Europe.* Paris: Editions France-Empire, 1981.

Guthrie, D. *A History of Medicine.* London: Nelson, 1958.

Hall, R. *Patriots in Disguise: Women Warriors of the Civil War.* New York: Paragon House, 1993.

Hamley, E. *The Story of the Campaign of Sevastopol.* New York: Gatewood, 1968.

Hankinson, A. *Man of Wars: William Howard Russell of the Times.* London: Heinemann, 1982.

Hanley, Sir E. *The War in the Crimea.* London: Seeley, 1896.

Hannavy, J. *The Camera Goes to War: Photographs from the Crimean War.* Edinburgh: Scottish Arts Council, 1974.

Harris, J. *The Gallant Six Hundred.* London: Hutchinson, 1973.

Hibbert, C. *The Destruction of Lord Raglan.* London: Longman, 1961.

_____. *The English: A Social History, 1066–1945.* New York: N. W. Norton, 1987.

Higginson, G. *Seventy-one Years of a Guardsman Life.* London: Smith, Elder & Co., 1916.

Hodasevich, R. *A Voice From Within the Walls of Sevastopol.* London: John Murray, 1856.

Holmes, R. *Acts of War: The Behavior of Men in Battle.* New York: The Free Press, 1985.

Hornby, L. *Constantinople: During the Crimean War of 1853–1854.* London: Richard Bentley, 1863.

Hume, J. R. *Reminiscences of the Crimean Campaign with the 55th Regiment.* Ludgate Hill, England: Unwin Bros., 1894.

Inglesant, P. *The Prisoners of Voronesh.* Ludgate Hill, England: Uwin Brothers, 1977.

James, L. *Crimea, 1854–56: The War with Russia from Contemporary Photographs.* Oxford: Hayes Kennedy, 1981.

Jocelyn, R. J. *The History of the Royal Artillery (Crimean Period).* London: John Murray, 1911.

Jones, D. E. *Women Warriors: A History.* Washington: Brassey's, 1997.

Judd, D. *The Crimean War.* London: Hart-Davis, MacGibbon, 1975.

Keegan, J. *The Face of Battle.* Harmondsworth, England: Penguin, 1978.

Kinglake, A. W. *The Invasion of the Crimea.* 7 vols. London: Blackwood, 1887.

Kmety, G. *A Narrative of the Defense of Kars on the 29th September, 1855.* 3rd ed. London: James Ridgway, Picadilly, 1856.

Knightly, P. *The First Casualty.* New York: Harcourt Brace Jovanovich, 1975.

Laffin, J. *Boys in Battle.* London: Abelard-Schuman, 1966.

_____. *Surgeons in the Field.* London: J. M. Dent and Sons, 1970.

Lake, A. *Kars and Our Captivity in Russia.* London: Richard Bentley, 1856.

Lambert, A. D. *The Crimean War: The British Grand Strategy, 1853–56.* Manchester: Manchester University Press, 1990.

Lawson, G. *Surgeon in the Crimea,* edited by V. Bonham-Carter and M. Lawson. London: Constable, 1968.

Lewis, G. *Turkey.* New York: Praeger, 1955.

Lincoln, W. B. *Nicholas I: Emperor and Autocrat of All the Russias.* DeKalb: Northern Illinois University Press, 1978.

Linderman, G. F. *Embattled Courage: The Experience of Combat in the American Civil War.* New York: The Free Press, 1987.

Lonn, E. *Desertion During the Civil War.* New York: The Century Co., 1928.

Lowry, T. P. *The Story the Soldiers Wouldn't Tell: Sex in the Civil War.* Mechanicsburg, PA: Stackpole, 1994.

Luvaas, J. *The Military Legacy of the Civil War: The European Inheritance.* Chicago: University of Chicago Press, 1956.

Lysons, Sir D. *The Crimean War from First to Last.* London: John Murray, 1895.

MacGregor-Hastie, R. *Never to Be Taken Alive: A Biography of General Gordon.* London: Sidgwick & Jackson, 1985.

MacMunn, Sir G. *The Crimean in Perspective.* London: G. Bell & Sons, 1935.

Manchester, W. *The Last Lion: Winston Spencer Churchill—Visions of Glory, 1874–1932.* New York: Dell, 1983.

Manning, C. A. *Russian Influence on Early America.* New York: Library Publishers, 1953.

Marjoulet, A. *Historique du 3E Régiment de Zouaves.* Paris: Librairie Militaires, 1887.

Marshall, J. *Reconciliation Road: A Family Odyssey of War and Honor.* Syracuse, NY: Syracuse University Press, 1993.

Marshall, S. L. A. *Men Against Fire.* Gloucester, MA: Peter Smith, 1978 (orig. 1947).

Masquelez, M. *Journal d'un Officier de Zouaves.* Paris: Librairie Militaire, Maritime et Polytechnique, 1858.

Massie, R. K. *Peter the Great: His Life and World.* New York: Ballantine, 1980.

Maude, A. *The Life of Tolstoy: First Fifty Years.* New York: Dodd, Mead, 1911.

Mayhew, H. *London Labour and London Poor* (Extra Vol.). London: Griffin, Bohn, and Co., 1862.

McClellan, G. B. *The Armies of Europe*. Philadelphia: J. B. Lippincott, 1861.

McPherson, J. M. *The Negro's Civil War: How American Negroes Felt and Acted During the War for the Union*. New York: Pantheon Books, 1965.

_____. *For Cause and Comrades: Why Men Fought in the Civil War*. New York: Oxford University Press, 1997.

Mercer, C. *The Foreign Legion: The Vivid History of a Unique Military Tradition*. London: Arthur Barker, 1964.

Mitchell, R. *Civil War Soldiers*. New York: Viking, 1988.

_____. *The Vacant Chair: The Northern Soldier Leaves Home*. New York: Oxford University Press, 1993.

Moore, F. *Women of the War: Their Heroism and Self-Sacrifice*. Chicago: R. C. Treat, 1866.

Moran, Lord. *The Anatomy of Courage*. London: Constable, 1945.

Morris, H. *Portrait of a Chef: The Life of Alexis Soyer*. New York: Macmillan, 1938.

Munro, W. *Records of Service and Campaigning in Many Lands*. London: Hurst and Blackett, 1887.

Ogden, R. (ed.). *Life and Letters of Edwin Lawrence Godkin*. New York: Macmillan, 1907.

Oliphant, L. *The Trans-Caucasian Campaign of the Turkish Army Under Omer Pasha*. London: Wm. Blackwood and Sons, 1856.

Osborne, S. G. *Scutari and Its Hospitals*. London: Dickinson, 1855.

Pack, R. *Sebastopol Trenches and Five Months in Them*. London: Kerby and Endean, 1878.

Paget, Lord G. *The Light Cavalry Brigade in the Crimea*. London: John Murray, 1881.

Palmer, A. *The Banner of Battle*. London: Weidenfeld & Nicolson, 1987.

Parish, P. J. *The American Civil War*. New York: Homes and Meier, 1975.

Parry, D. H. *"The Death or Glory Boys": The Story of the 17th Lancers*. London: Cassell & Co., 1899.

Parsky, D. *Sevastopol i Namyanuki evo Oboroni*. Odessa: Tipo-Litografia Shtoba Odesskovo Bocinavo Okpuka, 1903.

Peard, G. S. *Narrative of a Campaign in the Crimea*. London: Richard Bentley, 1855.

Pearse, H. (ed.). *The Crimean Diary and Letters of Lieut.-General Sir Charles Ash Windham, K.C.B.* London: Kegan Paul, Trench, Trübner & Co., 1897.

Pemberton, W. B. *Battles of the Crimean War*. London: Batsford, 1962.

Petry, A. *Harriet Tubman: Conductor on the Underground Railroad*. New York: Thomas Y. Crowell, 1955.

Pirogov, N. I. *Sevastopolskie Pis'ma, 1854–1855*. Sank-Petyerburg: Tipografia M. M. Stasivlevicha, 1899.

Porter, W. *Life in the Trenches Before Sevastopol*. London: Longman, Brown, Green, and Longmans, 1856.

Rable, G. C. *Civil Wars: Women and the Crisis of Southern Nationalism.* Urbana: University of Illinois Press, 1989.

Rawley, J. A. (ed.). *The American Civil War: An English View* (by Field Marshall Viscount Wolseley). Charlottesville: University of Virginia Press, 1964.

Regan, G. *Someone Had Blundered . . . : A Historical Survey of Military Incompetence.* London: B. T. Batsford, 1987.

Reid, D. A. *Memories of the Crimean War, January 1855 to June 1856.* London: Murray, 1911.

Rein, D. M. S. Weir Mitchell, Pioneer Psychiatrist in the Civil War. *Topic* 2:65–67, 1961.

*Report to the Rt. Hon. Lord Panmure of the Proceedings of the Sanitary Commission Dispatched to the Seat of the War in the East, 1855–1856.* London: Sebastopol Committee Reports, 1857.

Rich, N. *Why the Crimean War? A Cautionary Tale.* Hanover, NH: University Press of New England, 1985.

Richardson, R. G. *Nurse Sarah Anne: With Florence Nightingale at Scutari.* London: John Murray, 1977.

Robinson, F. *Diary of the Crimean War.* London: Richard Bentley, 1856.

Rodzianko, P. *Tattered Banners: An Autobiography.* London: Seeley Service & Co., 1939.

Rousset, C. *Histoire de Guerre de Crimée.* 2 vols. Paris: Hachette, 1894.

Royster, C. *The Destructive War: William Tecumseh Sherman, Stonewall Jackson, and the Americans.* New York: A. A. Knopf, 1991.

Russell, W. H. *The British Expedition to the Crimea.* London: G. Routledge, 1858.

St. Aubyn, G. *The Royal George, 1819–1904.* New York: A. A. Knopf, 1964.

Sandwith, H. *A Narrative of the Siege of Kars.* London: John Murray, 1856.

Seacole, M. *Wonderful Adventures of Mrs. Seacole in Many Lands.* Oxford: Oxford University Press, 1988.

Seaton, A. *The Russo-German War, 1941–45.* London: Arthur Barker, 1971.

_____. *The Crimean War: A Russian Chronicle.* London: B. T. Batsford, 1977.

Selby, J. *The Thin Red Line of Balaclava.* London: Hamish Hamilton, 1970.

Shaw, S. J., and R. K. Shaw. *History of the Ottoman Empire and Modern Turkey.* Cambridge, England: Cambridge University Press, 1977.

Shay, J. *Achilles in Vietnam: Combat Trauma and the Undoing of Character.* New York: Touchstone, 1994.

Shepherd, J. *The Crimean Doctors: A History of the British Medical Services in the Crimean War.* 2 vols. Liverpool: Liverpool University Press, 1991.

Slade, Sir A. *Turkey and the Crimean War: A Narrative of Historical Events.* London: Smith, Elder and Co., 1867.

Small, E. (ed.). *Told from the Ranks.* London: Melrose, 1898.

Smith, F. B. *Florence Nightingale: Reputation and Power.* London: Croom Helm, 1982.

Smith, G. L. *A Victorian RSM.* Tunbridge Wells, England: Costello, 1987.

Smoler, F. The Secret of Soldiers Who Didn't Shoot. *American Heritage* 40:36–45, 1989.

Snow, J. *On the Mode of Communication of Cholera.* London: J. Churchill, 1855.

Solomon, Z. *Combat Stress Reaction: The Enduring Toll of War.* New York: Plenum Press, 1993.

Stanislawski, M. *Tsar Nicholas I and the Jews: The Transformation of Jewish Society in Russia, 1825–1855.* Philadelphia: The Jewish Publication Society of America, 1983.

Steevens, N. *The Crimean Campaign with the Connaught Rangers.* London: Griffith & Farran, 1878.

Sterling, A. C. *Letters from the Army in the Crimea.* London: Robson, Leveyard Franklyn, 1856.

Stern, P.V.D. (ed.). *Soldier Life in the Union and Confederate Armies.* Bloomington: University of Indiana Press, 1961.

Strachan, H. *From Waterloo to Balaclava.* Cambridge, England: Cambridge University Press, 1985.

Strachey, L. *Eminent Victorians.* New York: Harcourt, Brace & Co., 1918.

Talbott, J. Combat Trauma in the American Civil War. *History Today* 46:41–47, 1996.

Tarle, E. U. *Krymskaia Voina.* Rev. ed. 2 vols. Moskva: Voennoe Izdatelstvo Ministerstva Oborony CCCP, 1950.

———. *Gorod Russkoi Slavy: Sevastopol v 1854–1856 gg.* Moskva: Voennoe Izdatelstvo Ministerstva Oborony CCCP, 1954.

Temperley, H. *England and the Near East: The Crimea.* London: F. Cass, 1964.

Thomas, D. *Charge! Hurrah! Hurrah!* London: Routledge & Kegan Paul, 1974.

Thomas, R., and R. Scollins. *The Russian Army of the Crimean War, 1854–56.* London: Osprey, 1991.

Thoumas, C. A. *Mes Souvenirs de Crimée (1854–1856).* Paris: La Librairie Illustrée (N.d.).

Tisdall, E.E.P. *Mrs. Duberly's Campaigns.* New York: Rand McNally, 1963.

Tolstoy, L. *Sevastopol and Other Stories.* London: Methuen & Co., 1912.

Troubetskoy, A. S. *The Road to Balaclava: Stumbling into War with Russia.* Toronto: Trafalgar Press, 1986.

Troyat, H. *Tolstoy.* Garden City, NY: Doubleday, 1965.

Trustam, M. *Women of the Regiment: Marriage and the Victorian Army.* Cambridge, England: Cambridge University Press, 1984.

Vetch, R. H. *Life, Letters and Diaries of Lieut.-General Sir Gerald Graham.* Edinburgh: William Blackwood and Sons, 1901.

Vulliamy, C. E. *Crimea: The Campaign of 1854–56.* London: Jonathan Cape, 1939.

Wachsmuth, I. K., P. A. Blake, and O. Olsvik (eds.). *Vibrio Cholerae and Cholera: Molecular and Global Perspectives.* Washington, DC: American Society for Microbiology, 1994.

Warner, P. (ed.). *The Fields of War.* London: John Murray, 1977.

Webb, R. K. *Modern England: From the Eighteenth Century to the Present.* 2nd ed. New York: Harper and Row, 1980.

Wellard, J. *The French Foreign Legion.* London: André Deutsch, 1974.

Wiley, B. I. *The Life of Johnny Reb: The Common Soldier of the Confederacy.* Indianapolis, IN: Bobbs-Merrill, 1943.

_____. *The Life of Billy Yank: The Common Soldier of the Union.* Indianapolis, IN: Bobbs-Merrill, 1952.

Williams, R. L. *Gaslight and Shadow: The World of Napoleon III, 1851–1870.* New York: Macmillan, 1957.

Windham, Sir C. A. *Crimean Diary and Letters,* edited by H. Pearse. London: Kegan Paul, 1897.

Wolseley, Field Marshal, Viscount. *The Story of a Soldier's Life.* Vol. 1. Westminster, England: Archibald Constable, 1903.

Wood, E. *The Crimea in 1854 and 1894.* London: Chapman and Hall, 1895.

_____. *From Midshipman to Field-Marshal.* Vol. 1. London: Methuen, 1906.

Woodham-Smith, C. *Florence Nightingale, 1820–1910.* London: Archibald Constable, 1950.

_____. *The Reason Why.* London: Archibald Constable, 1953.

Woods, N. A. *The Past Campaign.* 2 vols. London: Longman, 1855.

Wortman, R. *Scenarios of Power: Myth and Ceremony in Russian Monarchy.* Princeton: Princeton University Press, 1995.

Zürcher, E. J. *Turkey: A Modern History.* London: I. B. Tauris, 1993.

Zverev, B. I. *Sevastopolskaia Oborona 1854–1855.* Moskva: Gosudarstvennoie Uchebno-Pedagogiskoye Izdatelstvo, 1956.

# INDEX